# Any Kind of Danger

Building our connection with animals.
A veterinary surgeon reflects on animals of the planet

**Dr. Rowan Blogg**

**BALBOA.**
PRESS
A DIVISION OF HAY HOUSE

Balboa Press books may be ordered through booksellers or by contacting:

Balboa Press
A Division of Hay House
1663 Liberty Drive
Bloomington, IN 47403
www.balboapress.com.au
1-(877) 407-4847

ISBN: 978-1-4525-0371-4 (sc)
ISBN: 978-1-4525-0372-1 (e)

Printed in the United States of America

Balboa Press rev. date: 07/26/2012

# CONTENTS

Dr Rowan Blogg, Diplomate of the American College Veterinary Ophthalmologists, was the first registered veterinary specialist in Australia and pro bono vet for the Seeing Eye Dogs for 25 years. His books include four volumes of *The Eye In Veterinary Practice* and *Everydog* with co-author Eric Allan. In 1998 he was Professor of Veterinary Ophthalmology at Ross University.

*"Rowan has always been open to fresh ideas and is likely to be one step ahead of the rest in embracing worthwhile innovations. He is prepared to pioneer against resistance."*

Dr Eric Allan—Lecturer in Veterinary Practice, Charles Sturt University, Author of *EveryPuppy*

June 11th (Queen's Public Birthday), Dr John Rowan Blogg was officially awarded a Member in the General Division of the Order of Australia (AM).

The extinction of the formerly numerous King Island Emu is believed to have been caused by excessive hunting for food by the early seal-hunters who used specially-trained dogs to catch and kill the birds, killing 'several . . . every day' (Brasil 1914).

# PREFACE TO *ANY KIND OF DANGER*

Rowan Blogg is an Australian veterinarian of the highest distinction and I greatly admire his professionalism, which I observed for years at close range.

In *Any Kind of Danger* he has extended his work into the environment and moral philosophy by tackling the complex issue of how we exploit animals. In the 19th Century William Wilberforce and other pioneers argued that our treatment of animals is a measure of our humanity. Peter Singer's *Animal Liberation* (1975) stimulated international interest in the subject. Dr Blogg's book should do the same.

Rowan Blogg examines the role of wildlife on the planet, millions of years before our species became dominant, but how much habitat do we reserve for their natural life? How many species are under threat?

The world's population will stabilise at about nine billion in 2050—and this raises the fundamental issues of how much land, water and energy we will devote to raising animals for food. Is grazing an efficient or humane way of feeding our species? Industrial farming—out of sight and out of mind—involves inescapable cruelty. Chickens are raised on an A4 size space or smaller 'scratching area', confined in multi-layered cages. Do animals have a right of access to sunlight and paddock for at least the great part of their lives? How does a cow giving birth cope with a crowded cattle truck?

Do we turn our eyes away from the inevitable suffering involved in animal transport, especially life sheep exports? There are profound moral lessons to be learned from observing how we treat animals—and yet the issue will not be on the agenda for the next Federal or State elections.

'Vow for primary schools and kindergartens:

'We will learn all we can about animals of the planet so we can best look after their wellbeing. We will learn how to speak out against those who are not kind'.

Professor Barry Jones, AO, FAA, FAHA. FTSE, FASSA
Australian Minister for Science 1983-90

'We are in Dr Blogg's debt for this thoughtful, passionate book.'

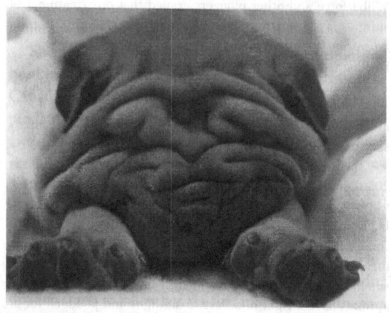

Do we easily recognize potential danger to the animals we breed? Skin folds near the eyes can allow displaced eyelid margins not easily noticed but later may cause serious corneal irritation and dryness. *Speak to a vet before you buy.*

*animals of the planet are not beneath us*
*—they are simply different*


*Are we wise enough to help animals*
*in any kind of danger?*

# ACKNOWLEDGEMENTS

There are so many people with kind hearts. Foot prints have trod the path of this book with me from animals in my childhood, including my first pony, Waverley Riding School to wildlife and academic veterinarians in Australian and American universities. People vivid in my memory include writers from The *Veterinarian magazine, the Australian Veterinary Journal*, and *The Age*.

Supporting family include daughter Sarah Blogg, son Dr James. twin sister Bev—no one helped me more—her husband George McCathie, their son Tom, granddaughters, Ella and Anna-Claire Blogg. My teachers, colleagues, vet nurses, Holy Advent Anglican Church, Armadale and the Cabrini Choir played a larger part than they realize. Before ophthalmology emerged as a special interest in the veterinary profession, medical eye specialists tutored me on the human eye.

Practitioners cannot function without family and the first of these I met starting as a country vet were the Dusty Rhodes family Maudie, Chris, Pene, Jan and Michael.

Many other people gave me their time such as David Connors, Mark Cleary, Luke Harris, Marianne Harris, Terri MacKenzie and Ian Westerland. Practitioner veterinarians, the salt of the earth who helped me, are almost too many to mention but included Drs Jack Auty, Jack Ayerbe, the Bryden brothers Doug and John, Brendan Carmel, Michele Cotton, Mark Curtis, Anita Dutton, James Gannon, Andrew Grant

Turner, Edith Hampson, Thomas Gordon Hungerford, Alain Marc, Jonica Newby, Shane Ryan, Alex Tinson, Chris Simpson, Catherine Tschanen, John Van Veenendaal and Tonia Werchon. Kevin Doyle, Jenny Cumming of the Australian Veterinary Association and Malvern Vet Hospital staff. University teachers from Australia and North America included Drs Virginia Osborne, Bruce Blauch and Kirk Gelatt. Friends form our life and quietly help: Cathleen Azzarello, Ben McGee, Nick McGee, Lyndal Turner, Adrian Chambers, Ian Mason, Sue Broadbent. Melbourne Zoo keepers of the Orangutans and Caulfield Writers Group. Staff of Computers Now, High Street Malvern, helped me technically. Rainer and Isabel Mccoy helped me find my path. The dedication of Jenna Wilson is acknowledged.

Holistic veterinarians helping to sort out fact from fiction, turned my clinical thinking to the broader concepts of health and away from the routine overuse of antibiotics which have become a human and animal health hazard.

For 50 years owners described to me the mystery of the human animal bond.

To all I offer my deep gratitude.

# DEDICATION

*To all who work for a more humane world*

To my wife and family, for their forbearance of my endeavors.

To slave abolitionist and RSPCA founder, William Wilberforce (1759-1833), who realized that we must respect other beings, and put aside financial gain as the main motive for what we do.

To my grandchildren, who can carry this concept of respect further so we can live in a kinder world for people, a world of no cluster bombs and where no newborn babies die of hunger.

To my mother, Sylvia, who showed me words, and my father, Valentine (Val), who showed me animals.

*And to our first teachers, the animals, on this planet before we appeared and who hold us together in compassion,* I dedicate this book.

## MORNING PRAYER
## FROM JOE MARSDEN

Headmaster of Malvern Grammar who influenced me and never realized it.

*Part of it, a little ungrammatically, went something like this:*

*.... Lord who hast safely brought us to the beginning this day; defend us in the same with thy mighty power; and grant that this day we fall into no sin, neither into any kind of danger.*

*Breeding with this pup will concentrate on selecting no nose wrinkles and shorter ears. Any slight deviation —out of line from nature's design—moves towards trouble and an animal life less happy.*

## Michael Has His Say

Michael was thrilled to get a puppy for his birthday. 'You must take him to the dog doctor for vaccination,' his mother told him. Michael eyes wide open, hung onto every word of my advice to make sure his puppy came when called. 'It is the first lesson and could save his life near a busy road,' I warned.

Back in the car driving home, the boy held onto his precious pup, his pup's feeding chart and packet of worm pills. Michael had enjoyed had the visit though was disappointed, 'But mum, the dog doctor was only a man.

# INTRODUCTION

## Respect in short supply

*The greatness of a nation and its moral progress can be judged by the way its animals are treated.*
—*Mahatma Gandhi*

**There are too many people on the planet
and too few wildlife.
And the too many do not care enough
about the too few.
But the too few have much to teach the too many.**

Once all earth dwellers were uncomplicated beings. Then *Homo sapiens came along.* Life on earth would never be the same.

Where would we be without our animals? We seem too busy and too distracted to appreciate that animals have intelligence and soul, suffer grief and pain. The natural world surrounds us, holding us together, teaching us the reason for creation and the power of empathy. We find that coming closer to different species is good for the soul. We need animals to bring out our most compassionate feelings. Perhaps it is the joy of finding how wild life can teach us to slow down, live simply and enjoy life. Many times I have been told by owners, "My dog knew I needed him; he sat on my bed for months when I was sick". Animals seem to know more about humans than humans know about animals.

My life with animals began when my father bought a pony for the family. I swept a thick body-brush over her shiny coat and fell in love with her instantly. This attachment increased through my teens and led me into a profession originally intended for the care of beasts of burden (*veterinus*, beast of burden, is the Latin origin of 'veterinary'). As a veterinarian, I observed the human-animal bond when I saw young children intuitively so close to young animals. Beautiful children, not yet taught adult ways, are our greatest asset.

My respect for animals slowly grew as did my acceptance that mankind does not need meat in our diet. After I turned 70, I became almost exclusively vegetarian, interested in avoiding cruelty foods; red meat, chicken and pork.

Animals need us and we need them. Most of all, they need our respect. What right do we have to treat them like objects that don't feel pain, don't feel emotion. What right have we to separate a mother from its child, to deny them fresh air and open spaces, to inflict pain and kill then inhumanely? Is this any way to treat innocent creatures that have so much to teach us?

Millions of people on the planet want to renounce all violence. Let's have more compassion.

*What we do to animals we do to people.*

Dr Rowan Blogg is a Melbourne-based veterinary surgeon, a humanist and a passionate advocate for animal rights. His most recent book *Any Kind Of Danger* draws on his own experiences and those of colleagues around the world.

Readers will hear of the dolphin who saved a whale, and how an orang utan rescued Dr Suce Urami from rape by two illegal tree loggers, this happening as 4,000 and more apes are killed with no protest from those who should care. They will read about the seeing-eye guide dog, Zappa, whose sense of humour was as good as his fun-loving owner's; Oddball, the livestock-guarding Maremma dog protecting the penguins; the cat, Fussy, who had to bite her sleeping owner's fingers to warn her the gas had not been turned off.

They will find out why Dusty, the decorated WW Two ace pilot, became a veterinary surgeon instead of a doctor and was a leading figure in the founding of a veterinary school; how Dr Shane became an elephant expert within 30 minutes; Dr Jim, a horse doctor in 24 hours; how Dr Jack correctly guessed the number of piglets which would be born as he drove his VW 100,000 kilometres each year. They will join Dr Bruce as he was nearly swallowed by mud on his mission to halt human TB, driving through 17 gates into cowyards and the same number out again. He then had to repeat the marathon to read results four days later.

Dr Rowan insists that we must give all planet dwellers more attention; we must not breed pets for fashion. Animals show the magic of migration to the world: they need their space. Where would we be without them?

Everybody needs a book such as *Hope for Animals and Their World, How Endangered Species Are Being Rescued From the Brink by Jane Goodall and others*. It is a prescribed text for a better world.

Dare we dream that our young children become so committed to animals—the lucky ones will learn horseback riding and the bush walking—that they will not be seduced by drugs or cyber-bullying? What constitutes too much electronic media?

*What must we do to help our children prepare for any kind of danger?*

*Encourage kids to be fascinated about animals, this might lead to a major life interest and thinking less about recreational drugs.*

We need to be animal guardians much more than just animal owners.

*We have been interested in animal breeding for our own ambition and not necessarily for the well being of the animal. Humankind is mostly driven by profit: to chase a show-ring prize or collect cash on the race track. Somehow we overlook that natural breeding is best and wild animals especially need genetic diversity to protect against extinction.*

## Family pets

Especially dogs have paid a high price of defective anatomy from human dominated un-natural inbreeding.

## Koalas

The koalas (pron ko ah' las) are under extreme pressure from loss of habitat, road kills, disease, and dog attacks. These are visible. Friends of the Koalas is one of many groups who believe in the future of Australia's wildlife, proclaiming now is the time for action. The free ranging and genetically diverse koala is needed for the long term survival of this Australian and world icon.

Utterly depressing 'is how writer Nikki Barrowclough describes the destruction of koalas, once in the millions through the Australian bushland. "Koala" was derived from an Aboriginal dialect of eastern New South Wales. The earliest known member of the koala family was a browser, and lived 15 millions years ago. The virtual absence of a tail, together with their stocky build and relatively long legs, gave the koalas a bear-like appearance, and led to their being incorrectly called, "koala bears".

Koalas once numbering in the millions, live in societies, and must be able to come into contact with other koala groups. They need large areas of suitable eucalypt forest, and if today's land grabs by developers causes the living areas to be split up and widespread, protected forest corridors are essential. Safe corridors however have not been provided and loss goes on. Some people who do not much care about wildlife will think hard about a dollars cost. No koalas mean less tourist trade.

We have known for many years koalas are special. Koalas need fear of people but visitors love to cuddle them. This is not helpful to the marsupial who must remain wild and independent of humans.

Koalas have a slow metabolic rate due to their high-fiber, low nutrient diet. Eucalyptus foliage is very fibrous and low in nutrition, and to most animals extremely poisonous. A koala's digestive system is especially adapted to detoxify the poisonous chemicals in the leaves.

Because they store little or no fat, koalas must sleep for up to 16 hours per day in order to conserve energy.

Koalas have enemies which include poorly informed politicians who do not diligently preserve koala habitat. Is there any sniff of corruption with land developers? Dedicated friends who have long been trying to help include Deborah Tabart, a veteran campaigner of the Australian Koala Foundation. She is supported by vets such as Dr Jon Hanger who isolated the deadly koala retro-viruses. Dr Jon is also stressed by koalas falling down with harvested trees, crashing into bulldozer blades and getting 'their limbs ripped off'. The Australian Zoo Wildlife Hospital vet Dr Amber Gillet is incensed by another loss, dog attacks. What are the dog owners doing?

Dogs, bush fires, disease and road kill, all obvious, hurt the bears. Dr Mark Powell, a vet once at Noosa says 'My grandchildren will probably never see koalas at all".

When frightened or in pain, koalas cry out. A volunteer driver said one injured koala cried and cried all the way to the vet.

The koala was suffering and called out. We look at bushfires, road kill and hear the dogs. The marsupial cries outto all of us. As guardians of the planet, we better be listening.

## Tasmanian Devil

Genetic diversity allows a species to adapt to changing climate. Lack of diversity is not easily noticed. The Tasmanian devil (*Sarcophilus harrisii*) is threatened with extinction because of a contagious cancer known as Devil Facial Tumor Disease. Low genetic diversity unnoticed perhaps 100 years ago has allowed the hideous cancer to ravage today's Devils. Dedicated activists today put their minds to saving the Devils. For low animal numbers the words are "early action". Had we been more aware before cancer spread it would have been easier to control.

## Fish

*The need for diversity can be hidden in the oceans. Overfishing silently eats away at genetic diversity of vulnerable fish. The market displays of fish tell us nothing of the tragedy waiting to happen.*

It was thought that even badly over-fished species would remain genetically diverse, because millions of fish remain even in the most depleted species. Some people however, count more carefully and are less optimistic.

Researching heavy fishing, Malin Pinsky and Stephen Palumbi of Stanford University in California found contrary to what was expected, state 'it looks like the effects of overfishing are widespread,. 'overfishing is just a few decades old, and if it continues it may lead to a further erosion of genetic diversity', Pinsky says.

Good work by caring people encourages others. Michael Alfaro and his many fish-counting colleagues of the University of California, Los Angeles, have found another ominous sign for fish stocks. "Humans are eating away the richest branches of the fish tree of life," says Alfaro.

Pinsky and Alfaro presented their findings at a meeting of the Society for the Study of Evolution in Norman, Oklahoma

**Speedy Evolution**

The team found that species with unusually fast rates of evolution in body size are more easily targeted by fishing.

**The bottom line is that people need to catch fewer fish** says Professor Paul Bentzen, a fisheries geneticist at Dalhousie University in Halifax, Canada.

*Can we become wise enough to limit wild animal extinction before lack of genetic diversity takes its toll?*

*Reference*

Barrowclough, Nikki (2012) How Much Can The Koala Bear? Good Weekend Feb 11, The Age Newspaper

*Further reading*

McCusker, M.R. and P. Bentzen. 2010. Positive relationships between genetic diversity and abundance in fishes. Molecular Ecology 10.1111/j.1365-294X.2010.04822.x.

Pinsky, M. L., D. Springmeyer, M. Goslin, and X. Augerot. 2009. Range-wide prioritization of cat-chments for Pacific 23(3): 680-691.

## References and further reading

Jane Goodall, Thane Maynard and Gail Hudson (2010), *Hope for Animals and Their World, How Endangered Species Are Being Rescued From the Brink,* Grand Central Publishing, Hachette Book Group, New York

Grandin T, Johnson C (2009) *Making Animals Happy, How to Create the Best Life for Pets and Other Animals,* Bloomsbury, London

Newby J (1997) *The Pact For Survival Humans and Their Animal Companions* ABC Books Sydney

# WHY THIS BOOK

The need for knowing more about other species and our own is paramount for all of us. We need to create the best balanced and healthiest young people we can. Pets help family cohesion and harmony. All species need that.

Animals feel more than we think

*Wildlife made homeless from habitat destruction or in poor standard zoos suffer in silence. More animals are noisy when in anguish but we do not listen.*

*Of 1.3 billion pigs worldwide killed in slaughterhouses each year, many scream, and the mother cow in the dairy paddock separated from her new calf stretches her neck to bellow out her pain. Animals suffer terror and we do not think about their grief.*

*What we do to animals sets a gold standard for how we behave to people.*

*People are cruel by default when they do not think beyond a butcher's meat display and a fast food advertisement. Some say our silence on cruelty is part of the crime.*

Animals are brighter than we are in many ways and express their love of life more readily. They nurture their young, care for their forest home, and endure loss. We realize animals are not dollar driven; they plan, invent, appreciate a sunset, contemplate and remember.

We do not regard sheep as brainy beings but Cambridge University has found a Black Leicester Longwool recognized about fifty sheep faces, also ten human faces and unlike this author remembered them two years later (Morell 2008).

A new Harvard graduate Irene Pepperberg in 1997 began her studies on a one-year-old African gray parrot teaching him the sounds of English. Virginia Morell recorded how Dr Pepperberg found not only was Alex a good talker but also came to know colours, shapes, and sizes and learned the concept of zero. Alex thought apples looked like cherries and tasted like bananas so he made up the word 'ban-erry' to describe them (Morell 2008).

We are in awe of what birds can be taught to say but also what they do. Australian research at Macquarie University decoded a language as sophisticated as that of Chimpanzees. Dr K. Lynn-Smith said *'chickens are the most underestimated animal on the planet.' The researcher* decoded a complex system of clicks and gestures that chickens use to talk about food, sex and danger. Flapping and squawking, migrating birds talk to each other as they follow a trail through the sky. The trail we offer avian species below on the earth is less inspiring. We confine domestic birds during egg production to be so crowded they cannot stretch their wings, let alone allow mother hen to show her chicks how to find seeds in the long grass. Animals have and need a harmony we can learn from but the sound of singing in the forests can easily be drowned out by chainsaws.

Dolphin cultures are as rich as ours. Echolocation is one sense giving cetacean awareness beyond human ken. People who work with dolphin trainers say the trainers are the pupils.

Most owners talk to their dogs. "He understands every word I say" is a popular comment by owners.

Human memory loss is a modern challenge. Not for dogs. Rico a Border Collie showed on German TV in 1991 he knew the names of some 200 toys. Hundreds of owners called to claim their dog had similar talents. One Border Collie had a vocabulary of 340 words and knew some 15 people by name.

Are we learning as much as Rico? There is a high impact meaning of CBD in the animal world. *CBD means Cruelty By Default.* Hand-in-hand with not thinking and not knowing, it is a wider CBD phenomenon than any business in any city.

We must learn to live at peace with other species. Animals with a different sense of the planet give and give to us. Concentrating on profit and power, humans are inclined to take and take.

Animals make us human, allowing us to find more peace within. When in their company, deep vibrations reach the heart. We are the forests and wildlife. Animals face extinction and it is time for us to face the music.

Young people are our greatest asset. Children need to learn about wildlife and as much as we can tell them about species of the planet.

In the words of Dr Catherine Tschanen (personal comm. 2010), president of Switzerland-based *Terre et Faune* has said *Within 20 years 40% of wildlife species of the planet will have disappeared.'*

Humankind likes war and killing. While war is a cause of famine and a basic instinct hard to change, there is something we can do now. ***It is time to recognize if we eat less meat we can feed more people.*** This is discussed in the chapter 'For Heaven's Sake Skip the Steak'.

*Further reading and reference:*

Carey, Adam (2010) Scientists Clucking Over Eureka Win, *The Age*, 18/8/2010

Morell, Virginia (2008) *Animal Minds, National Geographic*, vol 213, no 3

# HOW ARE WE TO LIVE AS ANIMAL CARERS FOR THE PLANET?

*First do no harm*—paraphrased from writings of Hippocrates (460 to 350 BC)

*Offer to children compassion for animals today and tomorrow their caring for other people comes more easily.*

*Owners know how to live: let everything that hath breath come into our care. Animals need company. If you are typically absent for the day consider owning two companion animals. Choose a companion animal for temperament before looks and watch body weight as a first health check*

❖ *Loyalty.* That's what domestic animals offer us. Simple, total, and constant loyalty. It is part of something strong, tough and tender—the human animal bond. Animals moreover are our teachers, and from them we learn about caring and unselfishness. In contrast, humankind is inward thinking, struggling to repay our debt to the animals.

❖ *All planet dwellers are entitled to a safe home* but what dangers are on the earth's surface? While trees cover 30% of the Earth, we are losing wildlife forest the size of England (13 million hectares) each year [World Bank]. Mankind's' driving force removing wildlife homes is financial, illegal logging is worth up to US $15 billion each year.

- ❖ The forest is home for many species, yet *eighty percent of original forests have been cleared or degraded* (Carr, 2007 UN environment programme). *We replace what we use leaving wildlife corridors pristine, unharmed and unmodified.* We hear of people who suffer in Mumbai; but not of animals from land clearing or of koalas whose eucalyptus leaves are spoiled by environment change.

- ❖ *Before we cut into a forest we need to check with wildlife conservationists.* Deforestation on a map does not measure the extent of loss. The noise is enough to disrupt their lives. Even before trees fall, distant chainsaws of the loggers interfere with wildlife.

- ❖ *List all wildlife species under threat and tell the local primary schools.* Eventually the young will have to deal with it.

- ❖ A human inheriting trouble, allows a cholera outbreak. Another leads his followers to slaughter infidels and enjoys the crime. People are not the only ones who inherit trouble. *Domestic animals suffer inherited disorders, many hidden in the young.* Beware of genetic errors and seek veterinary advice before buying or breeding. (Could we change history with a vet check of politicians?).

- ❖ *We must be concerned with how animals enjoy life, more than how they look.* So whiter coats look pretty? Pigmented animals however, better survive strong sunlight. Removing too much natural pigment is not common sense and moreover albinos do not see well and may not hear well. Some are cancer prone.

- ❖ Common sense guides us in all breeding. Consult www. vetsci.usyd.edu.au/lida. Can your selected breed come into the world naturally through the birth canal of the mother's pelvis? *A breed which can only be born by Caesarean surgery should not be conceived.*

- ❖ Does your chosen animal have a functional nose? *Smelling is the major canine sense.* A dog with no nose is similar to an eagle with no eyes. Furthermore animals with flat faces have shallow bony eye sockets which do not protect their eyes.
- ❖ Common sense is needed in all animal care. *In an emergency, you are the best person to be on the spot to save your animal friend.* Book a long veterinary consultation—perhaps at vaccination—to learn first aid. Take notes and perhaps one of your children.
- ❖ Ask your vet to show you how to examine body parts vulnerable to injury. *Learn how to examine animals in pain without getting bitten or kicked.*
- ❖ Animals hide disease from predators and hide pain from owners. Learn first signs of common illnesses so you can confine the patient when you suspect an animal is sick.
- ❖ Are we kind to all animals, should we create a factory farm with animals who all their lives do not feel sunshine on their skin or grass under their feet? What about a mother pig who cannot turn around in her farrowing pen?
- ❖ After the glamour of the Melbourne Cup, when the thunder of a hundred hooves has passed, how many slow runners who have given their all, have a happy retirement in a grassy shaded paddock to see out their days?
- ❖ A dog needs a run in the park at least once every day. Remember to pick up the poo.
- ❖ To protect birds and your cat, consider a caged backyard cat run. Outside the house, caging avoids cat-fight and road injuries.

- ❖ *Road Trauma*: before travelling, check for emergency wildlife phone numbers. Victoria: 1300 094 535; New South Wales: 1300 094 737 (WIRES—Wildlife Information Rescue and Education Service Inc., which is the largest wildlife rescue operation in Australia) and in Queensland, phone the RSPCA, local SPCA in North America. Place wildlife rescue numbers on your dashboard. When road trauma occurs, wearing a yellow coat or scarf and no dark colours, walk 200 metres or so against traffic flow on the side of the road. Wave a large white towel or torch.
- ❖ Factory raised dogs. Some pups are raised in conditions as bad as factory farming of poultry, pigs and vealer calves. Don't buy a new pup from a pet shop, adopt, more than one if a dog will be alone in your yard. All animals need to grow up free range as close as possible to mother.
- ❖ For a new dog or cat, contact petrescue.com.au. or local animal rescue service. Two dogs or cats are better than one. (There I've said it again).

*Reference:*
Carr Michelle (2007), *By The Numbers:* Forests G, *The Green Lifestyle Magazine*, July August 2007

# THE PASSING OF THE PASSENGER PIGEON

**1**

One hundred and fifty years ago the passenger, or wild, pigeon (*Ectopistes migratorius*) was the most successful bird in the world. Robust, adaptable, migrating and long-living, they represented 40% of all North America's birds. There was an estimated 3-5 billion passenger pigeons at the time Europeans discovered America. The birds nested in the northern forests each spring and summer, where a pair would raise just one chick from each mating. After a week of constant feeding, the parents would force their fattened youngster (called a squab) from the nest to the ground, where it remained until its first flight a few days later. In a large colony, hundreds of millions of squabs littered the forest floor, helpless to many predators. Local wolves, bears, foxes, boars, birds, rodents and snakes feasted on the squabs, but could eat only a small number before the squabs flew into the safety of the sky.*

In 1870, North American settlers could see some 2,000 million birds in one migrating flock alone. Watching from below, awed observers reported that the huge flocks passing overhead darkened the sky. The flights often continued from morning until night, and lasted for days, with the birds flying at an estimated speed of around 96 kph.

From ignorance, as the bird numbers began to decrease, passenger pigeons were confused with the mourning dove. The passenger pigeon's closest relative, the mourning dove resembled it in shape and colouring. However, the mourning dove is smaller and less brightly coloured than the passenger pigeon, and the iris of the adult mourning dove is dark brown, where it was bright red in the male passenger pigeon and orange in the female.

Once Europeans had settled, a classic horror story of extinction followed. Pigeons were trapped, blinded and pinned to stools as decoys—hence 'stool pigeon'. An average shooting club might kill 50,000 a week (Reader's Digest Assoc 1997). The extinction of the passenger pigeon illustrates to us what can happen when the interests of Man clash with Nature. Converting forests to farmland helped doom the bird.

The remaining passenger pigeons, some 250,000, were killed for sport in a single day in 1896. When Martha, the last of her species, died at age 29 at 1 pm on 1 September 1914 in the Cincinnati Zoo, the extinction of the colourful wild pigeon with a red iris was complete.

*http://www.damninteresting.com/extinction-of-the-passenger-pigeons*

*Passenger pigeons became stool pigeons*
*when pinned to stools and shot.*
*They were shot to extinction.*

# 2 RUN FAST, BREATHE FREELY AND BE WITH NATURE

Inbreeding is a problem for animals, as most are descended from a handful of progenitors. For many, the result of human tampering in the breeding process is severe debilitation, most commonly affecting the animal's vision, respiration and ability to walk straight.

Much of the blame for the genetic meddling in animals can be attributed to pet shows and parades in which animals are judged on certain fashionable physical attributes. The more highly regarded these attributes by show judges, the more inclined are breeders to breed animals with these attributes, no matter how inappropriate or unhealthy for the breed.

More education is needed before the registration of show judges and breeders. The BBC documentary *Pedigree dogs exposed* revealed how harmful and foolish breeding practices led to the skull of the cavalier King Charles spaniel being too small to house the brain, causing severe pain to the animal. Modern gene pools are severely limited regardless of how carefully a breeder selects which male dog to breed to which female.

Breeding dogs for show ring success is a disaster. We cannot breed without regard for nature's original design, guided solely by the opinions of a handful of judges. No matter how much you like what a modern breed has come to look like, function must come first. Breed standards have endorsed anatomical exaggeration, which has come to be considered 'normal'. But this concept of what is 'normal' does not take into consideration the dog's comfort. To encourage responsible breeding, and to improve the focus on animal health and safety, judges and breeders should have to pass a para-veterinary ('para' meaning 'near') training course on how a dog should be built to run fast, breathe free and be with nature.

Humankind has no doubt been responsible for some design triumphs. However, in the realm of dog designing we have been spectacular failures. Every breed has its health problems. What right do we have to wilfully change the original structure of a dog? We need to know much more about how the body works before we change how a dog looks. Moreover, misplaced enthusiasm can make us 'breed blind' and support a feature like a flat face which is not conducive to a canine leading a healthy and happy life. Such superficial changes are dangerous and unnecessary. Just because we can effect a change, does that mean we have the right to do it?

Exaggerations such as huge skin folds and the overlong ears of the basset are NOT beneficial to the dog. Who has the right to treat animals as a toy or an experiment? *The first and only rule of animal care is to do no harm.* The edict *I can do it therefore I will do it* has been disastrous for society and has been disastrous for the dog. How well I remember treating a basset hound who was brought to me by his owner because the dog 'seemed to be having a problem seeing'. I did not need to look far to determine that the excessive skin on the forehead and upper eyelids was so loose and droopy that the forehead skin was actually covering the eyes. I corrected the skin folds, treated the corneal irritation caused by the skin abrasion of the eye surface and made the dog more comfortable. He was now able to see, but I doubt that the owner fully understood that it was the breeding of these dogs that led to the problem. If basset breeders selected smoother faced stud dogs, one vision problem would be avoided and new breeders would get the message that 'wrinkles are wrong'.

The Shar-Pei was a fighting dog in China and was protected from bites on the face and neck by their numerous skin folds. They are no longer used as a fighting dog but, strangely, their deep, excessive skin folds are perversely thought fashionable. Notwithstanding the intrinsic dermatological problems associated with skin folds, the fashion gurus did not understand the problems they created. Each Shar-Pei has the potential for eye damage, pain and vision impairment, all needing correction by vets who surgically smooth out the forehead and face and restore vision. Unhappily, expensive surgery was essential to allow the eye and the dog to be comfortable.

Breeding for the show has highlighted the poor treatment of a faithful species which has no voice of protest. Inbreeding deformities were revealed to be an emerging disaster years ago (Blogg and Allan 1983), and today the problem is drastic. In some breeds, epilepsy is *twenty times* the human incidence, and in no breed is this more dramatic than the cavalier King Charles spaniel. Breeding for the show has also been responsible for pugs that are unable to breathe freely, German shepherds who cannot run, and bulldogs with skulls too large to fit through the mother's pelvis (Blogg and Allan 1983).

The dog shaped by nature rather than by human whim is healthier and lives longer. The St Bernard, a breed of dog that has been of tremendous help to humans, lives only an average of 4.9 years. It was evident in the 1960s that companion animal inbreeding was headed for trouble. In 2009, inbreeding was described as 'the greatest animal welfare scandal of our time' (*Pedigree dogs exposed* 2009). With a mix of ignorance and incompetence, breeding animals to ill health ranks as serious a threat to animal wellbeing as excessively confining poultry and pigs.

For millions of years, when a female egg was fertilised Nature allowed spontaneous change in the genetic makeup of progeny. Some of these changes did not support a good life and therefore Nature did not allow such life to continue—'survival of the fittest'. Humankind, interfering with Nature's plan, has meddled with natural evolution, resulting in a degraded animal anatomy. We now have dogs with heads too large to fit through the pelvis. noses too small to function, teeth which do not meet, and legs which cannot walk. Many dogs have an excess of skin carried in grotesque wrinkles. Skin is not always protective because there is not enough pigment to stop sunburn. In many breeds of dog, the ears and eyelids are too big, with eyeballs cloudy, too prominent and too dry. If breeders go against Nature, *persistently* selecting for one trait only—purely to win pet shows, for example—we end up with dog breeds with brain dysfunction (Grandin and Johnson 2005).

UK breeders helped us to see our errors with their Crufts dog show, showing us what happens when we inbreed or close breed for show appearance rather than for the health of the animal. The dogs may well look good in the show, but many carry a gene profile for hidden diseases. Hidden from *humans* the diseases certainly are. Mankind has not been up-front about the negative consequences of these kind of breeding practices. Jemima Harrison of the BBC has explained that 'there is a huge UK vested interest in dog breeding and this causes breeders to play down, minimise and sometimes downright lie about inherited disease' (*Pedigree dogs exposed* 2009).

Comparing a Crufts 'Best Dog In Show' with the original dog of 10,000 BC, the modern canine appears freakish. Genetically, it is. Modern pugs, miniature poodles, bulldogs and bassets are prominent examples of short-sighted breeding based purely on appearances humans find 'cute' or appealing. Now we must clean up the mess, although some breeds seem beyond hope. All is not lost, however. We must legislate against inbreeding show dogs, allowing common sense to rule. It is remarkable that we, the dog's caretakers, have allowed persistent and repeated close-relative breeding in families and then used progeny at stud.

All dog breeders must seek veterinary certification before licensing approval—*more education before registration*. If inbreeding is too hard to police, we might have to stop breeding some show dogs altogether. Without veterinary supervision, Crufts' 'Best Dog In Show' title has become invalid, although stupidity and ignorance have to be in the mix when we breed dogs with human disregard for canine wellbeing.

In contrast to show dogs, working dog breeding has been largely free of trouble. When we do not select for one trait on its own, our breeding of dogs who work for their existence is much better. Run, breathe, and be with nature sweeps over us as a breeding guide. According to Jemima Harrison, some retrievers have almost a 50% chance of developing cancer by seven or eight years of age (*Pedigree dogs exposed* 2009).

Unrestricted inbreeding produces poor health and worse—intense pain in man's first friend. Revealing no royal respect for the cavalier King Charles spaniel, a dog popular in royal courts of England during the 16th to 18th centuries, fluid filled cavities—*syringomyelia*—were later bred into the spinal cord of the dog and allowed to destroy nervous tissue. When cavities affected the brain in the tiny skulls of the cavalier King Charles spaniel, painful seizures followed.

*Syringomyelia* offered dramatic evidence of cruelty due to careless breeding, and has been described by UK vets as trying to fit the cavalier brain—let's compare it to a size 10 foot—into the cavalier cranium—a size 8 shoe. Mother Nature would not do that. Geneticists added *syringomyelia* to the many inherited disorders afflicting the dog. It now affects one third of the cavalier breed, adding agony to the discomfort of other inherited disorders.

Over the years, inbreeding has increased the number of diseases in dogs. Idiotic breed standards are one cause of the scandal. Sydney University Professor Paul McGreevy expressed it mildly when he found some breed standards go against the welfare of dogs. I would add some breed standards do so criminally.

British RSPCA veterinarian Mark Evans puts the cause of breeders' aberrant actions down to competition in the show ring. Of course we must change. People breeding dogs for dollars, such as puppy farmers and back yard breeders, disregard the long-term results of inbreeding, highlighting the urgent need of government legislation. Dogs need protection by government decree preventing any breeder from becoming licensed without studying the anatomy and physiology of their breed of interest, and having their level of competence proven by passing supervised tests.

Prior to buying and breeding, veterinary examinations with gene testing can help find affected dogs. A swab from the mouth may detect carrier animals. Beware, however, as some inherited disorders are only revealed later in life. We all need to know how to steer clear of affected breeds and make sure suspect dogs are not bred. Looking at the eyes, our care is found wanting. Bruce Robertson has listed some 80 hereditary or suspected hereditary canine eye diseases as part of the Australian Canine Eye Scheme (ACES) (Robertson 2008).

Close-relative breeding leads to show success but also to danger. For early disease prevention, breed societies can encourage genetic diversity, advising to breed away from a closely bred family instead of line breeding.

Breed standards must be about quality of life, not show ring acclaim.

*Shar Pei.*
*Do we have the right to breed wrinkled skin instead of*
*smooth healthy hair? The eyelids edges of this Shar Pei*
*are hidden but could be markedly turned in towards the*
*eyes to cause severe chronic irritation. Fashion too far?*
*There should be NO element of fashion in breeding how*
*our dogs look. You wear the latest fashion and leave your*
*pooch out of it.*

# 3 SNOW GEESE—FRIENDS AND FOES

*Snow geese breed in the Canadian Arctic and Alaska; as west as Siberia and as east as certain parts of Greenland. More than three million snow geese leave the far north for the winter.*

Azura, a gosling chick in a nest of eggs, hears her mother while she is in the shell.

She can discern her mother's talk above a thousand honking pairs in the colony on the open tundra of the Canadian Arctic. The geese find safety in numbers, as predators are intimidated by the noisy honks and are in awe of the strong flapping of white wings that span almost six feet (183 cm).

Instinct tells the unborn gosling to peck at what surrounds her and push open the cracked shell. Azura responds until at last she sees a sharp pink bill close to her. It belongs to the large head that has been talking to her through her eggshell. Azura sees her mother's pink feet and black wing tips and starts to follow her, the first moving object she sees. Azura can easily recognise one nestling from another at two weeks of age. She is a member of the species with the best vision of all vertebrates. At 3,000 metres in the sky above, humans cannot discern a bird with a three-metre wingspan. But Azura's visual acuity far exceeds that of people. She can see a hawk approaching in the sky at a distance at which the predator is invisible to humans.

Food is not a problem in the nest of goslings—green herbs are presented in the pink bill many times daily. Azura's yellow down, which covers her somewhat cylindrical body, slowly changes to white feathers, and her little yellow gosling flappers become white-feathered wings with black tips.

Azura grows and, not knowing as winter approaches where she will be going, intuitively prepares for a journey. As she gets older she jumps at top speed into the wind and is lifted into the air. Her jumps become longer and, once in the air, Azura's outstretched wings push air down and backwards and then up and forwards to produce low air pressure above the wing, sucking her body upwards. She develops bulky chest muscles attached to a massive breastbone. For the practice of moving feathers against the air, her muscles are ready to burn stored energy. Then one day Azura takes off. Migration has begun.

*Geese fly 5000kms to migrate and define loyalty. They pair for life. Migrating birds can fly in a state of reduced consciousness, a type of sleep. A 10 minute error in flying time can put a migrating bird 200kms off-target.*

Corresponding to those of a human arm, Azura's main wing bones are humerus, radius, and ulna. The ends of an avian wing represent our wrist, hands, and fingers. Feathers grow from wing skin and deal with a complexity of flight to a finer degree than aerofoils of commercial aircraft.

## Day and night travel

Azura and her fellow migrants fly in a 'V' formation, allowing each to see the birds ahead without being impeded by air swirls from their wing tips. An older bird leads at the front of the V. Flying through the day, Azura reads the landmarks below so much better than humans can. At night, chattering to her friends, she flies across the face of a moonlit sky (Elphick 1995).

## Sleeping on the job

### Bird rest while flying—Information from other migrant birds

Small songbirds get tired and avoid deserts, oceans or mountains during their migration. They usually lose 25 % of their weight during the migration. Sea currents form only during daylight, during which small birds migrate. In contrast geese, ducks and cranes migrate both day and night.

## Can migrating birds make up for sleep loss?

That some birds can really sleep while in flight is yet to be proved. Instead of sleeping for long stretches at a time, some migrating birds take several naps a day, perhaps only 9 seconds on average. Or they close one eye and rest half the brain.

Drowsiness and one closed eye sleep are less effective than normal sleep, but safer. Drowsiness is characterized by a partial shutting of both eyes that still allows some vision., thrushes and other migratory birds can reap some of the benefits of sleep only marginally increasing their risks of being caught by prey birds.

Research in 2006 showed to make up for night sleep loss, thrushes migrating distance of 5,000 kilometers mostly during the night, take hundreds of naps during the day, each of just a few seconds, Flocks of wild ducks take short naps during migration resting the whole brain. Or close one eye. Birds keep semi-alert by resting one half of their brain while their other eye and brain hemisphere remained active,

Migration is a team job. Ducks found at the head of the migrating line had half of their brain with one eye closed for one third of sleep time, while those in the middle of the flying line—feeling more safe—did this just 12% of the sleep time. When the situation is risky, birds were found to have more one-eye episodes (Stefan Anitei 2007).

During autumn and spring—the migration periods—thrushes reverse their typical sleep patterns, staying awake at night and resting during day. Instead of sleeping for long stretches at a time, the birds take several naps a day, of only 9 seconds on average. They too use one eye closed.

## Soaring into the heavens

Flight techniques, power and speed of the snow goose depend in part on hot air currents. Less effort is required if Azura rises ever upward on rising thermals, which are often visible as tufts of cloud. Snow geese are comfortable flying at heights of up to 1,000 metres, but cannot reach the height of bar-headed geese, which have been recorded flying above the summit of Everest. Whitman describes the flight:

3 SNOW GEESE—FRIENDS AND FOES

*At 29,028 feet (8,848 metres), Mount Everest is tall enough to intrude into the jet stream, a high-altitude river of wind that blows at speeds of more than 200 miles (322 km) an hour. Temperatures on the mountain can plummet low enough to freeze exposed flesh instantly. Its upper reaches offer only a third of the oxygen available at sea level—so little that if you could be transported instantly from sea level to Everest's summit without time to acclimatize, you would probably lose consciousness within minutes.*

The bar-headed goose, on average weighing five pounds (2.3kgs) and standing two feet high (61cms), gets its name from the two horizontal black stripes on the back of its white head. "They are powerful flappers, not soarers that just glide with the wind," says M.R. Fedde, an emeritus professor of anatomy and physiology whom I met while I was studying veterinary ophthalmology at Kansas State University's School of Veterinary Medicine. Fedde has conducted laboratory studies of the bar-headed goose's respiratory system.

Partly because of their massive wingspan, bar-headed geese have a disproportionately large surface area for their weight. "They can fly over 50 miles (80 km) an hour on their own power," Fedde says. "Add the thrust of tailwinds of perhaps 100 miles (160 km) an hour, if they are lucky, and these birds really move." Able to gauge and correct for drift, bar-headed geese can even fly in crosswinds without being blown off course. The same powerful and unremitting flapping that helps propel them over the mountains also generates body heat, which is retained by their down feathers. This heat helps keep ice from building up on their wings.

DR. ROWAN BLOGG

## Out of thin air

What's the secret to the bar-headed goose's aerobic success? "First of all, bar-headed geese are birds," says S. Marsh Tenney, an emeritus professor of physiology at Dartmouth Medical School, whose research on respiratory adaptations to oxygen deprivation includes studies of these high flyers, "and all birds are built for particularly efficient oxygen uptake."

The avian breathing system is uniquely structured. There are several sacs that temporarily store inhaled air that has passed through the lungs and then send it back through the lungs before it is exhaled. Thus, birds circulate inhaled air through their lungs twice—once more than earthbound mammals do—increasing their opportunities for capturing oxygen.

Birds can also pant for prolonged periods without constricting the blood vessels in their brains. So even when physically taxed, they keep their wits about them. By contrast, prolonged panting in people reduces blood flow to the brain, which primes them for bad decision making—hence the occasional unfortunate climber who blithely strolls off a cliff.

Bar-headed geese are "super birds", according to Tenney. "They do everything even better than other birds." They have a special type of haemoglobin that absorbs oxygen very quickly when the birds are at high altitudes; as a result, they can extract more oxygen from each breath of rarefied air than other birds can. Once their blood is stocked with oxygen, it rushes through capillaries that penetrate particularly deep into their muscles. Thus energised, their wings flap with seemingly inexhaustible vigour (Whitman 2008).

When the climate changes, we might ponder, how will the geese fly then?

The highest-flying bird ever recorded was a Ruppell's griffon, a blue-grey vulture with small white feathers on bulky brown wings stretching about three metres in span. On 29 November 1975, a Ruppell's griffon vulture was sucked into a jet engine 11,552 metres above the Ivory Coast, *more than two and a half kilometres above the peak of Everest* (Whitman 2008).

## Sense of direction

Azura the snow goose flies south, using innate senses to navigate to within 20 kilometres of her goal, after which she uses her bird's eye view of landmarks. Using the sun as a compass, small crystals of magnetite above the nostrils help her and her friends find the line of flight. Light from the sun through clouds is polarised light. People see this light in a rainbow, but Azura uses polarised light vibrating in one direction for navigation (Pye 2001).

Polarisation, by which electromagnetic radiation is seen passing through crystal, shows different properties in different directions. It is one of the fundamental properties of nature—we see it in the rainbow, in the dance of honey bees, in the colour of beetles, and the gloss of tree-leaves at dawn.

At night, if no clouds obscure the sky, Azura flies by the stars. She detects the centre of the stars' rotation using her star map. Azura is not aware of how she knows about small changes of gravity or the forces produced by the spinning Earth. To stay on track when the winds blow, she uses her sense of balance together with what she can see and feel. Her ears detect infrasound from the wind on distant mountains. Nearer to land, she hears frogs in the marshes, waves on the shores, and echoes of her own calls and those of other birds. Close to Earth, her sense of smell takes in pungent colonies of seabirds or the fragrance of sweet fresh meadows (Elphick 1995).

All sensory input to Azura's brain is modified by the bird's internal clock. She must know not only where to fly, but how long to fly and exactly when to stop. She can easily follow a large river to a resting station, but can she be sure about the food growing from the mighty waterway? She sees where other birds are and must rest there.

## Pollution

There is evidence the Mississippi River is in trouble. Poor quality drinking water and severe flood damage suggest the start of river death. Channels we design to straighten the path of the river and create new farming lands also decrease natural habitats, resulting in a corresponding decrease in the number of plant and animal species. Industries located on the banks of the Mississippi contribute to river decline. Factories dump pesticides, oils, and heavy metals such as lead into the river.*

River contamination is so great that in some areas it is not only hazardous to the plants and animals that live in the water, but also dangerous for the human population.

Contaminated fish and shellfish contain potentially deadly chemicals. Mankind tries to control the river, create drainage, dams, locks and channels, and building flood control levees to decrease the number of seasonal floods. Alas, these interventions increase rather than reduce the danger of major floods.

## Mississippi watershed is a precious resource

When the Mississippi reaches the Gulf of Mexico, it has nowhere else to go. Fresh water meets the massive expanse of salt water from the Gulf, and this slows the speed of the river until fresh water 'wider than a mile . . . off to see the world*' go no further. When the river slows, sediment settles and forms fertile marshland, some of the earth's most productive nutrient-laden soil. While delta formation occurs on almost all the world's major rivers, not all rivers receive sediment as rich as that carried by the Mississippi. The Mississippi River has the third largest catchment or drainage basin in the world, exceeded in size only by the watersheds of the Amazon and Congo Rivers.

Yet an invisible killer of the Mississippi is threatening wildlife: pollution. One way that scientists measure the pollution levels in rivers is by counting the number of fish that die as a result of contamination. It is easier to notice dead fish in the water than birds that fly away and die. When living in a diluted cocktail of heavy metals or chemicals, animals must struggle more than usual to survive.

## Feeding

Azura reaches coastal marshland and low-lying farmland bordering the Gulf of Mexico. She has avian company—other birds flying thousands of kilometres to be there, some with dark necks and clown masks. Wild ducks, shovellers, wild geese, gulls, teal and curlews pick their way through the tidal pools. For the survival of all these birds and the eggs they will lay in the future, river water must remain pure.

Azura must have enough summer food from the Gulf to lay down body fat for her return journey north, and also for the first two weeks she will spend on the summer breeding grounds of Arctic tundra. Once she gets to the tundra, if the climate turns too cold for Arctic vegetation, she will go hungry. Moreover, leaner times mean more hollow-flanked Arctic foxes will be hungrier and looking to feast on goose eggs.

## Mates for life

During her second winter, and before she is two years old, Azura pairs for life with a male goose (gander). Larger than she is, he protects her from predators and other geese. Soon there will be eggs of embryo geese. Nutrients in the pure tidal pools must ensure the health of Azura's future young.

When we look to the sky and see the V-shaped formation of honking geese, something happens in our soul. We experience an ineffable wonder at the beauty and glory of nature. Are we really going to let Man's careless polluting wipe their message of wonder from the sky?

*This chapter is dedicated to the memory of Lee (Julien) Duclos, good friend of many many people and wild birds. Lee believed animals have as much right to our planet as we have.*

In France, domestic geese are assaulted by another human extreme. Taking in grain by force-feeding for fifteen days with a tube down the goose's throat produces a popular 'fat liver' pâté (*foi gras*). Is this kind of luxury food, the product of cruelty, something we really need? Should we assault a sensitive bird four times daily when we do not have to? The Pope and the Dutch royal family protest while France produces three quarters of the world's foie gras in a growing market.

*http://greennature.com/article620.html*

*Animals in captivity are emotionally deprived but in the future, zoos may be the only place we can see what was once wildlife in their natural habitat. If we must have zoos for teaching, let our children see them free range in a natural forest if we can.*

Some call it "mass orang murder by deceit". We clear-fell virgin forest, home of orangutans, then plant palms for oil. We call it 'vegetable oil', a part truth sounding harmless to a poorly informed customer. Big dollars promote its use for a myriad of reasons in supermarkets. It is however far from harmless. Orangs suddenly have no home, and wander where they do not belong. Thousands die homeless, their infants stolen for human pleasure. More clear felling and a species is at risk of extinction.

# 4 THE VANISHING ORANGUTANS OF BORNEO

*Where is our respect for our closest relative, the orangutan (meaning 'man of the forest' in Malay), in west Kalimantan, Borneo? We clear fell the apes' forest home for timber, we create palm oil plantations, and when the orangutans are displaced, we steal their young for money.*

Deep in the forest Zylvia, a young female orangutan, enjoyed all the splendours of nature. Under her wisps of ginger hair, she was happy with all she heard, saw, smelled and tasted up in the trees. She loved her life high above ground, the sound of rain on the leaves she fashioned to protect her baby, and the feel of ripe figs and leaves she stuffed into her mouth. Swinging from branch to branch, her strong hold came from long sensitive fingers and toes. She swung from tree to tree in the old growth forest, made her bed each night in a two-metre wide nest woven of vines and leaves in the canopy.

Suspending herself from the branches, her large mouth took in fruit, fresh shoots and bark. With her gentle touch, she could pick up insects and bird eggs, with long fingers and thumb to hold her baby fast. Her feet were as useful as hands, each foot with four long toes plus an opposable long big toe as helpful as a thumb. She nursed her baby, content to be sharing a mother-and-offspring bond, closely together for 6 or 7 years, showing her how to fashion tools to get food, and other survival skills.

It was many moons ago that Nahum, a male orangutan with a large head and big mobile mouth, gave voice from deep in the peat-swamp forest. It was a long, loud call; a series of cries from his large throat sac, followed by a bellow, a haunting sound, across the valley. Soon he appeared. With long fur, he looked so different from Zylvia. Dark brown baleful eyes looked down. One ginger-haired arm languidly reached for a 15-metre-tall tree. Twice Zylvia's weight, Nahum had flanges either side of his head, which made his head seem twice the size. The orangutan's loud calls of "I am the boss" helped the male claim his territory. Nahum called females and kept out intruding male orangutans. Zylvia and Nahum were together for only a few days to mate.

With Nahum gone, Zylvia's life with her infant was no longer close to booming calls; it was just the two of them, mother and baby. Her ginger-haired infant had a gentle aura and instant baby appeal. Looking so different from the big male, the infant attracted the jungle hunter-traders, stirring a profound moral temptation in those wanting money. The hunter, with his shiny blade flashing in the light, wanted to go beyond his unlawful presence. He wanted to take the infant out of the forest; but a baby ape does not belong out of the wild. Her mother knew this and did not want to give her baby up. But the hunter-trader knew he could sell the baby in the Borneo market to buyers from around the world. Few cared the trade was illegal. Money was everything and bribes allowed the trade to flourish. A helpless baby wrenched from a mother. So much for assisting the helpless. So much for protection of the voiceless, for respect of genetically-related beings.

Zylvia could not move elsewhere—it was not in her nature. She raised her arms as she tried to protect her baby. The trader swung at the mother with his machete, slicing off Zylvia's fingers, which were held out in feeble defense. The machete swung again, severing Zylvia's hand. As the hunter raised his machete blade above his head, there was no obstruction between the jungle marauder and infant orangutan. Another blow at the mother's neck took off Zylvia's head. What horror was this in the peace of the forest? Bright red blood pumped onto the forest floor, spurting, spurting and spurting. Strong hands put the frightened little orangutan in a sack. *He was one of thousands abducted when their mothers were killed.*

Chimpanzees, gorillas, humans and orangutans together form the taxonomic family *hominidae*. The orangutan has 97% of our genes. Zoo-keepers regard orangs as highly intelligent. According to James Lee of Harvard University, orangutans are the most intelligent of all animals except Man, even brighter than chimpanzees (Randerson 2007). They also have imagination. A four-year-old orangutan can pretend to groom a doll, pluck bugs off its fur and feed the bugs to the toy. They show us we are not alone in our ability to invent, plan and contemplate. At the Great Ape Trust of Iowa, one keeper associated with orangutan Azy for 25 years said his ape-friend had a rich mental life, showing cerebral flexibility and being able to understand another individual's perspective (Morell 2008).

Gerd Schuster, Willie Smits and Jay Ullal spent many years helping and observing orangutans in the jungles of Indonesia and Borneo, recording their findings in the book *Thinkers of the Jungle*. One thing the men discovered is that the red apes are more humane than humans. These 'three wise men' describe the chainsaw massacre of the orangutans' forest home, and the slaughter and starvation of our closest relatives. Because they are far more gentle than the illegal poachers and loggers of the palm oil industry, it is easy to overlook that orangutans are seven times stronger than the average human.

A rickshaw driver, Becak, told the authors of *Thinkers Of The Jungle* about his nephew who worked as a woodcutter for a palm oil plantation. The nephew was one of many who cleared the native forest with screeching German chainsaws. The loggers knew which trees to destroy using the petrol-driven saw, but not much about orangutans, except the apes were slow, careful thinkers who took no risks to stay alive. No-one had told them how the cautious and careful forest dwellers, high in the trees, hand down their botanical knowledge from generation to generation. Or that orangs are jungle gardeners—many seeds only start germinating after passage through the orang intestinal tract. If the orangs die out, numerous fruit trees in the forest will die, as fruit seeds can only be spread through ape faeces.

Becak's nephew came to the last standing tree, at the top of which he saw an orang who had taken refuge. *Screech* went the chainsaw. The tree crashed down, and so did the red ape, pinned beneath a thick branch. The woodcutter hacked at the helpless ape. Other woodcutters came running, wielding their machetes. The pinned primate was close to death.

Suddenly a large orang appeared from trees nearby, grabbed the nephew's thigh in his strong ape hands and snapped the wood cutter's femur. The woodcutters freed the nephew and hacked the ape-rescuer to death. What the rescuer did was sheer suicidal madness. There were no trees close enough for him to escape to. He could have waited in his hiding place and gradually killed the woodcutters on by one. It was animal altruism in its purest form.

Willie Smits, who knows as much about the red apes as anyone on earth, acknowledges an orang knows each tree in his area of 300 hectares, and knows every plant from another. Orangs therefore have knowledge of around 1,000 jungle plants—which are edible, which aren't, which are health-giving and which are toxic. Smits observes that when an orang passes a tree of half-ripe fruit, he heads back to the tree on the exact day the fruit is ripe. The orangutan sense of smell, as far as we know, is as vestigial as that of humans. And how many of the 10,000 shades of green can they recognise in the forest?

Red apes rise from their tree nest at around 7 am, eat for three hours, perhaps upside down, and then take a nap. The mother-infant bond is closer than any other animal, the mother keeping her baby close for eight years. Their vision and memory is better than the average human. Orangs open coconut shells for which we would need an axe. Their jaws are as strong as a wolfhound's, their fingers perhaps seven times stronger than human fingers. Big males can crack open the fruit of *Neesia* trees, breaking through the almost 2 cm thick steel-tough shells into the highly nutritious kernel. (The distribution of *Neesia* is confined to South East Asia—western Indonesia, Malaysia, Thailand, and possibly Burma).

The three wise men ask how it is possible that 4,000-6,000 orangutans, genetically so close to us, are cruelly and wantonly killed without howls of protest in the media, boycotts, demonstrations in front of Indonesian institutions, wood, paper and palm oil companies? Their book also talks of the Dayak[1]* women who selflessly give round-the-clock care for the orphaned orangutans. When the young apes choose a Dayak surrogate mother, it will not go into the forest without her. Looks of love abound between red ape and Dayak carers.

Smits relates something which happened to an Indonesian scientist, Dr Suce Utami, working for Orangutan Survival. She would rather not talk about such an incident herself, but during her six months' observation of a large male orang, Willie said the story must be told. On her own, the scientist had been quietly watching the ape from a respectful distance on the forest floor. Suddenly, two illegal loggers attacked her, trying to rape her. The wild orang, who had ignored Dr Suce for months, climbed down from his tree, breaking off thick branches with

---

[1] * Various indigenous Borneo people

his strong hands as he marched towards the thieves. The ape put the thieves to flight. The shaggy red ape waited patiently, close to Dr Suce, until she regained her composure, and then climbed back to his treetop. An unsolicited act of kindness, rescuing a woman in serious trouble. It was all in a day's work.

Orangutans are the only great apes in Asia, and they need our care. But they are fast becoming an endangered species. As increased farmland is taken over for palm oil production, hundreds of orangutans, robbed of a home, have descended into villagers' vegetable gardens. There they are shot and killed. It is not just because multinational companies seek profit and palm oil plantations have been carved out of the rainforest. The local Indonesian has to make a living, feed his children. Palm oil brings in dollars easily, but at the price of taking the home from orangutans who have nowhere else to go.

The males, about two thirds the size of a gorilla, are found in tropical rainforests in northern Sumatra, Indonesia and in low-lying swamps of Borneo. The swamps sit on metres-deep carbon-rich peat. The palm oil and timber barons have made sure Indonesia is the world's third largest greenhouse gas emitter. Forest fires follow clear felling of timber. The government, and those with empty bellies wanting to sell timber, will not restrict the clearing of peat forests. In spite of a presidential ban on the clearing of peatlands, Indonesia's Forestry Minister has blocked prosecution of the illegal loggers (Forbes 2007).

When great slabs of forest are cleared, it is not as though we kindly place the orangutans outside the forest. Baby orangutans are often captured and sent around the world to be used as pets, even though they should never leave the forest. Pony the orangutan was found not in the jungle but in a brothel, chained to a bed. In the jungle, high in the trees, Pony was clever enough to craft tools to get her own food. In the brothel, she was humiliated day and night. She could not move about and smelled of her own excrement. Luckily, the Indonesian army set her free and she slowly learned to be an orangutan again.

At the supermarket, insufficient labelling means we do not know if the vegetable oil we buy is the palm oil produced through the destruction of the orangutan's habitat. The words 'palm oil' do not appear on the bread packaging, the biscuit packet or on the brightly labelled bottle. We consume palm oil not only in ice cream, noodles and chocolate, but also in products which keep our bodies comfortable, soaps, shampoos, cosmetics and toothpaste. Is this really worth the loss of hectares of forest, gone forever? Another reason we see cleared land is because we use Merbau timber in our homes. Merbau (Kwila) is a naturally oily hardwood with high tannin content. Very durable, it is resistant to termites and decay, and most commonly used for timber decking. But we should avoid buying Indonesian Merbau timber, as the animal price is too great.

Nobody knows the full price of taking out the next generation of orangutans. Will our demand for biofuels be the next threat faced by the red apes?

But there is hope, thanks to a lot of tireless conservationists, veterinarians and animal rights' activitists. Zookeepers Fleur Butcher and Jessica McKelson have visited Borneo, using their expertise to construct protective runs for the orangutans, educating the locals on how to weld metal and make money from the enterprise. Australian veterinarians Tim Rich and Tristan Mann have tried to educate locals in Borneo about alternatives to eating orangutan meat. They also taught Borneo orangutan keepers about treating the injured.

According to Jessica McKelson, "Indonesia needs an influx of conservation-minded people. Although President Yudhoyono is forest-minded, local authorities are not keen to follow their President's wishes and will need international urging to save the forests."

## Hope from the Bali Conference

At the Bali Climate Change Conference in 2007, Indonesian President Soesilo Bambang Yudhoyono launched an Orangutan Conservation Strategy and Action Plan from 2007-2017, saying, "As many as 50,000 orangutans have been lost over the past 35 years due to shrinking habitat, and if this continues, these majestic creatures will likely face extinction by 2050." The 10-year program is designed to save endangered orangutans from extinction by protecting tropical jungle habitat from logging, mining and palm oil plantations, according to the President. The plan aims to preserve up to 2.5 million acres of forest on the Indonesian half of Borneo island.

The plan will need world support beyond Indonesia to succeed.

Peter Garrett, Australia's Environment Minister at the time, attended the conference, and pledged Australia's support for helping Indonesia preserve its forests. What can we do to support the President of Indonesia in saving the forests? What can we do to help the school children?

The forest was in balance when discovered by mankind; we must keep it in balance. Trees. Even if the world is about to end, we must keep planting trees. As the famous vegetarian supporter of all primates Jane Goodall says **'the cheapest and most efficient way of slowing down global warming is to protect and restore the forests.'**

So much wildlife depends on it.

*Wildlife space is a sacred site. Avoid products of suspected palm oil origin. Can we stir supermarket staff to protest in groups to their supervisors?*

### Acknowledgment:
*Melbourne Zoo orang keepers Jessica McKelson and Fleur Butcher*

*The Orangutan Project in Australia estimates that 5,000
orangutans were slaughtered in the last 12 months in Borneo
and Sumatra due to the clearing of orangutan forest. In
Indonesia an area the size of six football fields of rainforest is
currently disappearing every minute.*

*Mother I need you, don't leave me! Baby orangs stay with
their mothers for years to learn what they need to know
to survive in the jungle.*

*Wildlife young belong in the wild, not in zoos. The rate at which we destroy their habitat, however, makes leaving them in the wild more challenging. There are thousands of caring people who look after vanishing wild life in free range zoos. Let us make sure there are passionate and dedicated staff who teach zoo visitors. Ask about volunteering.*

# 5 SPIRIT OF THE NORTH— POLAR BEARS ON THIN ICE

Polar bears, originally derived from brown and black bears, represent the world's largest land-dwelling omnivore, yet there are only between 20-25,000 of these proud creatures left worldwide, according to the Swiss-based World Conservation Union. Of these, 4,700 are found in Alaska, where more are digging snow dens on land instead of on sea ice. The mammal thrives in Arctic cold. Their fur acts as a miniature greenhouse, converting sunlight into heat, which is absorbed by the polar bear's black skin. A hungry bear can lope along almost as fast as a racehorse at 40 kilometres an hour. Running on ice is easy for a bear.

Polar bears can be found in Canada and Russia, while some live in Norway and Denmark. Wherever they are, polar bears need expanses of ice for hunting seals, beluga whales (also called white whales) and walruses. A huge bull walrus with tusks is no match for the savagery of the bear, though seals are the preferred prey for the bears, either on the ice or below it. When large prey cannot be found, polar bears eat rodents. The rodent's white fur camouflage does not fool the big bear, which easily picks up small prey by smell and acute hearing. The bears swim underwater to avoid detection while getting closer to their prey beneath the bergs. On land, especially in autumn, the bears feed on plants and, in the towns, sometimes on garbage.

The world of the polar bear is not a silent one. Adult polar bears, when agitated or threatened, indicate their feelings by hissing, growling, champing their teeth, and through soft chuffing. Prey species can learn too late to recognise an agitated bear. And that includes Man. People can spend too long listening instead of moving off. Bear talk can be a warning to stay out of range or be eaten alive. Polar bears are one of the few species on Earth that will hunt people down and kill us for food—behavior that contrasts quite starkly with what children learn about Winnie the Pooh.

This shaggy omnivore, three metres long and weighing half a tonne, commands respect. A mouthful may not be a young seal's head but a human face. Bear injuries on people are horrendous. The 19th century naturalist Edward Nelson recounted:

The Eskimo of Saint Lawrence Island and the American coast are well supplied with firearms, which they use when bear-hunting. In winter, north of the straits, the bears often become thin and very savage from lack of food.

Men went out from Point Hope during one of the long winter nights to attend to their seal nets, which were set through holes in the ice. While at work near each other, one of the men heard a bear approaching over the frosty snow, and having no weapon but a small knife, and the bear being between him and the shore, several times; each time the terrified Eskimo held his breath until, as he afterwards said, his lungs nearly burst. The bear suddenly heard the other man at work, and listening for a moment he started towards him at a gallop, while the man he left sprang to his feet and ran for his life for the village and reached it safely.

At midday, when the sun had risen a little above the horizon, a large party went out to the spot and found the bear finishing his feast upon the other hunter and soon dispatched him. Cases similar to this occur occasionally all along the coast, where the bear is found in winter.*

Yet in spite of the danger, the people of the north revere the white bear as a source of great spiritual power and wisdom. The bear is considered the 'Spirit of the North', and thought of as family.

But the existence of the polar bear is becoming threatened. Winters in Canada's Hudson's Bay are becoming shorter, with the ice breaking up two and a half weeks earlier than it did 30 years ago. These climatic changes mean the bears have less time to feed and build up fat for warmth, needed to raise their offspring. More alarming, cub survival has dropped, and mother bears may have one cub instead of two, as in the past. The bears are beginning to die out, even being described as an endangered species. There was a 21% drop in numbers from 1997 to 2004 (*The Washington Post* 27/12/06).

Not all agree about declining numbers, however. In the Davis Strait area, the population is up from 850 in the mid-1980s to 2,100 presently, according to biologist Dr Mitchell Taylor, who has been studying polar bears for 20 years. He states:

Climate change is having an effect on the West Hudson population of polar bears, but . . . there is no need to panic. Of the 13 populations of polar bears in Canada, 11 are stable or increasing in number. They are not going extinct, or even appear to be affected at present. It is noteworthy that the neighbouring population of southern Hudson Bay does not appear to have declined, and another southern population (Davis Strait) may actually be over-abundant.**

Press reports, while alarming, are difficult to verify. In September 2004, US Government scientists saw 55 bears swimming offshore in Alaska's Beaufort Sea. Was it a mass migration? Bears drift on bergs but do not regularly swim long distances. If they swim farther than their health or body fitness dictates, they tire and may drown. The scientists saw 'four bears die and some so hungry they were eating each other'.

As climate change slowly moves wildlife into places they do not choose to be, so politicians are moved by voters concerned about global warming. While politicians are thinking about what to do, shrinking ice moves polar bears from solid ice, tipping them into the Arctic Sea. They thus find themselves in deep Arctic water instead of on solid ice.

## Bringing us together

The polar bears are bringing us together. An international agreement on the conservation of polar bears was signed in Oslo on 15 November 1973 by those nations that have polar bear populations—Canada, Denmark, Greenland, Norway, the US, and the former USSR.

Signatory nations agreed to prohibit random hunting of polar bears and to outlaw the common practice of hunting bears from aircraft and icebreakers. The agreement also obliged each nation to protect polar bear denning areas and migration patterns, and to conduct research in the conservation and management of polar bears. Finally, the nations agreed to share their polar bear research. Scientists of the Polar Bear Specialist Group now meet every three to four years under the auspices of the World Conservation Union to coordinate ideas on polar bears throughout the Arctic. Who said we couldn't do it?

The Oslo agreement was one of the first and more successful international conservation measures enacted in the 20ᵗʰ century. Its legacy continues, with member scientists from each nation continuing to work together. They need to—the bears face new threats of not only climate change, but also pollution, industry and poaching.

Veterinary care is also needed. Cases of leptospirosis, rabies and morbillivirus have been recorded in the bears. They are especially susceptible to *trichinella*, a parasitic roundworm contracted by eating infected seals. Traces of heavy metals have also been detected in bears, as well as ethylene glycol (antifreeze) poisoning. Bears exposed to oil and petroleum products in the sea lose the insulation of their coats, forcing a dramatic increase in metabolism to keep up body heat.

*http://www.mnh.si.edu/arctic/html/polar_bear.html ** //meteo. lcd.lu/globalwarming/Taylor/last_stand_of_our_wild_polar_ bears.html*

**Read about** other bear species, and the dancing bears of Rumania tied in captivity, with rings in their noses denied a natural life at *WSPA e News*.

# 6 COMMUNICATION FROM A DOLPHIN

*To the dolphin alone, beyond all other, nature has granted what the best philosophers seek—friendship for no advantage.*
**—Plutarch, Greek moralist and biographer**

The beach was deserted. The Indian Ocean was bright blue and tranquil, the water gently lapping against the West Australian shore. I was standing waist deep and about to finish my swim. "Come in! Come in!" My wife's urgent cry sounded out of place. She was pointing out to sea. "Come in!" I turned and looked. Behind me was a dorsal fin heading straight in my direction. *What the . . . ?*

I was aware that I was in the presence of something which I could not articulate. I had not experienced something like this before. I had no time to think but I knew it was a dolphin and that I was safe. The dolphin somehow told me, though I was unaware of such telepathic power from an animal. Unaware that telepathy involves more than sending and receiving. It was more than thought transference. I felt a connecting and a knowing. Time had slowed. Here was a wild animal, on its own, visiting me. There was no dolphin pod in sight, just this single dolphin swimming towards me.

There were some long seconds, waiting to find if my instinct was right. *I better be right*, I thought, as I made no effort to leave the water.

Then the dolphin came to me, and I had my first close-up view of a streamlined three-metre shiny light grey creature with a short beak. Yes, it was a bottlenose dolphin—a *Tursiops truncatus*, I learned later. For those first minutes I was more interested in dentition than Latin. I had a glimpse inside the mouth—no great open jaws of massive razor teeth looking for a meal. Instead there was a set of friendly-looking conical teeth crowns. The eyes were larger than I expected. And what a blowhole!

Here was the first animal in the wild to ever have sought my company, circling me silently and serenely. I felt honoured as I stretched out my hand and spoke, asking what it wanted, if it was all right, what it wanted me to do. The dolphin seemed to indicate he was male and healthy. I could have sent my thoughts with no words. It is a human deficiency to talk when we do not need to. The dolphin was silent. The sight of me in my swimming togs earned me no squeaks. But no clicks of disapproval at last year's swimming wear style either.

The dolphin circled again. I was probably under sonar scrutiny, a holographic picture of my body energy being scanned. I wished I could have returned the compliment. I was aware that I was a veterinarian in part responsible for the welfare of this being. He swam to within one hand's distance of my outstretched fingers. If I had lunged forward I could have touched the slippery grey skin. But I did not want to touch. It would have invaded the dolphin's space. And I wanted the dolphin's company as long as possible.

For fifteen minutes the dolphin circled about, very self assured, coming in, going out, showing me each eye in turn and how to exhale through the blowhole. If there were words he wanted to say they were, "Hey, look at me" and "Peace—think about me, write about me".

Peace. When he turned once more and the dorsal fin came straight for me again, I hoped peace was the key word. I had heard that a butt from a dolphin nose is very uncomfortable. At more than 40 kph, not something you would look forward to. It is more than the gentle nudge they use to unearth razor fish buried in the ocean floor.

Later, in that marvelous Sea World on the Gold Coast, I learned from the dedicated staff that a dolphin once held a keeper under water long enough to cause concern—but not long enough for drowning. An average adult dolphin weighs 75 kg and can dive 300 metres deeper than a WWII U-boat. (Can I believe a killer whale dolphin, *Orcinus orca*, can go down one kilometre?) A bottlenose can hold its breath for six minutes. Not for me. I like being near the surface best, very close to another deep breath of fresh air. And I don't think I would like 75 kg on my back. I am glad the dolphin and I came to an understanding so quickly.

What about food? We have over fished, our excessive demand encouraging fishermen to do things they should not. Drift nets? Six minutes between breaths helps to explain how dolphins drown in drift nets. How often are dolphins killed because we do not think? Are we balanced about shark control? Shark nets are easy for the sharks to swim around and also easily kill dolphins. Pollution, alas, is an even greater threat (Scheele 1990). Is that what my visitor in the Indian Ocean wanted me to tell the world?

People who spend time with these former land dwellers remark on their sense of humour, quick learning of body language and words, emotional resilience and mental agility. It seems they are more aware of what we call the 'unseen reality' than we are. They have helped the autistic and the artistic—people who paint and who compose soulful music (Wyllie 1993).

It was time for goodbye. He held his head up and, with a wuff from his blowhole, swam out to sea.

Years later mercury killed dolphins on the other side of the Australian continent, in Port Phillip Bay, Victoria. In eight beached dolphins over two years, Monash University scientists found three times the level of mercury considered safe. Decades of gold mining pollution washed the metal deep into the harbour, where it built up in layers of sludge at the bottom. The stranded dolphins were high on the beach, away from the waterline, apparently disoriented. High mercury levels caused brain malfunction, bringing to mind the old saying 'Mad as a hatter', coined from the mental illnesses developed from workers handling mercury treated hats (Morton 2008).

Cetacean beings on this planet are at their best doing good things for others. Moko, a playful bottlenose dolphin, frolicked with swimmers at New Zealand's Mahia Beach, 500 kilometres northeast of Wellington. In May 2008 she responded to distress calls and helped the human rescuers. Not waiting for a photo opportunity with the local press to witness her compassion, Moko swam to help a disoriented pigmy whale and her calf. In spite of help from kind people, mother whale and calf were stranded four times on a sandbar. Human rescuers, unsuccessful at refloating the animals in distress, were thinking euthanasia. Moko pushed between people and whales, directing mother and calf to a deeper channel and safety in the ocean. "It was not unusual," said Anton van Helden, a marine mammal expert at New Zealand's National Museum. "Dolphins have long been noted for protecting people at sea." Dolphins have fun in the open sea and have a rapport with other beings, enjoying ocean rescue. "We've seen bottlenose dolphins getting lifted up on the nose of humpback whales and getting flicked out of the water just for fun."

Back to the mother and calf rescue. Malcolm Smith was among the rescue team and saw the two whales in obvious distress. Something went on between the two cetaceans, part inaudible chatter and part telepathy. Suddenly and willingly, the whales were following the dolphins along the beach and straight out to sea. "It was all over in minutes," said Smith. Moko achieved what human rescuers could not do (Layton-Bennett 2008).

Thirty-seven million years ago, cetaceans resembling whales and dolphins existed. Modern whales and dolphins swam the oceans four to five million years ago, developing bonds so strong that if one whale beached, others followed, preferring death to being alone and away from the pod. After millions of years, along came people who wanted control. Humans thought they were number one, in charge. If they were hungry and saw an animal they could eat, they would kill it. A harpoon into vital organs was one method of killing. Drift nets strong enough to hold a dolphin fatally away from fresh air was another. If all the drift nets in today's oceans were combined together they would be long enough to circle the Earth. Pods of dolphins in the way of tuna fishermen are dragged from the sea. In 1994, 20,000 dolphins were dying each year because they were swimming with tuna (O'Connor and Peterson 1994).

On top of all this is humankind's favourite method of killing—habitat destruction—is a threat less visible than nets. Pollutants flooding into the oceans kill cetaceans.

Swim well, my friend, safe from human poisons and refuse; and keep away from those drift nets.

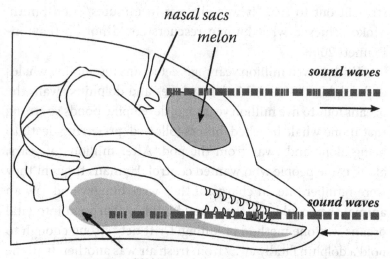

nasal sacs
melon

*sound waves*

*sound waves*

*Fat-filled cavity in lower jaw*

*Dolphins with three times higher than safe mercury levels have been found in Port Phillip Bay, Australia. In other countries where dolphins are not well thought of, after capture the cetaceans are eviscerated alive*

# 7 THE STORY OF SLOW SONG

*There is no way to kill a whale humanely.*
— *Sir David Attenborough*

We know whales by their songs. *LiveScience* staff writer Bjorn Carey writes: 'Whales sing at a low frequency, at the very bottom of the range of human hearing. You have to broaden your listening range.' Their voices are beautifully adapted for long-range transmission. Carey quotes Christopher Clark of Cornell University: '"They are acoustically prolific. By singing at low frequencies, whales are able to communicate across oceans—it's how they keep track of their pod and alert friends of a good place to eat".'

Using an underwater sound surveillance system more typically employed for tracking submarines, Clark and his colleagues zero in on specific whale songs and even track whales based on where the songs originate from.

At the 2005 annual meeting of the American Association for the Advancement of Science, Clark said: "If we went to the shelf-edge of Puerto Rico we could hear blue whales off Newfoundland, 1,600 miles (2,575 km) away."

But Clark and other scientists are concerned about the growing 'acoustic smog' in the world's oceans, particularly the waters near popular migration and feeding routes. Noise in the water is interfering with whales' ability to communicate with songs (Carey 2005). Many have not listened to the world of whales because Man the hunter wants a kill, not to hear a song of life.

The captain of the harpoon boat stood up in excitement. He had seen what he had been looking for, a fountain of frothing spray reaching up beyond the Antarctic Sea's surface. *Slow Song*, one of the world's largest mammals, was pushing out a jet of air and water through his blowhole. The captain of the powerful catcher boat called out, the engine roared, and the harpoonists were in hot pursuit. The whale, once able to avoid the ancient whaleboats of the traditional hunters, was no match for a motorised hunting group—spotter ships with modern technology and twenty men on board.

The crew knew little about their prey. They did not think about the fifty-million-year history of this air-breathing mammal, once land-living but now a dweller of the deep. Unlike ancient indigenous cultures, the crew had no ceremony, no ritual of respect and reverence for an animal larger than a dinosaur. The dinosaur had gone but the whale had survived for millions of years. Driven by the hunting instinct, the crew thought that *Slow Song* was there to be killed.

The captain knew more than most; he had looked inside a whale on the deck of the factory ship with one hundred and fifty crew anchored ten kilometres away. He had seen the quarry cut apart—'processed' they called it. The captain had been gobsmacked when he first saw the chest opened. Inside was something the size of a small automobile with big chambers—the whale's heart. Around the heart were massive lungs, shaped in the contours of the inside chest—giant pinkish sponges which held the air to carry the whale to the bottom of the sea. And the aorta carrying blood from the heart into the whale's abdomen—the captain realised he could fit his own body into this blood vessel.

Yet as massive as the chest was, it was nothing like what he had seen in the head, when he had witnessed the factory crew split open a whale skull. Unlike a dinosaur, the whale skull holds the largest brain of any animal. But the captain's mind was on other things. Never mind being awestruck; never mind that everything from the big cetacean could be sourced elsewhere—whales make money.

The method used to kill whales has altered little since the 19th century, when to penetrate the whale's body and kill by massive shock, the grenade-tipped harpoon was invented.

The surfaced whale, longer than a cricket pitch, was cutting through a salty swathe of sea, keeping pace with the boat at 16 knots (30 kph). The captain hoped this kill would be easier than the last harpooned whale, which could not scream its pain, but the injured animal took an hour and a half to die.

It was 1975 when a group of activists on an old fishing boat caught a Soviet fleet killing sperm whales off the Californian coast. One man, Paul Watson, stood on an undersized floating whale carcass in defiance of the Russians. Later, in 1979, Watson's vessel rammed and wrecked a pirate whaler. "Goddamn you, you whale-killing son of a bitch," shouted Paul. Next it was the Japanese fleet seeking 1,000 whales in the Antarctic summer of 2006—the very whales which migrate along Australia's east and west coasts each winter. Sea Shepherd with Paul Watson has sunk or put out of action ten Atlantic whaling ships.

Paul Watson, spirited founder of a group of extreme activists known as the Sea Shepherd Conservation Society, was born in Toronto in 1950. The muscular activist is greatly concerned at the indifference people show towards the extinction of plants and animals, and he is prepared to go where no other activist is.

In 1981 he secretly entered Siberia to document a Soviet food processing plant which was converting illegally harvested whale meat into animal food. Watson out-manoeuvred the Soviet navy around a pod of grey whales. He also slipped past the KGB. In 1985 he brought the Canadian seal hunt to near standstill by blocking the port of St John's, Newfoundland, announcing he would ram any sealing vessel that left the wharf. He has targeted Iceland and scuttled two ships owned by Iceland's largest whaling company in Reykjavik's harbour, though this had the unfortunate consequence of turning many Icelanders against the cause of saving whales. It is because of these kind of extreme tactics that Greenpeace, which Watson helped found, no longer wants anything to do with him.

But Watson makes no apology for his aggressive anti-whaling actions, explaining his feistiness as follows: "When you are dealing with a species as arrogant as the human race, you've got to be arrogant to believe you can change it." These days he continues to fight the anti-whaling cause aboard the Sea Shepherd owned vessel, the *Steve Irwin*, which in February 2009 collided with the Japanese whaling vessel the *Yushin Maru Nr 2* while attempting obstruct the ship's whaling activities. In February 2010, Sea Shepherd vessel *Bob Barker* collided with the Japanese whaling ship *Yushin Maru No. 3*.

Peter Singer, well-known philosopher and author of *Animal Liberation*, has the last word on the activist, calling Watson a 'hero' (Khatchadourian 2008).

Thanks to dedicated environmentalists like Watson, there are hopeful signs in the anti-whaling campaign. Japan's new cost-cutting government flagged plans to scrap the interest-free loans their whaling industry relied on. Nine-hundred and thirty-five minke whales could be saved from Japanese whale hunting in 2009 (Darby 2009). At least Japan is talking about it.

The thirty men from Greenpeace harried the catchers in inflatable runabout boats pushed along by outboard motors. They were clad in waterproof clothing but were unprotected from the powerful water cannons positioned on the catcher ship that could easily have knocked them into the freezing sea.

An injured whale, internally damaged, was hard for the hunters to see, as it could disappear into the deep. When the quarry surfaced again, the hunters aimed another grenade, this time closer to the heart. No-one on board realised the full extent of what they were doing. They didn't understand that man is capable of wiping out a species. No-one on the catcher ship bothered to question why they were killing this gentle giant when the Earth has alternatives to whale meat and whale oil.

The fact that *Slow Song* and his seven-octave song had swum half-way round the world to feed on fresh krill didn't occur to the captain. In the once safe Antarctic seas it was now completely defenceless against the power of a modern pursuit vessel's harpoon. *Slow Song*'s ancestors had moved from land millions of years before to escape predators. Now taking in air above the surface and breath-holding below it, he was cutting a graceful figure through the open sea.

An hour earlier he had swum up from the ocean depths impenetrable to humans. Needing fresh air, the Earth's largest creature had emerged to breathe out waste air through the blowhole positioned atop his head.

## Beaked whales dive deepest

The world of breath-hold diving has a new champion. Beaked whales, any of at least 20 species of medium-sized toothed whales, regularly plunge deeper beneath the waves than any other mammal. The beaked whale is among the most elusive of cetaceans, rarely spotted at the surface. To find out more about the life of the beaked whale, Peter Tyack and colleagues at the Oceanographic Institution in Massachusetts attached tags to whales in the Mediterranean in 2003 and 2004. The team found that Cuvier's beaked whale dives to more than 1,000 metres on average to hunt for the deep-sea squid that makes up most of its diet. While it is common for these whales to be submerged for between 20-30 minutes, the deepest recorded dive reached 1,882 metres and lasted for 85 minutes, making them the deepest diving air-breathing animals known (*Journal of Experimental Biology*, vol 209, p 4238).

In making their long journeys to forage in the deep sea, the beaked whales pass beyond the point where their bodies exhaust their oxygen stores, and switch from aerobic to anaerobic metabolism. "Deep-diving whales may take as much biomass out of the deep prey layer as all human fisheries," Tyack says. They are the only marine mammals known to routinely push past this limit during dives.

Beaked whales range in length from between four to 13 metres, and can weigh anywhere between one to 15 tonnes. Their key distinguishing feature is a 'beak', somewhat similar to that of many dolphins. Vier's beaked whale, also known as the goosebeak whale, is one of the twenty named species of beaked whale. It is so rarely seen that almost everything known about this small whale has come from studying stranded specimens. Cuvier's beaked whale has a tendency to strand more often than any other species of beaked whale. Stranded specimens have been noted in all oceans of the world except in both polar regions—an indication of an extremely wide distribution.

## Cuvier's beaked whale

Cuvier's beaked whales have a robust body and a small head which is about ten percent of its body length. Its forehead slopes to a poorly defined short beak, and its mouth turns upward, giving it a goose-like profile. This species has a depression behind the blowhole which ends in a distinct neck. Its blow is small and not very noticeable, and is projected slightly forward and to the left. One of its more interesting features is that the adult male has two large teeth, about five centimetres long, which protrude from the tip of the lower jaw. The males use these teeth in fights with each other over females. For their part, the females have smaller, more pointed teeth that remain embedded in the gums. The lower jaw of the Cuvier's beaked whale extends well beyond the upper jaw. Like other beaked whales, the Cuvier's has two deep, V-shaped throat grooves.

Cuvier's beaked whales vary greatly in colour. Its back may be rusty-brown, dark grey, or fawn coloured, and the underside of the body may be dark brown or black. As it ages, first the head and neck and then the body become more lightly coloured. The heads of old males are almost completely white. The back and sides of this particular species, especially the males, are often covered with double-lined scratches caused by the teeth of other males. Its sides and belly are covered with oval white patches.

The maximum length of Cuvier's beaked whale is 7 m, while the average male is 5.5 m in length and weighs 2,500 kg.

Cuvier's beaked whales are found in all the oceans of the world except the polar regions of both hemispheres. They prefer deep water of over 1,000 m and avoid shallow coastal areas.

The captain stood behind the harpoon gun, his legs apart for balance. As the catcher boat quickly drew closer to *Slow Song*, he took aim with great care. He knew how to shoot a harpoon and considered himself a skilled marksman. However, harpooning whales had taught him to accept the words of the naturalist Sir David Attenborough—*"There is no way to kill a whale humanely"*.

At fifty metres the marksman pulled the trigger. He was not on target and the harpoon glanced off, wounding skin near the whale's dorsal fin—skin sensitive enough to feel changes in the ocean currents. The catcher ship fired a second harpoon and then a third. The harpoon and its grenade entered *Slow Song* and exploded. The force of the explosion sent shrapnel through the whale's body. His major organs—heart, liver and lungs—were torn apart. The pain was excruciating.

Instinctively, the whale sought refuge by diving again to deep waters, perhaps to die alone and unseen, in slow agony. He was more fortunate than those whales speared without a rope attached to the buried harpoon. Injured whales not attached to the catcher drift in agony. But the strong rope pulled *Slow Song* back to the surface.

The captain fired again. This time a grenade exploded near *Slow Song*'s brain. While the whale felt intense pain, he could no longer see; nor could he hear his pod calling him or tune into the planet's magnetic field.

With the whale bleeding into the ocean for seventy minutes, the sea turned blood red. Life slowly ebbed from *Slow Song*. There was no more whale talk, no more noisy spouting nine metres "high" above the blowhole. The giant tail and fins became still. The gentle songs of the currents, the fish and the stars were silent.

It isn't just with harpoons that man kills whales. They also suffer the slow, silent death from poisons in the sea flowing in from factories and herbicides we put on the land. Only public conscience will stop pollution and global warming.

Although commercial whaling has been banned since 1986, 32,000 whales have been killed since the ban came into force*. In addition, Japan and Norway have repeatedly announced their long-term intention of continuing whaling and resuming commercial trade in whale products.

*http://www.panda.org/what_we_do/endangered_species/
cetaceans/threats/whaling/whales_killed/*

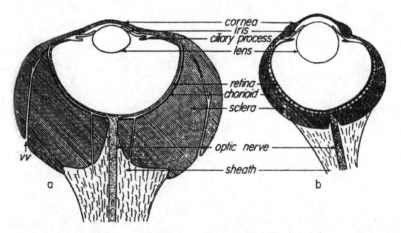

Whale eyes after Putter, Walls GL (1967).
*Thickened eye tunics around the light sensitive ocular layers allow deep diving cetaceans to survive deep sea pressures.*

# 8 REQUIEM FOR A JUNGLE GIANT

In 2005 there were reports from Africa that poachers and rangers had come to an agreement. There would be no more killing of the precious mountain gorillas. It was happy news. There would be no more groups of rangers standing sadly with heads bowed in the Congo's Virunga Jungle, silent witnesses to murder of man and beast. It was finally agreed that the big silverbacks (named so because of the grey or silver saddle of hair on the mature male's lower back) would be given a fair go. As a result of this gentlemen's agreement, we would have gorillas in our midst.

Now we hear differently. Hunting is a pre-eminent threat. So is loss of gorilla habitat. Renowned paleontologist Richard Leakey, who studies prehistoric times by examining fossils ('paleo' means 'ancient'), and others tell us groups of charcoal merchants have begun to harvest the gorillas' forest home in the Virunga National Park forests. The old trees are going, fuelling a $30 million per year charcoal industry, so much more in keeping with mankind's destructive ambitions for the planet. Where the forests are commercially harvested, so we must go, at least in our hearts and with our wallets.

Virunga, Africa's oldest park, is home to 700 mountain gorillas. A giant silverback alpha male called Senkekwe lies slaughtered. With the leader dead, the unity of the whole gorilla troop is under threat. Senkekwe is stretched out on a wooden frame of saplings and carried from the site of his slaughter to be amongst his friends, some of the 600 rangers patrolling the vast park. While the rangers mourn, the great ape's arms are stretched out in death, Christ-like, on the forest floor. There is a smell of death beneath the trees. To keep flies away, someone covers Senkekwe's face with a large jungle leaf.

One hundred and twenty dedicated rangers have been killed in the line of duty since 1994. Ranger Paulin Ngobobo, 43, lives in fear of his life. While he was lecturing villagers about the threat of forest destruction from the charcoal industry, men in military uniforms showed up (Johnson 2007). In front of his audience, they tied Ngobobo's arms on the wooden frame used for carrying the dead Senkekwe. The tallest soldier of the army troop removed his shirt to show his own muscled shoulders and then stripped off Ngobobo's shirt and flogged the ranger. At every bite of the whip, Ngobobo held his teeth clenched, silently counting each gorilla he had loved and lost. Counting the blood marked lines of red swollen skin on Ngobobo's back, a ring of soldiers restrained the villagers, who were asking who would save the gorillas from extinction.

Can anybody offer an alternative living to withdraw people from the cabal of charcoal merchants?

Two days later a gunman killed another of the female gorillas under Ngobobo's care. What is at risk in the jungle is more than the rangers' spirit. Do we stand to lose more than a great ape's life? Many observers of free living great apes, including Jane Goodall, Diane Fossey and others, have taught the apes to use human sign language. They have found apes to be free-thinking and self-aware. Apes form lasting social bonds, to have a rich social and emotional life. The apes plan ahead, surpassing some humans in their level of organisation and what they can do.

How deeply do they feel when one of their family dies? Dr Penny Patterson, of the California Gorilla Foundation, taught a lowland gorilla, Koko, more than five hundred words of sign language. This allowed Penny to understand Koko's request for a kitten for her birthday. When the kitten escaped and was killed by a car, the language researcher could feel deep compassion for her gorilla's high-pitched sobs (Kowalski 1999).

Compassion passes freely across species. At Brookfield Zoo, near Chicago, a three-year-old managed to climb the gorilla enclosure guardrail, falling two flights of concrete below the footpath level. He ended up unconscious among the great apes. Immediately one of the gorillas, Binti, with her own eighteen-month-old infant clinging to her back, cradled the boy in her arrns, carrying him to the nearest exit, where paramedics revived the injured boy (Kowalski 1999).

At Brookfield Zoo the injured boy was helped by a gorilla and lived. But in Africa, the killing of gorillas continues along with the demand for charcoal.

*With a canine mix of loyalty and independence, Maremmas are bred and trained to care for vulnerable beings (eg sheep or wildlife) at risk from wild dogs. Her protective power comes from a sense of territory, inherited from the wolf.*

# 9 THE SHEEP DOG AND THE PENGUIN

On Middle Island, close to the beach at Warrnambool, off the southwestern Victorian coast, there were about 2,000 fairy penguins in the 1900s. Foxes and local dogs gradually killed them off until only 27 penguins remained, when a sheepdog called Oddball, belonging to chicken farmer and animal activist Mr Swampy Marsh, came to the rescue. With her three canine maremma friends, Oddball had been out with the flock on guard protecting the farm's Rhode Island red chooks, allowing them to live free range. Her protective power comes from a sense of territory, inherited from the wolf. Oddy was one of four, as the dogs worked best as a group. One of the dogs acted as the leader, while the others stood by to help if needed. What was their thinking? Wolf-like habits prevailed—everything had to be in order on their patch.

## Original dogs chose us as friends, not we them

The maremmas (pronounced Ma-REM-mas) were bred in Italy to guard large flocks of sheep. Originally they lived day and night with the flock in their care, their white coats in harmony with the wool of the sheep. Their main attraction was their loyalty and independence. The young pups were reared in the farmhouse like many farm dogs, but with a difference. If the owners wanted them to become pets on the farm, they had to stay at home with them all the time. Especially if they are to make good pets, maremmas needed someone always at home. Similarly, they needed to be taken into town to become streetwise.

It is in their nature to be minders, and this trait was encouraged by Man with breed selection over many years to be one of the livestock-guarding breeds. Fortunately this has not been interfered with for the 2,000 years the dog has been in human company. Being typical dogs, they read our body language. If they tip over the flowerpots, they know we are angry by noting where our muscles are moving us and where our eyes are looking. As all dogs, and probably most animals, they have a psychic connection to people. Between 4-14 weeks, when the pup forms its social bonds, they are taught to be attentive to another species, such as sheep, but not people (Fox 1971). You can see a maremma pup sniffing a young lamb nose-to-nose in a sheep shed, though as dogs they are prevented from playing with livestock to be guarded (Coppinger and Schneider 1995). Living with livestock as an adult dog in the paddock, they are trustworthy but miss their owners. One maremma swam back to Swampy from Middle Island after three weeks because she missed him.

Maremmas are good at minding children, happily guarding against any kind of danger. Sometimes they are more than just good babysitters. One day an autistic boy who had never spoken, was walking down the street. Attracted to the big dog with an uneven coat, he wanted to stroke the first shaggy dog he had ever seen. His eyes bright and with a happy smile, the six-year old stroked the Maremma dog. And then the boy spoke his first words.

Maremmas are not aggressive, but they are fierce guard dogs for those they protect. The problem is they sometimes guard too obsessively. Strangers at your house must be cautious.

They should not march into the dog's space, but let the dog come to them. You must socialise your dogs; establish friendship early with a maremma. Farmers who do not make friends with their young dog will find the maremma will bark vigorous displeasure when a farm owner walks inside his own maremma-guarded paddock.

Other working dogs look to their owners for direction, but maremmas are independent enough to make their own decisions. If involved in something more interesting than being in your company, they do not obey or come when called. This upsets farmers who are used to an instant canine response to voice, whistle and gestures from their working dogs. The dog's different working style means farmers do not use maremmas as widely as they could to protect livestock such as new lambs.

Maremmas live happily with other animals, as long as they are the boss. They care most commonly for cattle, sheep and goats, but also for dogs, birds, chooks and other livestock. They can play a role in the care of threatened species. Maremmas are physical in their affection—they lean on you, and they may paw you to claim your attention. A claw scratching your hand sharpens the mind, suggesting you need to concentrate on talking to your dog. Maremmas are also playful, sometimes confronting for people not used to big dogs.

Training children and pups of all breeds when young is the best prevention of dog bites. When approaching strange maremmas or when they approach you, safety rules apply as they do to all breeds—avoid eye contact, let the dog come to you rather than you go to the dog; once in close, approach the dog from the side and allow the dog to sniff your hands.

An adult male maremma can grow up to 73 cm tall, the size of a miniature horse, and can weigh up to 45 kg. A female can reach a height of 68 cm and weigh up to 39 kg. The abundant coat makes the dog look bigger. They have a soft mouth when carrying a small animal, similar to retrievers. Their strong jaws and teeth appear daunting for a stranger receiving a traditional maremma greeting—a getting-to-know-you sniff in the crotch. Their voice is more daunting than their teeth.

One day a tractor broke down in Swampy's paddock, and was abandoned while Swampy walked to the machinery shed to fetch fuel and oil. One of Swampy's maremma dogs stood and barked at the parked tractor for five hours. A tractor did not belong there in the paddock. The tractor had to know its place—in the tractor shed.

Swampy himself could have problems; he was accepted in his working clothes, but should he be dressed up for social reasons, his expensive pinstripe suit and red tie were not to their taste. He was on the outer, regarded as a stranger until the dogs caught his smell.

Oddball was indeed a bit of an oddball; she thought the penguin flock were simply her old chook friends dressed in dinner suits. Swampy, who was her owner-partner in wildlife protection, could look after himself; he was down the social scale in shirtsleeves, but Oddball was sure all dressed up toffy bird friends needed looking after. She was governed by her ingrained sense of territory, a much stronger instinct than in most other dog breeds. The farm was her patch, and with maremma friends standing by, she had to be there to stop the penguin carnage.

There were adjustments Oddball had to make on Middle Island. The penguins casually came home at strange hours after dark, waddling up the beach in no apparent hurry, calling "Quack-quack-quack" to each other. That did not sound like Rhode Island reds. Then her charges disappeared into shallow, poorly protected sandy burrows. It was to her dismay that she discovered her new friends were day-night birds, with much of the noisy penguin activity taking place at night. When does a caretaker get her rest? What about a penguin having some quiet time after a hard day of flippers beating, feet kicking, flying for miles through the water, barely pausing before diving deep for krill? But these penguins didn't come home for a rest. It sounded more like they were getting ready for a party. Oddball saw penguins standing for power-naps—four minute sleeps, ten second sleeps. How uncomfortable. Hadn't they heard of sitting on perches for a sound snooze?

Oddball had *some* quiet pleasure; at least on Middle Island she was far away from a 4 am Rhode Island *cock-a-doodle doo*. It was a short-lived joy of silence, however. Her new friends did not stop talking as they walked from the sea. They chattered on at the burrows, giving out a *kak-kak-kak*, each defending their own private territory. Then penguin pairs got amorous, singing to each other in loud and discordant duets, one bird singing on the inhaled breath, the other bird on the exhaled breath. What a racket. Even copulation did not bring silence—it was a prelude not for sleep but for more song.

Oddball lived upstairs on her new island. Better to have your fostered group living in scooped out sand on a lower level. What was her owner Swampy doing? Camped some distance from the burrows, he slept out in the fresh air. Was it because he did not want to put up with fishy smells and penguin fights?

The livestock-guarding dogs show one species looking after another species, protecting pockets of Australian wildlife from predators. Can mankind be so committed to help other species?

Phillip Island penguins, after moulting, regularly enter Port Phillip Bay to feed before they breed. Fifteen kilometres off Queenscliff, penguins can become tangled in fishing nets. One night, 23 drowned after becoming caught in a shark net. *Twenty-three of our main tourist attractions struggling painfully underwater before dying in distress as a result of human carelessness.*

"Mass drownings are not the only peril. Some penguins come ashore tangled in fishing line, get caught in bushes and strangle," says penguin researcher Zoe Hogg. "Most bait fishermen take care, but the careless ones kill birds." Must shark fishermen put their nets where the penguins feed?

***Acknowledgement:*** Chris Wood

# 10 TO THE TRENCHES

*Men, who like to go to war, take with them other beings that do not.*

## Dogs on the front line

In 1915 a small terrier left his London home, running through the streets in search of his owner. He saw a group of soldiers marching towards Victoria Station and decided to follow them. Trusting his instinct, he jumped into a compartment and travelled with the soldiers to France. Having arrived, he followed the soldiers and managed to find his owner's regiment. This little dog was following a precedent set in the 19th century when a dog would accompany its master on a crusade. This story was depicted in a painting entitled 'The Wanderer sprang towards his Master with delight', which shows the great joy of a reunion—human to animal—whilst the bullets of war were raining down.

Communication between soldiers and their officers was important in wartime, and dogs played a crucial role in this respect, with all varieties of dogs being enlisted during the First World War. When telephone lines were broken and there was no wireless, dogs carried messages in metal cylinders attached to their collars. They leapt over trenches and ran across hazardous terrain, to the front line and back to base, facing the possibility of death on both journeys. As a part of their training for 'duty under fire', explosions were let off near their kennels.

Dogs were able to move five times faster than foot soldiers and were easily camouflaged, with dark coated dogs blending with the mud and being harder to detect. At Verdun, France, during the Great War, 17 soldiers were killed trying to deliver messages. When a dog was sent, it managed seven round trips before it was shot down. If they fell in a shell hole of filthy icy water, they would swim out and carry on their mission.

It was not just the dog's speed, it was its preternatural ability to find its way through the maze of trenches on the battlefield. The presence of the dog also acted as a morale booster for the soldiers, reassuring them that 'help' was on its way. One Airedale dog managed to cover three miles across trenches and shell holes in ten minutes. In New Guinea, during World War 2, US marines tested the speed of dogs versus humans in heavy jungle and heavy humidity. It took a man 15 minutes to emerge from heavy undergrowth, whereas a dog could do it in four and a half minutes.

By 1917, France and Britain had nearly 20,000 dogs at war. The Germans had 30,000—many of which had been acquired in Britain before the war. In 1919 it was estimated that German and British armies had killed 7,000 dogs.

## Pigeon English

During peacetime, pigeons are regarded as vermin, decorating public buildings with their droppings. It was a pigeon, however, that first related news of Wellington's victory at Waterloo. Pigeons are another example of animals providing an invaluable messenger service in the First World War. Although vulnerable to hawks and gale force winds, pigeons did not get bogged down in the mud and could fly long distances without a break. They could not be used in foggy weather, however, as they lost their sense of direction; and if they were not released before sunset they would roost during the night on their way home.

20,000 pigeons were killed in the line of duty during the First World War.

After being trapped in France, one US division of 500 soldiers was reduced to 200 in just 24 hours. A pigeon delivered the message containing this news, flying 40 kilometres in just 25 minutes. In 1914, as the German forces advanced, the head of the Belgium pigeon service burned 2,500 of his birds to prevent them from falling into the hands of the advancing enemy. He sobbed uncontrollably as he did so.

By the end of the First World War, there were 22,000 pigeons in service, looked after by 400 pigeoneers from Salonika to Mesopotamia. The British parachuted 16,544 pigeons into occupied countries, and only 1,800 returned. The 'war to end all wars' was of course followed by another one—the Second World War, in which a quarter of a million messenger-pigeons were active. Pigeons brought back the news that Allied troops had landed successfully on Normandy beaches in 1944 (Gardiner 2006).

## Battle horses

The sea of mud on the battlefields of the First World War claimed many horses as victims. One soldier could not get out of his mind the sight of six men and three horses slowly sinking in the sludge. Men struggled to free themselves, crying out to their fellow soldiers as the mud reached up to their chests and then rose above their shoulders up to their chins. The trusting horses, given to war by their masters, slowly sank with the soldiers—first their legs, then their heaving chests. As equine necks were lost to mud, horses threw their heads up to keep their quivering nostrils above the slush. Their eyes flashed with terror. The mud swept in until the horses could lift their heads no more. A spurt of silent bubbles in the deadly mire showed where a horse paid the ultimate sacrifice for doing his master's bidding.

## Still fighting man's battles

The nature of war has changed since the deadliest day in Australia's history near Fromelles on the night of 19 July 1916, in which 5,533 Australian soldiers were killed (McMullin 2008). We have developed much more efficient methods of killing since then, and we are still involving innocent animals in our battles. In the long running war in Afghanistan, Australian Defence Forces used a two-year-old life saver dog called Nova to sniff out improvised explosive devices. She was responsible for preventing an untold number of deaths, until the day she was killed by a military vehicle. The army tried to save her but the bomb-detection dog was too badly hurt and had to be put down. The soldiers grieved the loss of a good friend. The troops and the army chaplain buried her with military honours (Nicholson 2009).

Animals generally don't involve themselves in senseless killing. We have much to learn from them.

# 11 GALLOPING GOLIATH

Doping racing animals is illegal. The problem is, you don't always recognise when an animal has racing in mind.

There are no animals like Clydesdales. Bo had loved these huge and powerful animals since he saw them pulling strong wooden drays though the streets of Malvern. Their horse shoes made what we kids called *deeter dorter* sounds on the bitumen road, stopping and starting on voice command from the council sweeper walking somewhere near the gutter. Bo and his sister followed the horses, standing so close that they got splashed when the draught animals stretched out to urinate.

What could be a more commanding sight than a team of shiny bay and white Carlton and United Clydesdales, white faces all spruced up, black polished hooves on strong white-feathered legs. The team moved effortlessly in their black harness carrying heavy barrels at the Royal Agriculture Showgrounds.

Bo never considered Clydesdales as racing animals.

One morning, in a paddock at Echuca, Bo had the chance to treat one. A huge and handsome bay Clydesdale gelding named Goliath needed surgery. The gelding had a reputation for an eager showy gait. He was a willing worker, and his quiet behaviour when handled in the yard endeared the horse to those around him.

For months he had been in trouble with a large shoulder tumour, caused by a badly fitting collar. The swelling had not responded to antibiotic injections and now needed surgical removal. It should have been cut out a long time ago. Bo was keen to succeed, but there were a number of factors against him. Amongst other things, the new vet learned that general anaesthesia of large animals was more of a team job than he thought.

"It's a big job. Goliath will need a general anaesthetic so we can remove it all and control bleeding easily," Bo told the owner. "I'll give this anaesthetic by injection into his neck vein. I'll need your help."

The burly farmer, Max, nodded. He seemed to understand what would be required of him during the procedure. After the drug chloral hydrate was injected intravenously, Goliath would slowly and gently go down. There would be a lot of groggy horse to manage when Goliath was getting sleepy. Bo certainly needed Maxwell on the end of the halter rope.

Farmers are generally very practical people, and Max was no exception. Bo told him to hold the halter rope with both hands and arms slightly extended. When the anaesthetic starts to take effect and the horse begins to fall to the ground, the Clydesdale head at the end of the halter can be heavy. Not just heavy, but heavy as a sack of potatoes. The head could in fact hit the ground hard enough to fracture it or cause damage to delicate parts of the eyes. Preventing the head from hard contact with the ground is therefore an essential component of anaesthetising in the paddock.

For the procedure to be trouble-free, as the horse is being anaesthetised, tension on the halter has to be just right. Success depended not only on how much drug went in, but how gently the semiconscious Goliath was allowed to meet the ground. Max needed to hold just enough tension on the rope to ease the big draught horse's head to the ground.

"Put enough tension on the halter to be in control, place your feet slightly apart. That's right. Now lean your body slightly backwards."

Bo arched his back like he was on the bank of the River Murray pulling in a large fish.

"Play out the rope a little, pull in the rope a lot, play out the rope again. Something like reeling in a huge Murray Cod. Ya got that, Max?"

The owner nodded. He looked as though he was really listening. Bo was too young to realise that a nod from someone you are speaking to does not necessarily mean that person has absorbed the instructions.

Max was still nodding to Bo as the needle went into the horse's neck vein. Up went the bottle of anaesthetic, held high above Bo's head. The bottle had a rubber flutter valve on its narrow mouth, allowing air bubbles into the bottle while the chloral hydrate anaesthetic ran out. All was going well. Goliath began to show signs of becoming drowsy. Marked sedation was approaching. The horse was swaying from side to side. It was an ideal response to the chemical in the horse's bloodstream.

Bo was pleased with himself. Although he had barely begun practice, he had learned that careful instruction to owners pays off. He had a brief moment to feel glad he had taken the time to tell Max all about what he had to do. You need a farmer on side for a successful veterinary practice, he mused. Shortly it would be Max's big moment. Bo wondered if he had done anything like this before. Thanks to instruction and teamwork, Goliath would be down and out, lying gently on the ground.

"Are you right, Max? Hold the rope firmly now. Tight rope! Hang on there tight!"

Max's ability to absorb new information was unfortunately not as strong as his arms. Bo had failed to ask a vital question—Have you ever done his before?

Goliath gave one big lurch with his huge hooves, and Max, instead of holding fast at that moment, had a brain scramble. He let go of the halter rope. As he had not been involved in anything like this before (why did Bo not ask?), all instruction was forgotten. The end of the rope flew into the air. The Clydesdale took off through the fence where the two men were standing, drunkenly stumbling through the next paddock. With hooves lifted high like a hackney in the show ring, he cantered through the next fence and broke into an inebriated gallop across open space, heading for all points east.

As the draught horse moved off, Bo was too startled to act immediately. He did not have time to feel horrified. Almost too late he realised he must chase the getaway. He jumped into his Holden car to try to recapture the unwilling patient. It was an unequal race. The vet barely had a chance. Goliath not only had a head start but also was racing under the influence of drugs. Where were the racing stewards when you wanted them? Moreover, the big horse was avoiding the slower route along the track. Bo drove around fences, opening and closing gates. Goliath went through them.

Most clinical learning occurs after graduation. A new medic is typically in a hospital with many doctors. A new veterinary surgeon in country practice can be on his own.

The cross-country race, draught horse against Holden sedan, was no contest. When I made my class laugh telling how they cam learn from mistakes. Somehow Bo, my name as a young boy, stuck in the printing this story. I must confess it was I who didn't ask the farmer have you done this before? I was lucky the only harm done was to my reputation and farmers are so forgiving.

# 12 MOUNTAIN MEN IN THE BAR

The town of Tumbarumba, on the western fringe of the Bago State Forest in NSW, was a rough place populated mostly by timber cutters and cowboys. The families were rugged and so were the children. There were plenty of fights in the Tumbarumba pub, and it wasn't always easy to tell who had won. The men there were tough. One of them killed an injured horse with an axe, in full view of women and children. He could not wait an hour for a vet, or twenty minutes for a rifle. The axe was quicker. Horse lovers stood around, one mother hugging her child to shield her from the killing. Not shielded well enough, the child heard the axe blows and screamed at each crushing of the skull.

You were often out of radio contact when travelling through the mountains, so Dr Andrew Turner, the local veterinarian, found out about his next vet job from a red flag hung outside Judy Terry's motel. The red flag was a signal for him to go to a public phone to take messages about other work in the area. Few words were spoken in this town.

"Excuse me," Andrew asked two pretty twelve-year-old girls standing near the public phone, "could I use the phone?"

"Get f#@*ed," they said—a typical reply in this town in which expletives were not shied away from.

One local cowboy, Tex, rode his horse, Morton, into the hotel. Nothing too unusual about that. Then horse and rider went up the steep stairs to the first floor. It was easy enough going up—horses can climb steep stairs many at a time using their powerful rump muscles. However, in spite of spurs and Snowy Mountain curses, Tex could not turn the horse around and go down again. So the mountain men called the famous vet Bruce MacLean.

Bruce sedated the gelding. He had to be careful. Not too much sedative or Morton would collapse on the stairway too awkward for any hoof lifting. He needed just enough sedation to enable those at the bar to push and carry Morton back to the ground floor. Tex lifted each buckling front leg in turn to place an unsteady hoof on the next step down. Good guess, Bruce. The mountain men carried the drugged horse out the front door to stand and sway at the hitching rail. They had carried many men through the front door but this was the first drunken horse. The men then left Tex to look after Morton while they went inside for another round of drinks.

Dr Andrew the dedicated assistant vet helped Bruce finish his daily list. His working hours were long. A forty-hour week was too short to be thought about. He left home at 7 am and was back home at 9 pm to cook himself spaghetti and mince, washing it down with a cold stubby. The local cowboys did not always appreciate what Andrew did for them, or have it in their minds to give the vet or their cows a fair go.

Judd, who always wore black, was an opinionated black-bearded farmer of few words. Too few words, as a matter of fact, as he did not call Andrew for three days after his cow was trying to calve. Judd's delayed phone call was gross negligence. After such a long delay the calf, in the wrong position to be born naturally, had died and was going rotten. The cow now had toxins in her bloodstream. In veterinary terminology, the cow was septic, a victim of neglect from an owner ignorant of his earthly responsibilities to other beings. Judd offered no apologies to Andrew for not calling him sooner. Andrew spent three hours trying to save the cow by delivering the dead calf. It was a most unpleasant, foul job. It would have been much easier for Andrew to have asked Judd to shoot the cow as soon as he learned the cow had been so long in labour.

Ten days later, after a hard twenty-four hours' work, Andrew was feeling too tired to cook. He went to the pub for his evening meal. Two farmers were having a beer at the U-shaped bar. One of them was Judd. Andrew did not expect thanks for his hard work. Judd was immersed in his beer and did not look up to acknowledge the vet until he had put his glass down.

"Hey, Doc," Judd called out, "you know that cow you calved? She died."

Andrew left the bar. He did not appreciate a public sledging with only one side of the story being told, particularly when the untold side of the story involved the abuse of an animal. Andrew expected truth. He had tried very hard to help man and beast. He could accept the fact he got no thanks from Judd, as all he was concerned with was the welfare of the animals. In fact, his dedication to animal welfare was only strengthened after this incident. Andrew thought of the American Robert Frost's poem, ' . . . but I have promises to keep and miles to go before I sleep'.

*Ignorance and laziness are no defence against cruelty to animals.* Whether intentional or not, the animal still suffers. We have come along way with the improvements in our laws against animal cruelty, but we still have a long way to go.

# 13 THE FIRST CAESAREAN

It was no good. The black and white beauty was easy to identify, as she had a torn ear, but Daisy the cow could not deliver her calf. Try as I might, I could not ease or pull this calf out of the big Friesian. The calf's rear was much too big for the cow's narrow pelvis and birth canal. Stripped to the waist and groping about in the large uterus, I could not even reach the calf's back legs. In calf delivery, you have to know when to stop pushing and pulling. Too much trauma in the pelvic canal causes bruising and can be very painful for the cow.

It would have to be a Caesar. I was a little nervous, as many things can go wrong during surgery. Nevertheless, I had observed plenty of Caesars, equipping me with the calm and confidence to be able to help this cow. Arthur, the dairy farmer, was not the slightest bit fazed. He was probably the best dairyman in the district. I wanted to do this operation on Daisy while she was standing in the bail. Cows do better standing than lying on an operating table. Lying on their side, cows do not belch, causing them to bloat; and trapped gas in the rumen is fatal if not relieved.

I injected anaesthetic into Daisy's flank and blocked the spinal nerves running to the site of the proposed incision on her left side. I scrubbed the skin with Betadine. Next I put the surgical drapes right up to the edge of a proposed bold incision, big enough for the calf to get through. My hand was steady as I held the scalpel and made a gallant cut, as though I really meant business.

Who was to know it was my first Caesar? You must be careful but not timid when cutting through cowhide. No keyhole thinking. An easy error is to make the incision too small for the emerging calf.

*I hope that cut is in the right spot to reach the calf inside,* I thought hopefully, trying to reassure myself as blood trickled onto the drapes.

I pulled the underlying muscles apart with minimum cutting so the deep wound could heal more quickly and resume normal function soon after surgery. As Daisy shifted her weight restlessly, the incision moved under my hands. The cow felt no pain.

I was relieved to find the incision was in the right position, and I could reach the womb easily. Inside the cow, the rumen, the biggest stomach in ruminant animals, takes up most of the abdominal space. The rumen is the fermentation vat where bacteria convert grass to food. It is from this large stomach that when the animal is inactive the partly digested food, in a remarkable reflux, is returned to the cow's mouth as cud for thorough chewing before being (omit re) swallowed again.

I wanted to find the organ holding the calf—the uterus; not the rumen, which can get in the way when operating near where the calf is. It is also a trap for the unwary, who may confuse the massive rumen with a uterus bulging with a calf. And it would not look so good delivering a bucket of digested grass to Arthur in return for his Caesarean fee.

I could feel the calf now, moving about in the uterus so carefully exposed. It is not nearly so good if the calf is dead. A new little heifer pays for my fee. I cut into the most prominent part of the shiny wall of the uterus so the calf could be more easily reached. It was a big incision in the womb for a whopper of a calf. For a moment I was envious of medicos, who like a small wound and a big fee. Vets live with the opposite. I pulled the wet calf out through the flank. Bringing such a big new life into the world is something medicos do not experience.

Arthur and Sonia, his wife, were bright eyed with pleasure at the big calf Daisy had delivered. Dairy people love their cows. Cows are more than milk factories—they are valued companions. Try walking among a dairy herd and you will discover tranquility. Learn your cattle breeds, however. Beef cattle with calves are not such good company. A shake of the head and aggressive steps towards you means move away. *Fast.*

Arthur and Sonia were both helping, their hands easing the calf down out of the incision to the milking shed floor. I put a pessary—a compressed anti-bacterial suppository—into the womb. I sprayed hormone on its distended shiny womb surface to cause the uterus to shrink. I then started stitching everything that needed sewing together.

I was feeling relieved at the safe arrival of the calf. Daisy had not gone down on the dairy shed floor as some cows do during surgery. I checked inside Daisy and my instrument tray to make sure I had not left anything inside that I might have wanted to use again. It is embarrassing if you reach out for your favourite forceps and realise at that minute they are sitting inside another cow you attended to some miles away. A pair of special forceps is never so useful if it is grazing out of your reach in a paddock somewhere.

Daisy's calf was a great looking heifer, a beauty with strong limbs, large dark eyes and long dark eyelashes. What is more appealing than the newborn? She wobbled to her feet and was soon looking for a drink. One animal, with the magic of birth, becomes two. I have never got over the wonder of watching a new life come into the world. It reaches as deeply into my soul as any other part of my life experience.

I now had two very large wounds to suture—womb and skin. Twinges of envy for keyhole doctors returned. But these pangs would not be endured for long. I was in a hurry to get to the next sick cow. I finished suturing and hurriedly packed up. Instruments were put into a bucket of soapy water—thank you, Sonia—for cleaning, ready for the autoclave. You experience a bit of a come down after the high of a calf delivery. You need an assistant because cleaning up seems a bore. I had no attentive vet nurse to clean up but enjoyed the company of the farmer-hosts.

"No thanks, I won't stop for tea. Keep the wound clean. Scrub off any discharge firmly with cotton wool soaked in Betadine. You can take the stitches out in two weeks."

My advice later proved inadequate. At that moment my mind was on the fact that Arthur and Sonia were an experienced team I could trust. "Call me if you see trouble." There, I said it again.

I jumped into my car and was off to the next job, down the road six kilometres to a cow down with low blood calcium, not very aptly called milk fever. My mind had left Daisy. I was now thinking of how to look after an unconscious cow with an intravenous injection of calcium to stop her dying.

I saw Arthur at the sale yards one month later. He was smiling from afar—always a promising sign. Better was to follow. He was generous in his praise.

"You did a beautiful job. Beautiful job."

That was high praise from Arthur. He usually only said things once. But Arthur had more to say in the same enthusiastic tone.

"Three days after the operation, hungry crows sat on Daisy's back and picked a hole through the wound into the rumen."

"Wha-what? Right through, Arthur?" I was aghast, and did not share any of Arthur's apparent satisfaction.

"All the way. Now, whenever she coughs, a fountain of liquid grass shoots out. Up to the sky like a volcano. Fermented grass sprays out everywhere. People passing by lean on the fence to watch. Oh, but you did a beautiful job, a beautiful job." Arthur smiled with pleasure, remembering my great work.

My professional dismay was slightly lessened by the fact that bloat, a fatal stomach distension of gas, is sometimes relieved by making a surgical hole from rumen to skin. But this operation is not usually undertaken by crows in the paddock.

After my next Caesar, I suggested tighter supervision after an operation—a cow rug had to be kept on until the wound had healed. A rug after surgery was a good idea for the cow, but it meant no-one could then see my great work. I had to accept that my light was not only hidden under a bushel, but also under a cow rug.

I later learned about the emotion of cattle birth and death when a calf was slaughtered and roasted by bandits in Central America. For many weeks, until the rainy season came, the cattle herd gathered in a circle where the calf had been butchered, *loudly lowing their grief* (Kowalski 1999). Cows make the same loud calls on dairy farms after their newborn calves are taken away. Humankind wants the milk more than the rightful owners of the life-giving liquid—the calves. As a young vet I did not realise that cows had strong feelings. After calving, cows want their young with them. I just wanted to finish my surgery efficiently and get to the next farm.

What had my casual approach to Daisy's wellbeing taught me? Think, boy, about right and wrong. Think in advance about what might happen. I could have put the calf out of Daisy's reach so that it couldn't suck but where the mother could at least see her newborn. Successful outcomes are all about being wise before potential problems have a chance to be realised. Learning to predict the possibility of trouble and grief was to make me a better vet. *Why should we ever be casual about what animals feel?*

# 14 THE UNSPOKEN BOND BETWEEN ANIMALS AND PEOPLE

The atmosphere of the Dandenong Ranges surrounding me brought back sad memories of when I acted as host to Robert Brodey DVM, an exceptional Canadian veterinary surgeon with a strong passion for birds, who died in a car accident after he returned home to the American veterinary school where he was teaching. We had met in Manhattan, Kansas, where I was teaching, and he came out to Melbourne with his wife so they could see a superb lyrebird in its own forest. The Canadian was ahead of his time in his deep connection with wild birdlife.

I was not fully aware of just how shy lyrebirds living on the Australian east coast are. We had to move so quietly to see their brown-grey chicken-sized body. I got my eyes ready to catch a blur as they ran and dodged rapidly through the dense forest underbrush. I wanted to show my visitor the touch of reddish yellow on its tail, neck and wings, but it would not be easy to pick up. One of the dangers faced by these ground dwellers who roost in low trees at night is an attack from a cat.

Cat owners must confine their pets inside at night, or in caged runs outside when they leave home during the day.

Although I had asked the advice of a local naturalist, I was apprehensive about seeing the bird. Was I on the right track? Then, when we heard the sounds of different bird species singing, quickly followed by a chainsaw and a barking dog, I recalled the lyrebird is a great mimic.

The lyrebird's name comes from the shape of the male's tail, the sixteen feathers of which, when spread out and on display, resemble a lyre, a stringed instrument of the harp class played during recitations by the ancient Greeks.

The Canadians were smiling. We were getting close to a bird, and we were hearing calls that had been passed on from generation to generation. These birds are not only able to mimic sounds they hear in the forest, but sounds going all the way back to the time of the early settlers.

I acted casually, as though finding lyrebirds was easy, but I had followed to the letter the detailed instructions from the Australian birdlife naturalist I had consulted. As we walked silently along, the vet's wife broke her stride and bent down to pick up a one-centimetre paper fragment, which she carefully put into her knapsack. This was a lesson for me from a deeply committed naturalist.

All of a sudden it happened. We stood in complete silence upon seeing two shy brown-grey birds softly clucking to each other. They were scratching for worms and spiders in the leaf litter covering the Sherbrooke Forest floor. I called finding the birds good luck, but on reflection it was more than that. I held my breath, wondering how long we could watch before the birds ran away, using their wings to jump up onto rocks and into branches to find solitude.

Here I was again, years later, in a reverie, returning to the tall eucalypts in the Dandenong Ranges. I drove up the steep drive in search of a dog and a woman called Kate, a stranger to me although I had looked after her father and his guide dog years ago. I was soon meeting Kate and her latest seeing-eye bitch, a mixed breed of golden retriever and labrador. I started to talk to Kate but her dog, no longer in her dog-guide working harness, wanted to talk to me, pushing her head at my hand, asking me to pat her. I found my animal connection.

Kate was born with cataracts—cloudy lenses carried in the genes of her family for four generations. In spite of blindness, she had the courage to marry and have a family. Here was a mystery—why had the genetic lottery from her husband and herself kept their children sighted? It was her good fortune that the parental gene mix did not produce cataracts in her own two children. As a twelve-year-old, Kate had had much more eye trouble. Cataracts were removed, but sixteen eye operations later, disease of her retina cost her the last vestige of sight. Undeterred, she gathered a sighted family around her, with a helpful husband, Ian, who never said 'you can't do that'. Blind people may become over sensitive and can easily feel abandoned by society. So lack of vision strengthened Kate's affinity for abandoned animals.

The unsighted mother, described by some in the workplace as handicapped, overcame being written off because she was blind, and being told, 'We don't want you here, there's no work'. She succeeded in finding work as a customer service officer with her local shire.

Kate spoke freely about what it is like to have a handicap. She does not like to use her guide dog in the house, and this has a downside for her family. Occasionally Ian forgets his wife is blind when he leaves a ladder directly in her way without thinking. Kate, sporting painful bruises on her shins, gets a reminder—Ian is not just a loving husband but a handyman working inside the house.

I sat on a stool in Kate's kitchen. Kate's current guide dog, Qiana, brought me a dog blanket in her mouth while her owner talked about the many animals she adopted. "They were dumped here," Kate said passionately. "People don't try to understand animals." Kate has adopted a cat, a horse, a goat and chooks, all courtesy of people who could either no longer care for their animals or because the animals arrived from owners who had died. We might ask, who did the adopting—Kate or the animals? Feelings between animal and a foster parent travelled freely both ways.

Sighted people take their vision for granted, and many think that disadvantaged people do not matter. You don't have to worry what change you give a blind person. When people are 'different' and perceived to be handicapped, they are at first glance considered to be a lesser person. People often equate a handicap with not being bright, so why not short change those who cannot see? When Kate is counting money, coins are easy to feel but a blind person has to know exactly what dollar notes she has in her purse.

Kate recalled the time when bad news was emotionally too much for her. After her doctor told her she had the extra health challenge of cancer, Kate went to the paddock, crying. Blindness and now this! Her loyal quarter horse picked up her distress, came up close and stood beside her. Kate knew horses felt for their owners—that's how performance horses jump the hurdles and win races—and she could show her grief freely to her horse, out of sight of her young children. She stood with her horse for a long time, her sides heaving. The horse nudged her arms, her side and her chest.

Kate's closeness to her animals reminded me that we are composed of birds and beasts, rocks and grasses, because in one way or another all biological matter is related.

One day a new guide dog, Quarry, arrived. "We bonded from day one; I adored him. This endearing soul was my best mate." I was already won over to Kate's bond with animals. It was not the words or how she said it, but what went unspoken that reached into my being. Kate, with her unsighted eyes earnestly gazing at my face, spoke words with more strength than most I have heard. "Our connection was deep, exactly what you might think, and we *totally* bonded."

I was moved to tears by Kate's spoken and unspoken communication. In her emotional attachment to her dog, she had journeyed into territory where words were not enough. Here was the spirit of kindness, the bond of life, the invisible energy cord between dog and humans, the spirit holding humankind and animals together. I usually do not show such emotion to people I have just met. I kidded myself she did not know I had a handkerchief at my eyes, but I confessed

Who knows when the first animal-care person emerged? When mankind began to farm instead of hunt for food, early vets became involved. Healthy meat production was a priority. Animals were confined and, no longer free to roam and choose healing herbs, needed higher levels of care. There were more diseases to be controlled. Slowly it was appreciated that people needed more than food and clothing from animals. We needed someone to be with, such as dogs domesticated as long as 15,000 years ago (Lagoni, Butler & Hetts 1994). The dean of one American veterinary college has said that animal-to-man bonding is the prime reason for a veterinarian's existence.

nevertheless. "You're making me cry," I said, though I was sure she already knew.

Kate's bond with her guide dog was strong but the frailty of life was about to reveal itself. At seven years of age, Quarry copied his owner and grew a malignant cancer. Quarry's neoplasm was behind his ear. Kate's vet gave his opinion—the next cancer growth would be deeper. When would it spread to his spleen? It could be life threatening without warning. Quarry's diagnosis affected Kate at a deep level.

Quarry had four operations and could need more surgery together with chemotherapy. Kate had her dog but she didn't have her healthy dog. A cure seemed impossible. It was as though Kate loved her dog too much. "I could not work my dog almost at his retirement age in that state," she said. There was pain and bravery in her words. She tried to explain her deep sadness as I sat on her kitchen stool. Qiana, her current seeing-eye dog, came from behind and nudged my legs. Perhaps Kate's words alone could not tell me of the pain a blind person feels when breaking the bond with a canine guide, so the dog was telling me as well.

It was a loss of closeness, but happily not of the physical body. Kate felt grief but Quarry did not die. He was with Kate's boss, who loved him dearly.

Invisible energy leaves us to spread through space. A psychologist has pointed out some of the mystery of how people pick up our ideas and emotions. Only 7 percent of our thoughts are communicated verbally. Ninety-three percent of our thoughts and feelings are communicated with no words (Lagoni, Butler and Hetts 1994). We suppress our inner senses although they are equipped to perceive non-physical data.

Little wonder dogs are so well informed about our feelings; and Kate conveyed so much of her feelings about Quarry. The energy of unspoken words from a blind owner and her dog was in the air. I made no obvious achievement that day, but was inspired by this courageous owner fighting cancer, with her similarly afflicted guide dog.

The unspoken or telepathic bond between man and animal isn't necessarily restricted to our domesticated pets. Stacey O'Brien, a biologist dedicated to wildlife conservation, was asked to adopt a newborn barn owl chick with a disabled wing. Before he had his eyes open, Stacey was his foster mother and offered a new definition for the phrase 'close to another being'. Stacey held the chick, caressed him, talked to him, and preened his feathers. She christened him Wesley. The two used telepathy in their life together, and for their nineteen years Stacey fed him fresh mice, the bones of which Wesley would regurgitate and cough up.

The owl understood Stacey's key words; but more than that, the biologist described their communication as spiritual. Wesley would seem to know about something Stacey was planning to do to him or with him two hours or two weeks before she did it. If a promise were not honoured, a disappointed Wesley would squawk in protest. Stacey read his moods through his black eyes, which could express mischief, innocence, ferocity and love. The owl moved his skin under his feathers and Stacey read the feather pattern—how the feathers were sitting. Stacey knew so well what he was about to do. She listened and knew her chick's feelings. Wesley became her teacher. His twitters and chirps meant approval. Hisses and clicks were the sounds of disapproval. She learned the 'way of the owl' after many hisses and clicks.

Her grief when Wesley died was deep. Stacey became gravely ill and contemplated suicide. But she had received so much unconditional love and loyalty from the wild bird that his love lingered and sustained her. She is now a wildlife rescuer for many species, but none are so close as her barn owl with the large, dark mischievous eyes.

*Acknowledgement:* Sue Broadbent

# 15 DIVINING THE AURA

At the 2004 Australian Veterinary Association conference in Canberra, Tonia stood before the assembled group of holistic veterinarians. Holistic medicine is an approach to health which considers the whole being rather than just treating the symptoms of illness. The term 'holism' was coined by the South African politician Jan Smuts in the 1920s. In veterinary medicine, we use the word 'signs' to describe what animals show, instead of 'symptoms', which describe what people feel. The longer I was a veterinarian, the more sense holism made.

Tonia held two 100 cm lengths of thick fencing wire, each bent at right angles into 10 cm and 90 cm arms. Around the vertical 10 cm portion of the wire was a 10 cm sleeve of garden hose. When holding the two pieces of bent wire, they were sitting freely in the two lengths of hose. There was no direct contact with the two wires. Tonia held the hose pieces containing the short arms so that the long wires at 90 degrees were horizontal. In contrast to a divining rod, there was no direct connection from wire to hands. The long part of the wires, with no finger pressure, could move horizontally as they pleased.

Tonia asked me to stand up, move to the floor near her and think about the worst thing that had happened to me. Put on the spot, I came up with a betrayal I had experienced by ambitious veterinary colleagues, when 70 pages of ophthalmology notes I had written were plagiarised and distributed to Melbourne

University students under another author's name. It was not the worst thing that had happened to me, but it was the worst example to come from a leading university failing to show our next generation how we should work together, regard each other better. Academics allowed an uncaring attitude, far from the 'band-of-brothers' feeling of my veterinary student years at Sydney University in the 1950s. Since that time I had come to understand the huge challenges in looking after all species, each one with special needs. 'Let's help each other' was the spirit required to give all animals a fair go.

With thoughts of this betrayal in my mind, and standing one metre away from Tonia, the two wires fell together. Little energy from my body was shown by the wires. Indeed, when Tonia stood close to me, my energy, measured by her freely held fencing wire, showed my aura was spread just beyond a metre from my body

"Now," said Tonia, "think of the best event in your life."

My mind travelled back 12 years to the Royal Women's Hospital and two humidicribs. One twin granddaughter was in one crib and the other snug in a second crib next to her sister. Tiny hands clenched, little white hats on tiny heads, the smallest tubes of oxygen disappearing into tiny nostrils. The wires in Tonia's hands flew apart.

"He's having a good time," Tonia quipped, moving an extra two metres away. The wires were well separated even at the greater distance.

"He's having a *really* good time!" Her voice was full of joy as she moved further away, now four metres from me. The wires showed no signs of wanting to fall together. There was so much positive energy across the space between us.

"Let me try that," I said. In the face of this mystery, my manner was not as polite as it could have been. It carried an element of strong disbelief. I knew energy emanates from all beings, but I had never seen such a demonstration. She had just revealed my invisible self. Was it my non-physical reality?

Tonia gave me the wires as I turned to a member of the audience, Nicki, an attractive veterinary acupuncturist who practised in Prahran. Nicki thought it was ridiculous, that it couldn't be true. The divining wires I held in my hands, with their piece of hose covering, fell together. Where was my empathy, my touch? You would not be able to rely on me to find water in the arid outback. Was there any magic in my soul? Did I have sensitive healing hands? I could play no part in sorting out how our energy and thoughts could help healing.

Next came a change of heart. Nicki was thinking of a pleasant experience, letting me see a positive aura. The wires flew apart. *It does work*, she decided. It was Nicki's turn to be having a good time. But what's this? The wires suddenly fell together. Perhaps, after all, I did not have Tonia's skill, her insight. Nicki noticed my puzzled disappointment and later explained the behaviour of the wires. In the midst of her joyful thinking, she turned to less happy thoughts, of being bullied at school. That's when the wires collapsed together dramatically.

Some people can see the energy aura around another being, describing it as a fuzzy yellow light, sometimes coming from the fingertips. Since the 1940s, when the Russian Semyon Kirlian used photography for identifying the electrical corona, or aura, which he examined in health and disease, auras from people and plants have been on photographic record. We can feel the positive influence from our friends and charismatic people, but we seldom have such a dramatic demonstration of the power of thought.

Tonia used her wires to pick up changes in the energy of sick animals. She would hold the wires towards the ailing animal . . . "Hey Mum!" her young clients would cry out as the divining wires moved. "Look at what the vet's doing!"

Wires flying apart were a more dramatic show of energy and joy than hairs standing up on the back of my neck when I heard a soulful song. If I had been thinking more about the joy we get from animals and less about uncaring colleagues, my aura would have been stronger. The wires would not have come together.

Let's help each other. It's not an original concept. Animals help each other, and us, all the time.

# 16 FIND THE HAPPY MAN

I first met Zappa, an eight-year-old shiny black golden / cross, in the foyer of the Seeing Eye School at Kensington, in Melbourne. Zappa led Steve Nicholls to meet me, the visiting veterinary eye doctor. I had not met either before, and when you shook hands with Steve you felt well met. Steve was the sort of man I would like on my side in a cricket team or on a football field.

We chatted for a while in the foyer and then went into a quiet corner of the school office to sit and talk about life. Before we began a serious discussion, Steve took Zappa's harness off, removing the inverted U-frame which connects blind people to their guide dog. As soon as the last piece of harness came off and the animal was free to do as he wished, Zappa exuberantly threw himself at me, wanting to get on my lap. It was only his good manners and training that stopped him showing more affection. I had met Zappa ten minutes before when he was on duty, but now he acted like an old friend, almost throwing his arms around my neck. I felt honoured to be greeted so warmly.

Zappa could not have known I had been around seeing eye dogs nigh on fifty years. Or could he? Was he living each moment, just being happy?

"Is he like this to everyone?" I asked.

"To most, but not all," Steve replied. "He pulls back when meeting people who give out the wrong vibes, and his manner can sometimes warn me to be careful with some people."

Few people greet another being as Zappa did. We humans share the planet, but it often feels as though there is an invisible barrier keeping us apart. I looked at the beautiful animal, one moment full of communication and now, after such exuberance, once more settled down, a working animal near Steve.

The guide dog was bringing back my memories of the Seeing Eye School when it began as the Lady Nell Centre in Malvern in the 1960s. I reflected that all the seeing eye dogs I had met in my surgery had been restrained, usually on duty with a trainer or newly trained blind owner. They were very much business visits, quickly in and out, with no time wasted. It took me years to realise the haste with which vets see people and their pets in clinical practice, while necessary to be able to get through the day's work, was far from ideal. I appreciated the bond of dog to blind owner, but to feel the spontaneous joy from Zappa was a gift for my soul.

"Let's go for a walk and I'll show you how he works," Steve suggested, and we went out to pace the streets of Kensington.

Steve spoke quietly to his dog. "Forward, Zappa." The dog strode out at fast pace, lifting his front paws like a show pony, and I had to speed up to keep up with the pair. The dog moved with confidence, and seemed proud to be leading the way. A challenging threat to Steve's safety came quickly—crossing a road at traffic lights. I was aware Steve was in potential danger every time he crossed a road.

"Find the crossing," Steve instructed, and minutes later Zappa put his nose against the pole holding the crossing lights. Steve then leant down, ran his hand along his dog's head to his nose and felt where the button was to turn the lights green. He then listened for the rapid *click-click-click* of changing lights. What about Zappa's colour discrimination of traffic lights? While he listened I was thinking a change of colour was no guarantee of safety. Standing at the curb, dog and owner were guided by clues other than colour.

Dogs see some colour but their eyes do not register red; their retinal cones can detect violet and yellow-green, but not wavelengths of red hue. It is not just the eyes, however—colour vision also involves sensitive cells in the brain.

Zappa relied more on his training than what the lights were doing. How would I cope without sight, and with thoughts of a car swooping around a corner? Zappa did not look at the lights, and took us across the road in a manner which told me he was unworried. It was all in a day's work. Crossing the road was a team job. Steve can feel when people move beside him onto the road. Indeed, if the coast is clear his dog might take him on a jay walk—but a carefully guided jay walk. Unfortunately, some drivers out there show no patience or sensitivity to a person standing beside a dog in harness.

Dogs not only help us cross the road, they can help us heal. Many owners discover their most loyal companion is their dog, observing, "He was beside me for nine months when I was sick and helped me recover."

Once we crossed to the other side, Zappa was striding along in his business-like mode that suggested, "I am in the moment walking with Steve—no distractions."

"He's not always like this," Steve says. "Sometimes he tells me through the harness—telepathically, if you will—he would like to look into, say, a jeans shop. Zappa will go in, look around, then come out again."

Walking the footpath some minutes later there was a distraction when Zappa was put off by barking—it sounded like terriers—inside a galvanised iron fence. He suddenly slowed his walk. His tension was due to previous experiences. Owners, when they let noisy little dogs run out at seeing eye dogs, do not consider how much their dogs can worry a dog trying to work. Steve thought some owners needed admonishing for "interfering with his eyes", and should have enough common sense to restrain their pets at all times inside and outside the house. He was right—all dogs need constant discipline more than affection.

We walked on happily, with Steve explaining his dog's joy. "Zappa thinks he's going to the railway station. He loves trains."

We did not make it to the station, for we were only on a demonstration walk, and turned back for home. Zappa was disappointed, and slowed his walk, as though saying, "Don't take me home yet, Steve." But the go-slow ploy did not work. We were on the home trail.

As the dog led us home, Steve began his story. "I was thought to be clumsy as a young child, always bumping into things. I wore prescription glasses but struggled with school work."

*Seems bright to me. Pity no-one looked at his retinas, I thought.*

"Some months later it seemed the edges of my retinas were not working, although no-one noticed I had tunnel vision. I had no peripheral sight and could not see well out of the corner of my eyes."

Peripheral sight alerts an animal to moving danger. In the wild, for hunted animals like antelope and deer, it is essential for survival.

Steve went through school and into his teenage years without his vision problem being diagnosed.

"I found out I had an eye disease after I got my car licence. They did not suggest an eye exam in order for me to get my licence, and so I passed my test. Then I had ten side-impact accidents in eighteen months."

Ten prangs! I was taken aback but thankful Steve was still alive.

He went on. "Because of so many accidents, I went to court and the judge ruled that I should have my eyes tested."

Seems like a good idea after ten side-impacts, I mused.

Steve obeyed the judge's direction and went to see the eye doctor. The ophthalmologist looked into Steve's eyes and had no hesitation in his diagnosis. The disease is called *retinitis pigmentosa*—'Ret Pig' for short. His retinal blood vessels, the optic nerves in both eyes, were ailing. The doctor explained the retina was getting thinner and losing its organised layers; they were becoming jumbled together. The doctor explained this and then gave Steve the verdict—he would be blind by the age of 24. *Spare me the details* was Steve's first reaction, full of the confidence of youth to fully take in what was happening.

When Steve had had time to think it over, the young man was shattered to learn what the doctor had told him. No cure! All he could think of was that he was going blind and there was no cure. He was slowly going to see less and less! All he wanted was to be a free, carefree, doing anything he wanted. Blindness was too much to contemplate. Steve denied his diagnosis and did not let on he had a disability. He tried to manage, but work was very difficult. His boss did not understand why Steve was having trouble. Steve said nothing. No-one told the boss about Steve's increasing loss of sight from Ret Pig.

'If healthy, the eye looks and the brain sees'. Light receptors get into action and, when hit by photons of light, send impulses to the brain, which interprets the images. Rods are more plentiful in the dog retina because of a dog's need to see well at night. If the rods are ailing, night vision is seriously handicapped. Ret Pig affects the rods, the night retinal receptors in the thin layer of tightly packed cells lining the inside of the back of the eyeball. Ret Pig is somewhat like the canine disease Progressive Retinal Atrophy (PRA), an inherited retinal thinning in dogs. Mankind has carelessly allowed inherited disease to lessen canine vision and their joy of running in the meadow. However, due to breeder and veterinary vigilance, disorders such as PRA, although spread through many dog breeds, are no longer a threat to the breeds used as guide dogs.

Years later Steve and his dog went back to his old school, and he advised a Year Seven student who was night blind with Ret Pig that it took him fourteen years to come to terms with the fact that he had to learn to live as a blind person. "Tell everyone about it; it will be a weight off your shoulders," Steve told the boy.

Steve told me what it was like to be blind. As vision receded, he became too afraid to leave the house. Unknown to him, his mates thought Steve needed a guide dog, and they learned the blind had a choice of two schools in Melbourne offering dogs. They contacted Seeing Eye Dogs Australia (SEDA), which for 45 years had offered visually handicapped people independence. Within two months 'his dog would know his favourite shops by name and he could be taken there on command'.

Steve's heart lifted. He spoke to the director, Phyllis Gration, wondering if he would be accepted. "Do I need to be assessed before I get a dog? How long should I wait?"

"Don't be silly," she replied. "We'll give you a dog right away!"

Phyllis explained that seeing eye dogs cost $25,000 (in 1999), but involved no payment from the blind new dog owner, thanks to the generosity of donors. This included six weeks' live-in training to learn how to use a dog. The school had a one hundred percent safety record over its 45 years.

So in 2000 Steve's life was suddenly changed. He spent six weeks in residence with Zappa learning the ropes. 'Invisible rope' is as good a term as any to describe how man is joined to the dog, the oldest domesticated animal from 15,000 years ago. Steve got a dog for his vision, but Zappa was to become a social lubricant as well, helping Steve recover from a severely rough passage in his life.

Steve has vivid memories of his first solo walk with Zappa. The dog had the harness on, but Steve was walking free for the first time in his adult life. "I got Zappa when I was 34, and before that time I depended on other people to go anywhere. I was a bit like a recluse. That's all changed. I have confidence now." Steve, with his dog, moved about like a footballer on the field without the leather in his hands.

Animals have senses we have lost or never had. Zappa's smell and hearing are so much better than Steve's. Due to an innate sense of location, when he and Steve are separated, the dog also has a feeling of where his master is. We do not fully understand animal powers. In the wild they must heal themselves or likely die. Infra-red detectors in a dog's nose offer an extra sense for dogs to find their way around.

"I'm never home. Zappa gives me an independent life. I don't have to be on someone's arm, and love life with my seeing eye."

I did not have to hear Steve say it to know that he loved life. I could tell he felt free, ready to run out on any field and kick a goal.

"I would not go out at night until I was in my late thirties; now I do. At night Zappa works differently. He's closer to me. I feel him nearer to my leg."

The night vision of the labrador mix breed is better than that of a sighted person partly due to a dog's eyeshine layer behind the retina. Steve appreciated the fact that, with his dog, he could join friends as they were walking in the dark when there is no moon and no street lights. Because of Zappa's superior night vision, Steve's friends are safer walking with him and his seeing eye than they are on their own.

Zappa loves to be the centre of attention. Steve says, "He seems swollen with pride when he walks with me. He knows he is special." His manner seems to say, "Look at me, I'm proud to guide Steve around. Steve speaks with some pride too. "He's my eyes, my life and my best buddy. People must think I'm totally crazy. I have a conversation with Zappa when walking down the street. His personality is very similar to mine—we are both a bit cheeky, outgoing, and we both love a challenge."

Hearing Steve and watching Zappa reinforced my belief that we have much to learn from animals. Especially from guide dogs serving us so closely.

Steve recalled his first trip to Safeway with his seeing eye. It was Steve's second day out with his new dog. They had never been to a supermarket before. Zappa was ready for action. Before he put on the harness, Steve felt his dog was dancing on his toes. Up one aisle and down the other. Shopping was easier than he anticipated.

Then the checkout girl asked, "Are you going to pay for what your dog has, sir?"

"Pay for what?"

Steve realised Zappa had been up to something while he was distracted selecting goods from the shelves. Now he realised his dog's body language, well transmitted through the harness, had changed while Steve was preoccupied. The young man felt Zappa's face. His good friend had helped himself to a soft toy and was displaying it in his mouth.

"He loves them," Steve explained to the checkout girl. He kept the toy, a trophy of his first shopping trip.

For dogs guiding blind people, the main command is "Find". Steve had discovered a dog will sometimes find without being commanded.

"Find me the lift," he asked Zappa when shopping with his mum at Knox City.

"How can he find the lift?" asked Steve's mum. "He has never been here before."

Zappa found the lift with no hesitation.

"That's what he's been trained for, Mother."

"How do you know to follow?"

"You've gotta have faith in your dog. You must trust him. If you say 'turn right' and he turns left, *you go left*. He goes against your command for a very good reason."

Mum thought of her son often going against her directions. She now had two in the family.

Zappa responds to seventy commands, but must have some time being his mischievous self. He will sometimes playfully resist getting into a taxi with his owner. Instead, with no harness on, he bounces on the road, tail wagging, clearly indicating he'd rather walk. He can be playful on public occasions. At a lecture or school gathering, he can throw dignity aside, choosing to sit on Steve's lap in the front row, tail wagging, looking behind him at the audience. If there is not enough attention coming his way, he has been known to roll on the floor, moaning and groaning, putting his paws in the air. Steve looks the other way. Who brought him? He is used to being upstaged. Beyond his carefree approach on formal occasions, he is also smart and hides when the vet calls.

Sometimes Zappa gives his own command. He loves bananas. He does something better than speak the words, "I like the greengrocer". He takes Steve there. Tail wagging makes sure Steve knows his dog likes bananas, which are put in the backpack for Zappa to eat when he gets out of harness, back home. Steve has to interpret Zappa asking in his own way, "Buy me a snack and then we can go to work."

Zappa loves public transport. On a crowded tram Steve says, "Find me a seat." The dog nudges people's legs. Put in words the nudge would be, "Give my dad a seat. Now!"

Seeing-eye-at-your-service gets its way. People move and Steve sits down.

Zappa has a sense of fun. He will go round and round a roundabout, just to try Steve out. "OK, big joke," says Steve. What is Steve's answer to his run-around? He gives his dog a pat on the bottom, a gentle word, and then they carry on. It's so easy to forgive a dog.

Steve and Zappa spend much time visiting schools, the sick and elderly. They enjoy time off, and went to Magnetic Island for a holiday. It took Zappa no time to learn where everything was at the resort.

"Want any help, Steve?" asked the manager.

"No thanks, just give me and my dog ten minutes."

Soon Steve's voice rang out in the corridor. "Find the restaurant." Then "Find the pool." Later it was "Find the bar". When they are on holiday, it was "Find the man and his dog having a good time."

Steve does not need time in the sun to reflect on the fact the working bond depends partly on himself and his trust, not just the dog. "The relationship between Zappa and me is such that he totally understands my every movement, and all he wants in return is a big cuddle and for me to tell him he's such a good boy. When I say 'good boy', the tail will wag as if to say, 'I know I am, Dad'. I truly LOVE Zappa for coming into my life."

# 17 THE CAMEL WHISPERER

Captain George told me with delight his story of carrying wild camels to North America.

The first rumours about the possibility of carrying camels were heard when the ship was travelling on the eastern coast of Canada and the United States of America, discharging cargo from Adelaide and Brisbane. Whispers passed quickly through the crew when Captain George was advised that he might be asked to carry wild camels to the Philadelphia Zoo. During the loading voyage down the eastern coast of the United States, any sailor charged with a minor transgression received from the captain a light-hearted threat to give him the job of looking after the beasts of burden.

Some six weeks later, when the ship docked in Adelaide, Captain George was officially asked by his company's agent to take camels on board. Not just camels, but feral, wild camels not used to man. He hesitated because his ship, the Nottingham, was refrigerated and all his previous animal cargo had been frozen carcasses. Although he was naturally anxious to please the lords and masters of the company, he spluttered and blustered about having no experience whatsoever with camels, let alone wild beasts.

The young animals would be carried on deck in specially constructed boxes. Their wellbeing, however, would depend entirely upon Captain George's crew—a crew that knew nothing of the ships of the desert except that camel meat tasted like beef and was low in fat. In spite of this ignorance in relation to the camel, the captain heard himself saying some minutes later, "Okay, I'll do it, but only if I have a stockman or camel handler on board." Later he thought this remark was either foolhardy or brave. He decided it was brave, especially after cables, phone calls and below deck mutterings of crew dismay. The lords and masters added to his joy when they sent news that a stockman was unlikely to be granted. This news was digested with some apprehension. Crew mutterings grew worse.

One morning there was a knock on the captain's office door. Upon being given permission to enter, there appeared Jim, the third officer (always referred to as 'Three O' on board the ship) looking somewhat diffident.

"May I, sir," he said hesitantly, "look after the camels?"

"Good heavens, yes." God bless you, thought Captain George. He was surprised but concealed his enthusiasm.

The captain was invited to inspect the livestock at the holding paddock where the stockman vendor conducted his business. He asked his third officer, Jim, to accompany him. Captain George and Jim looked over the holding paddock fence, which was surprisingly high. Captain George did not realise camels could jump and flip themselves over a two-metre fence without much difficulty.

And there they were—frisky, shy young wild camels, one male and two females. Not yet fully grown, they had been recently caught in the desert north of Adelaide and west of the Flinders Ranges. The camels were obviously flighty and not used to people. Just the cargo you would want to carry with an inexperienced crew.

Jim was looking at their humps, having just learned that the humps store fat.

These camels had firm humps, so Jim knew they were well nourished. He would watch the humps during the voyage. Not enough tucker and the hump loses tone. From what he had been told, the humps would flop almost from side to side if food had been lacking in the desert. Jim made another mental note—big water troughs would be needed. Camels conserve water by not sweating much but can drink 100 litres at one go.

The first Australian camels came from the Canary Islands. The camel's job was to carry food, clothing and, in hard times, water to outback settlers and miners. The camels Captain George and Jim were looking at were descended from camels brought to Australia by early Afghan traders. Feral camel numbers in Australia have increased steadily. Sometimes they ransack tourists' cars for food. One camel put its large lips into a tourist car and tried to nibble the sun visor. According to current estimates, there are up to one million feral camels in Australia, with most roaming in the southern part of the Northern Territory. This represents considerable export potential.

Camel transport has its place in outback history. Copper was mined in the Flinders Ranges between 1853 and 1914. Animals hauled the road wagons prior to steam engines. When the British government wanted uranium for defence purposes, camels were used for transport to and from uranium deposits until 1940.

While soft-footed and gentler than cattle hooves on the delicate inland topsoil, feral camels still trampled fencing and damaged swamps. Once the backbone of inland exploration, camels have long since been replaced by cars. This was starting to occur even before the Alice Springs to Darwin railway, the Ghan, was laid down. Camels were the attraction before the Ghan became one of the great train journeys.

Camels are highly sought after not only by American zoos but also by Middle Eastern countries because they are mostly considered disease-free. Camels have large pads on their brisket (under the chest) and well-formed carpal pads to protect their knees. This allows them to be couched down chewing the cud during the long desert dust storms typical in Africa. More than dust flies in the Gobi Desert—animals take cover when black sand storms carry rocks flying through the air.

I talked to Dr Alex Tinson, an Australian vet and author who has looked after camels in India, Mongolia and the Middle East. He has been stuck in fierce sand storms in the Gobi Desert and vouches for how severe they can be. Alex doesn't like the storms but he loves camels. "They live off the smell of an oily rag yet supply low cholesterol meat, milk, and are great transport. Lawrence of Arabia wasn't the only soldier to find that out in the First World War." However, Alex is concerned about diminishing numbers. The world has too few camels. "Australia is the only place on earth where camel numbers are increasing. Highly toxic illegal mining and callous hunting for sport are the latest threats to this species in Africa." He is not happy that camels are sometimes hunted for food in parts of China.

Alex appreciates camel racing and compares the camel and horse. The camel is like a diesel engine and, less injury-prone than the horse, goes on endlessly. "The horse goes in bursts like a fast car full of gas, but legs can give in and the horse may then conk out."

In 1890 there was held a 100 mile race between a horse and a camel. The horse only just won, but could not fully savour the victory, dying that night. After the race, the camel coped well with his defeat and the death of a fellow long-distance competitor by walking home the 100 miles.

Captain George did not know any of this and asked the vendor if care was difficult. The stockman replied, informatively,

"Oh, no worries. All you have to do is give them a bit of hay and a drink of water each day. When you change the bedding and clean up the shit each day, look out you don't get splashed by the male. His dick points backwards." The stockman had a roguish sense of humour. As an afterthought, he nonchalantly offered some vague misinformation. "Whatever you do, don't let them lie down for more than twelve hours. If they lie down as long as that, they will never get up again." He was right about camels lying flat out for too long, because they get bloat. Sitting upright on their brisket is safe, however.

The stockman glanced at the captain's face, full of great concern, and smiled sympathetically. The stockman was smiling because he was glad to get rid of the camels. He observed that giving confined animals enough movement was not easy. For legs and bodies to keep healthy, the camels needed exercise. The more he learned, the more worried Captain George became, hoping his crew was up to it.

"Bloody hell," exclaimed the captain. "Camels!"

The conversation with the stockman warmed up—he was becoming almost helpful. "The one thing they have going for them is the fact that the Australian dromedary camels are the healthiest camels in the world. Mostly disease-free. That is why they are so acceptable to the American zoos. But I have to tell you that these darlings bite, spit, kick and pass lots of wind. Watch out for kicks—they can break your leg."

Jim, who had been standing there saying very little, then confessed that, after those first whispers of the possibility of taking camels on board, he had visited the zoos in all the ports on the eastern seaboard of America and ports in Australia to see camels and talk to their handlers. Such dedication astonished the captain. More than that, he was very relieved. At last all he could say was, "Carry on, Three O."

The camels were loaded in Adelaide, all in an open wooden pen with a sand floor and a partial shade shelter on the afterdeck. The word got around. In Sydney, a newspaper photographer came on board for an opportunity to photograph their beautiful heads, peering with imperial hauteur under their hooded eyelids and showing off long eyelashes. Not seen by the cameras under the large upper lids, camels had their own wide angle view of the world, with oval-shaped pupils designed to help them scan the horizon.

Next day a large photograph of the camels appeared in the Adelaide morning newspaper. It was labelled 'Three P & O Captains', to hoots of delight from the crew.

The ship's passage for three camels with their own third officer was almost a month long across the Pacific Ocean, sailing through the Panama Canal to New York. Jim had other duties in addition to tending to the camels. He had two four-hour watches every twenty-four hours, as well as noon sights for navigation. But in his time off from ship duties, he saw to the camels' care with devotion and tender loving attention. Mindful of the danger from both ends of the wild camels, he constantly changed their bedding and cleaned out manure, always talking to his humped friends. He had named the kicking, biting, spitting, wind-filled darlings Jezebel, Tinkerbelle and The Sheikh. The camels began to know him and change their shy, feral ways. Jim was slowly beginning to groom them. This was some accomplishment considering how wild his charges had been.

Disembarkation was planned for New York. Though the Philadelphia Zoo was to be their home, quarantine regulations demanded a detailed examination in New York. The longshoremen unloading had great trouble getting the camels into their lifting boxes from the deck to the wharf transport. As the camels baulked at the strangers they kicked, spat and farted their displeasure, showing off wonderfully to their apprehensive audience. To say the longshoremen were exasperated was a polite understatement.

Finally, Jim could remain a simple onlooker no longer. "May I help?" he asked. He climbed into the camel pen, soothed them, speaking slowly, whispering in their ears and rubbing their necks for a long time—long enough for them to settle and stand quietly. Then he coaxed them, one at a time, from the pen into the lifting boxes, much to the astonishment of an admiring ship's crew and the growing numbers of longshoremen.

"Hey buddy, look at this Aussie guy" was murmured among the ranks of those who had to unload the strange livestock. The American consignee, the buyer of the camels, was a short-tempered man not known for his gentle speech, commonly referred to as 'the impossible old bastard'. His difficult, demanding and critical manner was well known. He was always derogatory about the condition of the animals he had bought. He liked threatening to sue shipping companies. On this occasion he later told the captain,

"I have never seen wild animals better handled or in such beautiful condition. They looked immaculate, with not a hair out of place."

Captain George smiled broadly. Before the delivery, Jim had spent hours grooming the camels with more than his usual care. The 'impossible old bastard' shook Jim's hand and discreetly gave him an envelope containing a very considerable wad of money. The look on his face and a suggestion of tears in Jim's eyes showed his sadness at the parting. Was it just a suggestion of tears? The wild camels had become his good friends.

Some months later, Third Officer Jim visited the zoo in Philadelphia. There they were, now fully grown into marvelous animals. He called them by name. The camels still bore the names Jezebel, Tinkerbelle and The Sheikh. They turned and gently loped up to him and attempted to nuzzle him. Jim said that with those big, mobile lips and lugubrious looks they were talking to him. He stroked their faces and rubbed the base of their ears. He was smiling back but behind the smile he felt emotional. He was pleased to be alone with his camels and he was glad the crew did not see his display of deep feelings.

# 18 ANIMAL SENSES

*The best and most beautiful things in the world cannot be seen or even touched. They must be felt with the heart.—*
**Helen Keller**

We know very little of the enormous capability of animals and are in awe of their different sensory achievements of sight, smell, memory, how they survive harsh conditions, how deep they dive, how high they fly, how they migrate across the planet with only Mother Nature as a guide. Horses who help disabled riders and instinctively stop when the rider slips in the saddle. A timid cat who never showed his face in front of children until his owner was in danger and then chased the menacing kids away, the cat who had to bite the fingers of her deeply sleeping owner to tell her she had left the gas on in the kitchen (Grandin and Johnson 2009). How bees with a special dance tell their friends where the best flowers are.

Animals feel and suffer from family separation, from pain, grief and terror. People close to animal species tell us of the lighter side. Dogs, cats, elephants, dolphins, monkeys and other primates have a sense of humor. But wildlife when they lose their habitat, suffer in silence and the human invasion continues.

## What Do Our Animals See, Smell and Hear?

We know little about animal senses, especially the mysterious inner senses such as clairvoyance, clairaudience and intuition. But it is the eyes, more than any other organ, that have shaped the evolution of animals, where and how they live (Land & Nilsson 2002). About 540 million years ago, after what seemed to be the sudden appearance of a variety of complex animals, the phenomenon known as the *Cambrian Explosion* (Land & Nilsson 2002), vision was the one sense that dominated life on Earth. Evolution slowly created healthy eyes for all living animals, adapted to a variety of different light levels. Yet so much of vision is as mysterious as the energy of the universe. So much is unseen and unknown. What we do know, however, is that life on earth would have been very different if eyes had not evolved into so many forms.

Owners interested in taking care of their animal's eyes usually first look at the cornea. Animals in the air or on land have the cornea as a powerful light-bending surface with air on the outer side and aqueous eye fluid on the inside. Under water, when fluid exists on either side of the cornea, the bending of light is not so marked.

Apart from vision, human senses are poor compared to most animals. Some animal vision, however, is better than ours—especially that of birds. To work out how well animals are able to live in the jungle of their life, we need to consider not just sight but all animal senses. Some senses are poorly understood. We humans tend to consider sight as the most important of the senses. We therefore tend to talk up vision's significance in animals and overlook how other senses allow animals to communicate with each other.

Animal eyes are placed in two main skull positions in the head, either at the side for self protection from predators or at the front for hunting prey.

Domestic animal differences from human eyes include:

❖ There is a third eyelid which when prominent can hide serious injury

❖ Dogs' bony orbits around the eyeballs claim space for massive jaw-closing muscles may lack good bony protection around the front of the eyes

❖ Most species including wildlife have eyeshine to help night vision.

Humans have a sensitive central retinal area called a *fovea*, responsible for acuity and close-focus vision, which cats do not have, possibly because their eyeshine layer (tapetum, see *Night vision* below). Eyeshine is so helpful when the sun goes down, and scatters bright light to the retina.

We cannot simply compare animal sight with human vision. People consider vision our major sense, but it is much deeper than the eyes. It represents an understanding of the soul.

## Design for vision

Serious owners and breeders need to study all parts of the eye. As anatomist Gordon Walls told us, every part of the vertebrate eye means something. Except for the brain, we cannot say that of any other organ. All mammalian eyes are similar but are adapted to diverse species and there are points of difference to the human eye. For example, dogs, cats and horses have large corneas in order to be able to gather light in the dark, as well as to enable them to move quickly.

The ostrich has the largest eye of any land-dwelling creature.

## Do domestic animals see as well as we do?

Close vision is not as good and colour sense is less developed in animals who do not eat ripe berries. The animal range of colour appreciation varies with their needs. Night vision is generally superior to ours due in part to a reflective shield—the tapetum—sitting directly behind the retina. The reflection shows as eye shine, most easily seen reflected from a torch on the eyes at night. Nocturnal animals see color poorly but some birds have four visual pigments in the retina for color detection.

## Q&A

Q: What are the first things we look at when we think about what animals might see?
A: We first note how large the eyes are. Big eyes are for fast movers. Cheetahs, horses and birds of prey have vision for speed. Kangaroos have large eyes to graze and move at night. What a contrast to the slower moving koala living quietly among the leaves. The very large raptor eye helps to explain how the African vulture, from a height of 3,000-4,000 metres, can see whether its prey is dead or alive! (Duke Elder 1958). At that height, in spite of its 3-metre wing span, we cannot even see the vulture in the sky.

Q: To learn about an animal's vision, what do we note next?

A: Observe where the eyes are in the head. A hunted animal, like a rabbit, has eyes at the side so it can more easily look behind. Horses, cattle and deer can look behind when their head is down while grazing. A grazing stallion can see around his body except for a blind spot at his tail. A hunting animal, such as a cat, has eyes at the front, as does a thatch-weaving orangutan, who uses hands to strip a palm to eat the pulp of the plant.

## Bird's eye view

*Birds possess the best vision of all the vertebrates, and can detect ultra violet light invisible to people.* Avian eyes are supreme, superior to all other living beings, including humans. A falcon can see a pigeon eight kilometres away. The owl's eye, even though evolved for night vision, will detect a hawk in the day sky at a height at which the hawk is invisible to people (Duke-Elder 1958). Domestic hens scratching in the field can see grains of wheat hidden on the ground. Birds have extraordinary powers of recognition, being able to recognise each other at two weeks of age. Tiny robins (*erithacus*) can recognise their mates at 27 metres when partly screened by trees. Pintails (*dafila*) can identify one another 274 metres away (Duke-Elder 1958).

## How far can animals see?

Animals generally have less use for close vision than we humans, relying more on their close proximity senses such as smell and hearing. Head cocked, a wolf or cat listens for sounds in the grass or the burrow. A cat's hearing is extremely keen, and they hear the faintest sound made by their prey out of sight in the undergrowth.

Animals require movement to be alerted to look at something, and vision relates to what they have to do. A wild dog kept in a zoo may see no further than the bars of his cage. *Recent genetic studies of the dingo (Canis lupus dingo) suggest the ancient dog, from China and Polynesia originally, (http// www.cosmomagazine.com/news/4774/dingo-origin-predates- neolithic-expansion) travelled partly by land to Australia 4,600 and 10,000 years ago.* Some say, once a domesticated dog of indigenous people returned to the wild when the dog arrived in Australia.

Generally, dogs see owners 500 meters away. Police dogs see moving objects 900 meters away but recognise the same object stationary at only 585 meters or closer. Spaniels can have visual trouble at 10 metres. Even gun dogs do not see a stationary rabbit 20 metres away. Greyhounds—one of the 'gaze hounds'—have the best canine sight, but like foxhounds at the hunt, they need the prey to move or they can miss the fox.

## How large is the visual field

What do animal eyes mainly do—help to find a meal or avoid becoming one? Where the eyes are positioned on the head— whether at the front or side—tells us if the animal is prey or predator. Cats and dogs, as predators, have eyes at the front. Unlike prey animals, they must turn their head to look back. The side-positioned eyes of the grazing horse see almost 360 degrees around the body, even enabling the horse to see behind itself when the head is down. However, horses have a small blind area at the rear, so to avoid being kicked in the stable, you need to talk to the horse as you are approaching.

## Eyes look and the brain sees

The mother will search the horizon to teach her pups to look afar for signs of movement and danger.

The way the mother teaches its young to look reveals to us another truth. We are so captivated by the beauty of the eye that we can easily overlook the vital fact that vision is a brain function. What we see is interpreted in the head. Vision has many mysteries. People with multiple personalities have different vision for each personality. We are still discovering new sight areas in the brains of animals.

## Colour vision and light scattering

*Objects reflect light of different wave lengths to varying degrees. This is the basis of colour. Animals see colours they need to see to find food. Polarization (light scattering) which people are unable to detect, is common in animals and used in navigation.*

The animals well known to us who seem to have full colour sight are primates and birds using three visual pigments—they eat ripe fruit. and they need to see red. Other animals around us do not see red and use two pigments. They see two main hues, yellowish green during daylight and bluish purple in the moonlight. Bright moonlight is about a millionth as bright as sunlight (Land MF & Nilsson D-E 2002). Seeing grass uses the yellowish—green ability, and getting about at night they use bluish-purple receptors. Twilight vision and colours use less. Animals see well in reduced light because of the reflecting tapetum and pupils made much larger.

Animals, when watching TV, do not see what we do. Dogs see our red and green as shades of grey. Cats and people have three cone types, but these cones have in the retina do not give the complete answer to colour vision. There are colour sensitive parts in the eye-to-brain pathway and in the brain itself. Animals may distinguish closely related shades of grey better than we do.

Vision fits life needs. Observing an animal's lifestyle teaches us about animal colour vision. Does the animal eat ripe fruit? If the answer is yes then the animal sees colour. Are we looking at a nocturnal animal? Then there are plenty of low-light receptors called rods in the retina. Bear in mind some animal vision, such as night or distance vision, can be better than ours. Although we say 'colour', strictly it does not exist in nature. Colour in the strictest sense or more correctly 'hue' exists only in the mind. *The colour of a surface depends on the kind of light by which it is seen.* Objects cannot reflect only a single wavelength, and hence have no pure colour (Walls 1967).

Our pets live in a world of pastel tones, and the colours they see depend on how bright the light is. For our pets, colours of the day are more like what we see at dusk. Dogs have two sorts of colour receptors, called cones, but form and brightness are more significant than colour. Two hues blue and yellow are probable in dogs. Canine colour vision is similar to that of people who are red-green colour blind. Human blue-green is more like shades of grey to our pooch, and our green lawn is a duller grey-green to almost whitish. The dog is sensitive to violet and yellow-green but not to red. See chapter 'Find The Happy Man'.

By training two horses to select identical but different colored boxes containing oats, a professor and director of Frankfurt Zoo worked out that horses can see blue and green, but can by far more easily distinguish yellow (Grzimek 1968). This finding is reinforced by jockeys' opinions. *Yellow on a horse's steeple is a good idea for horse and rider safety.*

How do seeing-eye dogs guide their owners when they are not sensitive to the red traffic lights? Those clicks we hear at a set of traffic lights indicate when the light has changed colour.

Knowing when to move out onto a busy road is a team job of the sightless person and dog supported by canine training. Two hues, blue and yellow are probable. The dog is assisted in its role by the blind person's ears and common sense. Pedestrians crossing a road of horse-drawn traffic beware, horses see yellow best. (Elderly people beware, if you cross a road away from traffic lights especially at dusk, wear or wave a yellow or white scarf or wave a large white handkerchief).

Grandin T and Johnson C 2005 Scribner, New York

*Further reading*

Land MF & Nilsson D-E (2002) *Animal Eyes*, Oxford University Press, Oxford UK

## Night vision

Animals do not need lights when racing at night—the floodlights are in place for the spectators. The most dramatic difference between our own and our animal companion's eyes is the shiny shield called a tapetum (from the Latin *tapete*, meaning 'carpet') inside their eyes. The tapetum is located immediately behind the retina and gives a brilliant reflection which we refer to as 'eyeshine', best seen in dim light when the pupils are large. Light is reflected back through the retina when the rods of the light-sensitive layer get a second chance to record photons. A cat's tapetum reflects 130 times more light than the human back of the eye (fundus). This 'sun' shining from a cat's eyes was the reason why the ancient Egyptians worshipped domestic felines. Killing a cat carried the death penalty—a penalty which today's vets are grateful no longer applies.

Seeing better in the dark is also helped by larger pupils, better nerve impulse connection between retinal neurons, and increased rhodopsin (visual purple) in the retina. Seeing better may take 30 minutes or more in the dark.

Following combat, cavalry in the field at dusk learned the value of equine night vision. When soldiers had completely lost their bearings in strange territory, they put the reins on their horses' necks and the animals would take them home (Grzimek 1968). Soldiers needed a torch at night but a horse moved about safely in low light because of reflection back onto the horse's retina courtesy of a second exposure to the light receivers. The daytime slit-like horse pupil dilates so much more than in the human eye, thus more light reaches the reflective tapetum.

## White of the eye

The white of the eye is called sclera. The white around the cornea contrasts with a brown or hazel iris colour and attracts us to other people. In contrast, animals should not show as much white. Alas, we do not seem to be able to stop interfering with nature's design of animal eyes. The cat and dog eyelids should hide most of the sclera—as should the lids of other domestic animals. *Obvious animal scleras (whites) means the eyes are too prominent, the corneas too exposed.* It is one of our breeding follies that we breed dogs to have large eyes like people. Big eyes are more easily damaged and dry out more easily. Dryness is very uncomfortable and slowly causes reduced sight when pigment covers an exposed cornea. Pain and vision loss are the cruel results of our whim to have animals look like us. *The eyes of our beloved domestic pets need to be protected, showing small whites as we see in animals living in the jungle. NOT as those big whites we see in popular cartoons.*

## Third eyelids

Animals have an extra eyelid sitting in the corner of the eye near the nose (medial canthus). Called the third eyelid, it is not to be confused with the chakra of the third eye. Transparent third eyelids flick over the eyes of the bird diving into the sea—it is protective and acts like a windscreen wiper for the eye surface to help provide and spread tears. If it is not pigmented, it can become sunburned. Third eyelids of domestic animals are never removed unless cancerous. Lack of eyelids skin pigment allows infection (called 'pink eye'), sunburn and skin cancer.

## Cancer eye

Squamous cell carcinoma of the eyeball or eyelid skin is called 'cancer eye'. It is most common and costly in cattle.

## Tear film

Corneas need constant protection and lids that gently fit against the eye, serving as a frame for the first layer of the cornea, a liquid covering called the tear film. The lid edges must sit exactly on the cornea, neither folding in nor turning out. Unfortunately, many dogs have either droopy or rolled in eyelids. Sometimes both on the same lid! Poor lid fit is one factor causing the most commonly overlooked cause of eye discomfort, dry eye. Poorly-fitting animal eyelids are monuments to our stupidity in breeding selection. Ask your vet.

## Equine vision

Horses see with both eyes until they are a metre away and then turn their head to use mainly one eye. They treat every object in peripheral view as suspicious, and this is at least partly responsible for rider death and injury from shying. Reassuring words to your spooked horse can lessen shying and save your life. For repeated shying, think eye check.

A horizontal pupil guards bright-light vision in the horse with over-hanging brown bodies resembling small dark grapes, mostly on the top of the pupil. In contrast to a circular pupil, the oval shape with the little grapes on its border seems to completely close down the slit pupil. When the head is down grazing, the pupil's brown bodies shade the retina.

The horse eye has potential danger. With few warning signs other than a pupil that will not get large (dilate) in the dark, the iris in a horse can be savagely inflamed. An immune-mediated inflammation of the blood-rich eye layer behind and including the iris is called uveitis (*you-vee-i-tis*). It is a sneaky disease that, untreated, results in blindness.

## Keeping in line with nature's design to retain our pets' sight

We need to change our thinking about small nosed Pekes, Pugs, Chihuahuas, Boston Terriers and flat-faced cats such as Persians. A small nose means a crowded mouth and shallow eye sockets with poor to no bony protection of the eyeball. When choosing a new animal, select a breed with the head shape of the Kelpie, Dingo or Corgi; *not* a breed in fashion, such as the latest prize basset with excess skin drooping from its face. Do not choose a breed for fashion.

*Fashion in breeding is the enemy of good sense and animal comfort.*

## Before you buy

When we get older we need glasses—not so our animals. Unless diseased, with good lid fit their eyes generally last for life. By careful selection of stud animals, and good genes, we can avoid retinal atrophy (an inherited degeneration of the retina). Eyes are also under threat from head skin wrinkles, facial hair. And turning onto the eye, weak lid closure and lids that are too droopy may not protect the eyeball.

*Before you buy ask your vet about inherited diseases, some may not appear until later. Look at the family and breeder reputation before purchase. A reputable home can offer great value. Avoid 'the latest colour' and avoid what might become an aggressive dog.*

Lack of protective pigment around or in the eye leaves the eye vulnerable to destructive UV light and allows sun damage. Unpigmented eyes eg white bovine eyelids in the paddock without shade, are more likely to develop a wretched cause of discomfort, 'pink eye'. Furthermore less pigmented cattle eyes are prone to the world's most common cancer called 'cancer eye'.

If we support breeding that retains the original wild animal head, shape and colour, we are likely to breed more comfort. The original design is cheaper because it will require fewer visits to the vet. *Keep in line with nature's design.* There you are, I've said it again.

"Scandal of not knowing before breeding, not thinking."

Pekingese                    Chihuahua

*Pekingese and Chihuahua skulls. The small plastic balls in the Chihuahua skull are in place to hold the skull in shape post mortem. Some breeds are created with grossly deformed skulls a long way from nature's design. Neither skull has a protective bony orbit and this puts the eyeball so much at risk from injury and drying. Imperfectly formed bony orbits should be declared illegal.*

Animals move around in their world by combining vision with smell, touch, hearing and inner senses. They remind us that we know very little about the reality of nature. When we want the best in treatment for domestic animal eye disease, the first piece of common sense says it is not a person's eye we are treating. Many people forge this fundamtental, and give animal vision the same significance as human sight. Some animals see less than people, but many avians see more, bird's vision is so much better than ours. Animals use much more than their eyes to get about.

## What about other senses?

Dolphins not only have larger brains than we do, but use echolocation, a sense we can only imagine. The duck-billed platypus finds worms with its eyes closed, foraging in the mud with its large, sensitive bill. The bill can locate worms, their favourite food, by detecting energy vibrations. The first description of this animal by colonialists Down Under was not believed. Some thought some crazy Australian had glued a duck's bill onto a furry creature with a fat tail. In keeping with later dual traditions of a doctor's passion for wild animals and the enjoyment of life, one ophthalmologist, Dr O'Day, probably sent the unusual platypus retina from Australia to London preserved in Scotch whisky (Duke-Elder 1958). The specimen plus the liquor seemed to attract more than scientific interest.

Elephants feel vibrations in their feet and hear sounds of such low frequency that we cannot hear when they are calling to each other. We can guess that the elephant, with its massive ears, relies on hearing sometimes as much as sight. Beware on safari—you must make no noise. The elephant hears but may not see you and might do something dangerous out of fear. The nimble horse has a larger eye than the slower elephant. The zebra is equipped with an eye larger than that of some whales, to enable zebras to gallop over the African savanna and escape predators.

A hint of sight linked with other senses is suggested by research carried out at Harvard University (Pascual-Leone 2005). The brain changes with every perception and every action. An experiment in which subjects wore a blindfold for five days showed that the brain is much more malleable and fluidly organised than previously thought. The visual cortex, traditionally thought to be the part of the brain that controls vision, may not be devoted exclusively to the eyes at all. Within two days of the blindfold being in place, the visual cortex could be stimulated by performing tasks with fingers. The visual cortex is also stimulated when we listen to tones or words. Links from body parts like fingers to the seeing part of the brain are already in place but are not used as long as the eyes can see. When the eyes are blind, the brain grabs whatever messages it can, providing blind people with information required to help them get about (Pascual-Leone 2005).

## Smell

Fortunately many animals have a major sense to fall back on when vision fails. The big nosed animal sense of smell is vastly superior to that of humans. A bloodhound can detect human odours from a fingerprint left out in the weather for days. Olfaction is the first sense developed by the newborn animal and guides baby to mother's teat.

To work out how good the adult sense of smell is, we are guided by the size of the nose. Bloodhounds, horses, bears, elk and pigs have a strong sense of smell. The smell-sensitive lining inside the nostrils is much larger than is obvious from the outside. The nose contains scrolls of cartilage covered by olfactory nerve endings, providing an enormous area to absorb odours. *What a crime to breed out the sense of smell by selecting a flat face.* The dog with a reasonable nose has about 220 million scent receptors compared to five million scent receptors cells in people. As my esteemed colleague Dr Paul McGreevy put it 'to sniff is to be a dog'. In addition to the nose, there is a pheromone detector, the vomeronasal organ on the roof of the mouth behind the upper incisor teeth. Pheromone therapy is used for separation anxiety. Scent hounds include basset hounds, bloodhounds, and beagles, used for picking up smells on broken vegetation, footprints of the lost or hunted, sniffing drugs and the smell of cancer. *Human Lung cancer is detected on the breath by sniffer dogs with 99% accuracy.*

Although some animals can smell distant food and enemies from afar, rabbits close by in a burrow are easily detected by their odour.

In contrast to people, a large nose may be more important than vision when an animal moves around in the house or paddock. Following fashion rather than animal needs and welfare, we have seriously interfered with head design by breeding some animals with a flat face and virtually no nose, which has severely restricted the animal's ability to live as nature intended.

# 19 COCKY GO TO BED

I was discovering that birds are much smarter than I had first thought. I recalled the budgerigar Bertie coming in to see my neighbouring vet, Ruthie, with a chronic high-pitched cough. The cough had a distinctive sound. You can hear it mid-winter on public transport. She was surprised to find the lungs were clear. The owners of the bird were becoming anxious because the cough was resistant to all known therapy. After many weeks of unsuccessful treatment, the husband accompanied Bertie into the examination room. While waiting for the vet to re-examine the budgie, the husband coughed. His cough was identical to the little bird's sound. Bertie was suffering not from an unusual infection but from a copy-cat cough.

Recognition of the cleverness of birds was supported by years of scientific avian research in the US. One such landmark study described a (Caledonian) crow bending a piece of straight wire into a hook; not simple bending but repeatedly changing its angle so the shape was an exact fit to get food out of a tube (Weir *et al, Science* 9 August 2002: Vol. 297. no. 5583). These observations, published in *Science* magazine, shocked people who had not considered that a bird, for whom wire is a foreign object, could have used wire as a tool to get food.

But birds can do more than bend wire into special shapes. They have reasoning skills. No-one told me this when I was a student. While still in my twenties, though many years after

I had graduated in veterinary science, Dr Irene Pepperberg, not a veterinarian and therefore not shackled by conventional veterinary ideas, realised her twenty-five-year-old grey African parrot, Alex, had the level of learning of a four—to six-year-old child. Through a mixture of reasoning, intuition and perception, the parrot solved problems. While I was trying my hand at the puzzle of animal diagnosis, African Alex solved the puzzle of words and could answer questions about objects he had not seen before.

Alex didn't just learn simple words like 'cat' and 'dog', but concepts like colour and shape. Dr Pepperberg showed Alex a square piece of blue wood and asked him what colour it was. "Blue," Alex answered. "What shape?" asked Dr Pepperberg. "Four corner," Alex replied without hesitating (Grandin & Johnson 2005).

A good clinician is one who asks the good questions. In all my clinical years I had never thought of asking such questions—especially of a parrot. Alex was able to answer the colour and shape correctly and with ease, but he certainly was not the only smart bird with a vocabulary. Another grey parrot, living in New York City, has a vocabulary of over five hundred words (Grandin & Johnson 2005). Sounds like a difficult pet for any house in which one wants to hold one's own.

Animals have been listening to me for years, usually accepting my words in silence. From time to time I have wondered what animals think of me. It is not often a vet gets an animal opinion straight from the horse's mouth. It was Robbie Burns who picqued my curiosity about how animals see us. As erring fellow earth dwellers?

O wad some Power the giftie gie us
To see oursels as ithers see us!
It wad frae mony a blunder free us.

It was a while before I realised 'the giftie' was God, from whom all things are given. If birds could speak freely, what would they say about the care I provide them? I had not sought their opinion regarding this. Could animals help me to avoid diagnostic blunders?

I am fascinated by the appearance and behaviour of the patients I look after. The giftie has surrounded us with such a diverse range of beings. The colours of parrots enchant me. What will Earth be like if our animal care becomes less adequate and giftie does not intervene in our removal of more rare species?

What do the animals think? I had waited years to get feedback from the animals, and Cocky the cockatoo finally provided me with the opportunity. He was a brightly coloured psittacine, his magnificent red and green contrasting starkly with the other grey-brown animals I had been seeing that day. He came in sitting on the shoulder of Cyrus. The close bond between the two was obvious. Talk to one and you talked to both. I introduced myself while Cocky took the chance to gently spread his wings. What a stretch. There was just enough space in the consultation room.

"Settle down, Cocky," Cyrus admonished his companion.

"Settle down, Cocky," mimicked the cockatoo.

I began to take a history. "How old is he?" I asked, expecting something like ten years. Most animals I treated were teenaged or less. I had some skill estimating ages. You can easily tell when an animal is approaching its early twenties.

"He's forty-six," said Cyrus.

I felt a surge of pleasure that at least for this consultation I was not into juvenile medicine. At last I was treating someone my own age.

"He has something wrong with his eye," Cyrus told me.

Sure enough, there was a copious grey-coloured discharge from one of his eyes. I filled a five-millilitre syringe with sterile saline to gently irrigate the discharge from the eye. It would give me a chance to better examine the cornea. I examined with my slit lamp, as I needed to know if discharge had been covering a corneal injury.

Next I looked at the back of his eyes, the part where the retinas are that we call the fundus, meaning base. I had to examine in the dark to reduce corneal reflection so I could look past the cornea. To make the room dark, I pulled down the blind.

"Cocky go to bed," said the parrot, fanning his topknot of erectile feathers.

## Anatomy

Birds have a special eye anatomy. The eyeballs are very large relative to the rest of the body, and keep their shape with pieces of cartilage in the outer eye-wall, called sclera. Vision is essential for bird survival—much more significant than in people. Blind birds die. Partial blindness will keep birds out of the air and vulnerable on the ground. To protect the large cornea, birds have large upper and lower mobile lids and an almost transparent third eyelid called a nictitating (winking) membrane. The eyes are kept protected, wet and clean by constant eyelid action in the sky or forest floor, and by the third eyelid cover when under water.

A change in the need from protection from the air to protection from the water can take place in an instant. I saw pelicans diving vertically at full speed into the Caribbean Sea off Saint Kitts and Nevis. Moments later a head with what seems an empty bill appears above water. A slow *flap-flap* of the large pelican wings gets the bird airborne. Flying high again, the pelican is ready for another dive. A pelican's eyesight might not be the sharpest of all birds, but is sharp enough to see fish under water from its diving height.

The avian pupil is unique in domestic animals because the circular hole in the iris is under voluntary control as well as responding involuntarily to light. In ancient Rome, 'belladonna' described lovely ladies with big pupils resulting from the ingestion of a preparation of the same name made with the leaves and root of the deadly nightshade plant. Birds don't need drugs for beauty; they can make their pupils large at will.

## Shooting

Scientists worry about reduced numbers of songbirds. Do we need to shoot for sport? Do we want a silent world? Or do we accept bird migration needs our care to remain one of the wonders of the world? You want to shoot something which cannot shoot back? Line up ten drink cans in the nearest paddock and take aim.

In 1966 at Kansas State University, a veterinarian arranged for an officer of the US Armed Forces to set up a cocktail-hour shoot out for me. The light was fading when he placed a pistol in my hands. Holding the handgun up to eye level, as they do in the Midwest, I hit every can, probably because I had consumed several cans before the contest. My host, with cool military precision, hit three. After my score, I hurried inside in case I was asked to repeat the exercise. It was the only time I was requested to shoot for Australia.

## Migration

Propelled by an ancient faith deep within the genes, a bird of matchbox size can fly from Alaska to New Zealand with no food and without touching down. Shorebirds fly 240 hours without stopping from the tip of South America to the coast of New Jersey, a brief fight from New York City. Many migrations take place at night, 'marked by the stars', following 'a path graven in their genes' (Weidensaul 1999).

Birds show us the wonders of instinct, which allows them to soar the winds from one hemisphere to another, 'stitching the continents together' (Weidensaul 1999). Heinricks, a reviewer of Weidensaul's *Living On The Wind*, points out that bird migration is 'the most riveting and miraculous phenomenon of the planet'. According to radar count, during migration one million hawks fly across Cape Cod in one day. Habitat degradation and deforestation will reduce these numbers. *When we drain wetlands vital as stopovers, we kill exhausted birds.*

## Disease cures and causes

Poultry supplies chicks for vision research, helping us to learn more about a most mysterious malady—glaucoma. Researchers used continuous light to discover unremitting light makes the eyes of a chicken oversized. Called 'light-induced glaucoma', it is unique to birds. Glaucoma, although causing an enlarged eye in its later stages, is not a single disease but describes many disorders which induce raised eye pressure. Glaucoma offers a diagnostic challenge when it sneaks under our guard. To prevent sight loss in humans and animals, early glaucoma diagnosis is of great significance. Waiting for an eye to become larger than its fellow eye from sustained pressure is a recipe for blindness. *We try to be wise before the event.* When visiting a health professional, make sure you get your eyes examined. *As a routine eye measure, please check your eye pressure.* (I offer in rhyme to give your sight a good time—and perhaps you will better remember.)

Bird, or avian, flu placed a global focus on birds. The H5N1 virus is a serious health risk, especially to younger people. The disease becomes a possible greater risk when the virus mutates. Avian flu is most fatal to children aged between 10 and 19 years, with an overall fatality of 56% (*The Age*, 3 July 2006).

Should we keep birds in a cage or commercial flocks imprisoned so close together? Poultry is the most abused domestic species. The McDonald's hamburger chain has made a start to modify factory farming, requiring its egg suppliers to double the living space of their hens, though the space they request is still less than the Europeans have specified as humane (Singer 2002).

Poultry living in geographic isolation (if this is possible in today's world) can be somewhat shielded from avian flu. However, animals kept in an overcrowded space, wherever it may be, can suffer infectious agents causing not just avian flu but inflamed eyes due to the herpes virus—called 'pearly eye', it is associated with a cancer called Marek's disease. The birds, cramped and unable to walk, become blind and paralysed.

Quite apart from disease control, a walk in the sun is a necessary part of animal life. Healthy birds need free range. Living at least part of life in a big barn offers some uncaged freedom. But for birds in the open, beware of predators.

## Back to cocky

As a first approach to treating Cocky's eye discharge, I began to tell Cyrus about a natural antibacterial herb. In thrall to constant marketing pressure from the pharmaceutical companies, we use far, far too much antibiotic. I told Cyrus what I thought about natural therapy and how we need to know more about herbals and homeopathics trying to reduce the number of superbugs emerging in our human hospitals. This was a comment I made

to veterinary students when lecturing on natural medicine—
*Don't use a sledgehammer when a tack hammer can do the job.*
Unfortunately, by the time I spoke to emerging vets in their
later university years, they had already been indoctrinated into
the culture of 'sick animal means antibiotics'. "No it doesn't," I
would tell them. "A sick animal means a thorough examination
of the animal and its surroundings."

We need experience to choose between an initial 'no-
antibiotic' approach with an antibacterial of softer clout, and
heavier antibiotic therapy. Save the antibiotic for an animal
really needing it, not as first treatment.

Cocky stood on the table, looking at me eye-to-eye, and
began to talk, nodding his head up and down, up and down,
speaking to me earnestly. *Gabble-gabble-gabble, gabble-gabble-
gabble.* The bird looked wise but the words seemed a little
nonsensical to my untrained ear.

"What's he doing now?" I asked.

"He's imitating you."

As Cyrus walked out into the waiting room with his pet on
his shoulder, Cocky turned his head back to me and said, "See
you later."

I had passed his grading. What better acceptance could
I have? Furthermore, he understood what I was about and
expected to see me again.

That evening, as shades of night were falling, I was walking
along the road at Flinders. The chatter of the birds became softer
as they settled on the trees. A squawking flock of cockatoos flew
past, telling the world of their presence. They were too noisy and
could not hear me as I called, "Cocky go to bed."

# 20 THE DANGERS OF A PART-CLOSED EYE

## Shut-eye for the doctor

Closed lids can hide a blinding disease, and can indicate the eye contains a foreign body, or worse, the eye has suffered chemical burn. Learn how to treat a part-closed eye when remote from a vet eye specialist and without the assistance of a second pair of hands. It is a good idea to ask your vet to show you how to cope with suddenly part-closed eyes. If the eye burn is caused by a substance like cement, your quick action on the spot may save the eye. Once in the vet's waiting room, do not wait your turn but ask for immediate help from reception.

Dr Joe held his Australian cattle dog, Banjo, in his arms. This was a little unusual as Banjo weighed in at 25 kg, the weight of a suitcase you would carry for your widowed aunt. Banjo was no easy armful, and Dr Joe, with his serious expression and matter-of-fact manner, did not seem the cuddling type. The doctor, a busy general surgeon, certainly looked unhappy. Banjo did not look so happy either, with one of his eyes firmly half closed.

"The eye looks bad; I did not give it attention when I should have. I just didn't realise this could happen when a dog is simply poking about."

The doctor's eyes told me of his distress. Not many people who come to see me admit their error and ignorance.

143

Banjo would require a general anesthetic for me to examine him. While I was pulling Pentothal into a syringe, Dr Joe continued his story.

"Been up north. We let Banjo out for a run on the way up, and this is what happened."

"*What* happened?"

"When Banjo came back from exploring he looked fine, except he had one eye slightly closed. It did not seem a big deal; he was away only a few minutes. I did not take much notice."

Banjo had gone for a toilet break and had explored a house-building site near the river picnic area. Someone had left a bag of powdery cement near where a house floor slab had been poured. Banjo got too close and it all happened in minutes.

Banjo jumped into the back of the car, ready to travel the next 200 kilometres. The good doctor's mind set on travelling north, he did not pay too much attention to the blinking closed eye. But those 200 kilometres and two hours without treatment were fatal to the eye's vision.

I talked to Dr Joe about what owners can do to prepare themselves for applying first aid in the event of eye burn.

*Signs may be subtle but owners need to know emergency therapy for health disasters before the event.*

Nasty stuff, cement. It burns due to its high pH. Alkali burns on the eye are worse than acid maliciously thrown in the face. Anything with alkali content can burn deeply. In contrast, acid precipitates protein of the cornea, and in this way is self-limiting. Wet cement, or wet mortar, is dangerous to animals because it is alkaline. Serious injury is often overlooked because the dog is stoic and does not tell an owner of his pain. To the casual glance, it appears as though he is merely not holding the eye fully open. But a partly closed eye like this can fool you. *Lids jammed shut means the eye is in great pain. Alkali penetrates deeply and seriously damages the internal eye.*

Ammonia from fertilizers, refrigerants, fireworks, builder's plaster, white wash, and line-marking powder used on sports ovals can be a hazard (Blogg 1987). You and your dog may leave your mark on the world by walking across wet concrete, but do not linger, and wash off all cement immediately. Calcium oxide, also known as lime, is the caustic ingredient in cement. It generates heat when diluted with water and can produce a thermal or caustic burn.

Cement burns are not a recent phenomenon, and their effects have been known for centuries. Eye burns can be so severe that we must keep lime and cement away from man and beast. *Do not store cement mix anywhere it might be discovered by children and animals.*

Dr Joe now realised that the small lid-closing sign was the big warning. Banjo quickly needed the eye to be washed out. It is difficult to wash out all the cement from an eyeball. Because of the serious nature of eye burns, if you cannot get to a vet immediately, you must be prepared to plunge your pet's head in a creek or bucket of water to wash out foreign particles. Hold the dog's lids apart and push the head under water several times with the dog's eyes wide open. Plunge quickly so the dog does not feel as though he is being drowned.

When Dr Joe took Banjo to the vet at the next big town, the young vet did not realise that cement had already burned deeply into Banjo's cornea. This was perhaps not the vet's fault, rather the negative consequences of a crowded syllabus. Universities need many practitioners on the staff who can advise and educate students on practical scenarios vets encounter.

Banjo's eye had lost vision. It had turned white and shrunken from inflammation inside the eyeball. Dr Joe was consumed with remorse. "I didn't know. I wish I'd had a first aid saline plastic bag in the car." Dr Joe has since learned to take precautions prior to the event. Next time, his dog's half closed eye will receivte quicker treatment.

What kind of occurrences might critically affect an animal's eyes, and what owners might have to do, it is not easy to determine. As animal carers, it is our duty to ensure our pet is not suffering. Animals often do not communicate their concerns; therefore there is a need for constant vigilance.

A savvy, well-informed owner can prevent the worst effects of chemical eye burn. Before a pet runs among buildings or through long grass, it is a good idea to ask your vet to show you how to cope with a suddenly closed eye. The actions of the person on the spot will determine whether vision in the burned eye is saved or not.

If you suspect something nasty like cement in the eye, can you do something yourself to help the eye or should you rush to the vet and ask for an eyewash? Try both. Bear in mind, *an owner's first aid knowledge on washing the cornea and the hidden eye-lid linings sitting on the cornea is the best vision saver.* The vet may not have been taught about such eye emergencies at vet school.

If you don't think you are capable of pulling the lids back and o it a look, steel yourself to get over it. The most common cause of a part closed eye is a grass seed or maybe a thorn. If your dog has been running in the grass and presents a part closed eye, think grass seed. Grass seed awns are not always obvious and might only be seen by careful looking as thin yellowish fibres hidden behind the third eyelid.

If your dog has been near a building, put squeamish feelings aside and inspect the eyeball. If the eye is an angry red, wash the eye for approximately ten minutes. Use a garden hose if you must. The second best option is to drop in a copious amount of artificial tears. *Tear substitutes should be in every first aid kit, along with the 500 ml plastic bag of saline.* Rest your hand on the top of the dog's forehead and place your other hand, in the shape of a 'V', under the dog's chin. Hold the bottle of artificial tears away from the eye so it will not touch the eye when the dog moves. Dive bomb tears onto the eye from a two-finger width distance above as you rest your hand on the patient's forehead. A second pair of hands will help with holding the lids apart. Slowly use the whole bottle. A passenger can do this as you drive to the vet.

Wassat? You cannot open the half closed eye to have a look and there is no hose available? Try tap water squeezed from a handful of water-soaked cotton wool held above the eye. Pull back the lids and wash the eyeball from the copious flow. Come on, gently pull the lids well apart, not by the lid edges but by skin traction a centimeter or so away from the eyeball. More and more water please.

Learn common health disasters, some have subtle signs. Use an animal first-aid book and write in the book the wisdom of your vet

I told my students how important it is to empower owners through teaching them how to identify common eye emergencies and offer first aid. Owners must not rely on someone else. An owner's quick response and aid can save a dog's sight. The owner is the ambulance officer, the on-duty emergency person and the on-the-spot eye-carer.

Banjo's specialist surgeon-owner punished himself and had the last word looking at his one-eyed dog. "Unlike many human patients, animals by nature accept what happens; they rely on us and do not ask us to help them. It is up to us to save them from pain. We can do well to think perhaps of younger days hearing Lord Baden-Powell and his spot-on advice to his boy scouts—*be prepared*."

# 21 A GREEK TRAGEDY

It was a long time ago, 7 pm one evening in 1975 when what sounded like an emergency struck. Just what you want when you have too many people crowded into the waiting room.

Benni, who never turned away any sick animal or any client, whatever their circumstances, who shared owner pain when tragedy struck their pet, came from the Gold Coast, in Queensland, where his family bred cattle dogs. His parents were so proud the day Benni was accepted into the Veterinary School of Queensland University. His dad, full of joy, phoned every one of his friends. "My son got in!"

Now Benni was the new vet, working in his first job. He had come south to Melbourne in response to an ad in the Australian Veterinary Journal. The journal can tell you about a job offering more money than the new vets are getting on the Gold Coast, but you need grapevine information to tell you about the type of person you are about to work for. Had Benni tapped into the grapevine, he would have quickly learned that Cleveland was not the best employer. Some described Cleveland as a bit of a bully—a bully who could not easily see the best path to tread. He dominated his staff until payday. On payday he left them alone. The staff discovered when Cleveland left them alone, his chequebook left them alone too. Rarely did he pay his staff on time. And he liked to watch his staff as carefully as he watched the dollars. But despite all this, being a new graduate, Benni was very keen to do what he thought was right for all concerned, especially his new employer. Benni thought of each task as a make or break challenge.

The emergency Benni currently faced involved a member of his family's favourite breed, an Australian cattle dog, Lemnos, with snakebite. Very hard to diagnose, is snakebite. The thick cattle dog coat usually hides snakebite puncture wounds. In this instance, however, the owners saw the brown snake bite the dog. Benni went into top gear. Not a moment could be lost. Saving the cattle dog's life was paramount. His parents would be so proud. Benni had to order antivenene from supplier Lyppards, which he quickly did. Never mind the cost of $700. This was urgent.

Top priority was given to Lemnos in spite of the fact that the other people in the waiting room were less than understanding, offering groans of disapproval. But Benni did not hear them. Upsetting clients who had been waiting for hours was not always a good way to go, but Benni saw a stricken dog needing his care.

While waiting for the special delivery of antivenene, an IV drip was hooked up. Into Lemnos' bloodstream went vital fluids. The special delivery of anti-snakebite serum arrived by cab from twenty kilometres away. In went high doses of antivenene. A tube placed in the windpipe assisted the breathing. The well-dressed Greek owners—brothers Nick and Spiros, who had an air of well-groomed prosperity—were pleased with the prompt attention. The white coats and emergency flurry of care impressed them. Better care here than they could get back home in Athens, they thought.

Early signs indicated that Lemnos seemed to be doing well, if 'well' can describe a dog who has recently been bitten by a snake. Smiling appreciatively, and happy to leave their dog in the care of professionals, just before they walked out the door the two Greek brothers warned, "We do not pay if he dies."

What's this? No money without successful snakebite therapy? Benni now faced a dilemma. He had spent $700 of his boss's money, and he had collected no fee. The Greek 'do-not-pay-unless-he-lives' approach sounded like goodbye to his first job. No-one told him it would be like this in vet school at Saint Lucia.

Benni and staff worked hard, watching Lemnos in between looking at the other patients. However, the snake poison gradually took over. During the night, although Benni was in constant attendance, slowly, like an evil tide sweeping in, shock and powerful snake venom killed Lemnos.

Early next morning the Brothers Grimm knocked at the door. Can we see Lemnos? The owners' wallets had not yet been opened. How could Nick and Spiros understand how hard Benni had tried? Lemnos had to live first—only then would dollars be paid. It was not yet a good time to tell them the sad news. Nick and Spiros pushed their way into the treatment room before Benni could say what he wanted to say. What was Benni to do?

He had no better idea than to show Lemnos on the treatment table to his agitated owners. While the brothers were looking for signs of life, Benni held the breathing bag under the table, connected to the dog's chest. Squeeze and release, squeeze and release. With the endotracheal tube in place, the chest was moving up and down, up and down. Benni applied the stethoscope with a flourish and listened intently over the heart area, his expression one of deep concentration. "Hmmm, seems to be OK there." Benni exuded confidence to Nick and Spiros. The Greeks needed to be confident before getting their wallets out. Benni needed to be confident to hold onto his job.

The owners left, paying $1000 on the way out. Benni's job looked a little more secure. Two hours later the owners were phoned by the nurse, Maggie, and told of the patient's demise. Lemnos was taken to the local tip for burial. But Benni's trouble was not yet over.

Benni had been convincing, but not so convincing. Another phone call. Could Nick and Spiros pick up the body so they could determine the exact time of death? The dark cloud over Benni's future veterinary career—and his acting career—had moved a little but was still hovering, blocking out the sun on any future performance. Benni fought back against the forces of darkness. "We gotta get that body. Quietly, unheard, unseen. Can't be in broad daylight."

Benni and support staff planned a midnight visit to the local tip wearing mining helmets with lights on top. What a wise move. But it was not easy searching in the dark. It was too dark to see. What would passing cars think about moving lights amongst the rubbish? What would night strollers make of subdued voices rummaging in the tip?

"Can't see anything here," said the team. More searching through more smelly rubbish. And still more searching. Must be here somewhere. But the midnight search and rescue was not in vain. At 2 am the departed Lemnos was discovered. As the team pulled away at plastic bags and decaying vegetable matter to uncover the body, Margaret, the veterinary nurse, mused, "What overtime will Cleveland be paying?" There is nothing as good as a joke in a smelly setting in the pitch black in the middle of the municipal tip. This was the Australian Comedy Festival at a surprise venue.

Lemnos' body was taken back to the surgery and laid out for the autopsy. But the grief must have been too much for Nick and Spiros, for they never did return to found out the time of death. The precise time of death was thus never recorded. And

Cleveland remained happy with his new vet. Benni not only kept his job but went on to become a highly dedicated and sensitive veterinarian.

This sort of thing would not happen today, times they are a changing.

*Acknowledgement:* Story from Mark Curtis

# 22 BLIND DOG FOR AN EX-POW

A thin retina affects more than a canine friend due to our cavalier attitude to animal disease, more than 90 dog breeds go blind from inherited Progressive Retinal Atrophy (PRA)—the degeneration of the thin light sensing layer, the retina, in the back of the eye. Dogs with PRA at first lose night vision, while retinal loss is slight. The ten healthy retinal layers gradually thin to a jumbled three, or less, diseased layers. Retinal disease is mostly painless for the dog, though in rare cases of chronic PRA the lens can fall out of place, which can cause the animal a significant amount of eye pain. And if our lack of care causes just one instance of this pain, then that is once too often.

Dogs can carry PRA in their genes. Although apparently unaffected, their sight intact, these PRA dogs used for breeding spread the blindness. Even though we have known about PRA since 1911, careless breeding perpetuates this form of vision loss. Today, in some breeds, DNA analysis from a swab inside the cheek can identify carriers of PRA. Though PRA arrived by chance, it has been spread in dog breeds by mankind. Now we need vet eye specialists looking at retinas in 90 dog breeds in an attempt to limit PRA from producing more blind dogs and giving more owners heartache.

## Doug

The room was hushed. Someone who carried himself like an officer and looked like Douglas Fairbanks was holding the audience with a song. Doug Lush was singing 'I'm Glad I'm Not Young Any More', with a different twang to the American. I was hearing pure Australian with a lilt of Maurice Chevalier.

The applause was enthusiastic when the song ended all too soon. I sensed a strength and compassion in this upright elderly man who was glad of his years and looked so young.

## War

Doug, who loved songs, athletics and poodles, was a veteran of the Singapore defeat by the Japanese in World War Two. What was it Australians said to each other at the time? 'Singapore is too far from Europe to engage British military minds. The War Office in London fighting an enemy close at hand has other things to worry about.'

The Japanese, following Hitler's success in Europe, declared war on 8 December 1941, and quickly occupied French Indochina. The Allies thought invasion would come across the China Sea, so did not prepare 'Fortress' Singapore against the possibility of Japanese troops swooping overland down the Malayan Peninsula. Doug was among troops of the Sixth and Seventh Divisions. So quickly were they shipped to battle, he told me later, that they had no jungle equipment or camouflage. They arrived in the jungles of Singapore not in jungle uniform but in desert gear, ready for the Middle East.

The war in Singapore started when Japanese bombs sank the *Prince of Wales* and *Repulse*, two ships of the British Navy in the Singapore harbor. The raw Australian troops soon learned the rules of combat—the enemy shot or bayoneted all wounded. But it was not until later they found out about 40 Australian nurses, moving away from carefully aimed Japanese rifles, were shot in the back as they walked out to sea. One young nurse played dead and survived to tell the story.

Japanese troops came out of the jungle to capture Doug and 3,000 men. Most spent three and a half years in the notorious Changi Camp as prisoners of war, with not enough food and too much disease. Lieutenant Doug Lush told me such privation got to the young men, with many dying of malnutrition and dysentery without a sound. Men in their twenties went off their food and quietly died. Doug, a competitive 120 yards hurdler in his twenties, was tougher than some younger men. He did what he could to help boost the spirits of the troops when morale was low.

## A vet as a medico

One of the men captured with Doug was a Dutch veterinary surgeon called Hans 'Dutch' Eykmann. In the absence of a medico, this vet in Changi scraped many leg ulcers of the captured troops. With no anaesthetic but friends to hold the patients down, Dutch applied a red-hot poker on the scraped ulcers. He would never have done this to a dog without an anaesthetic back at his practice, but the circumstances were different, and ulcer cautery helped keep the captured troops alive. Dutch the vet stood in each morning at sick parades hoping to influence the guards, trying to protect men too sick to work.

'Sarute me prease. How many time bowel move? You say only eight time? Eight not many time. Go out from camp. Work on road.'

To work on the road meant a bowl of rice. No work meant half a bowl for the day. Work near the golf links carried extra memories. Consigned to the pick and shovel party around the Singapore Golf Links, it was not a half bowl of rice for them, but no rice at all.

Dysentery stopped for many men only when they died.

## Untrained anaesthetist

Doug found new duties looking after his men. Lieutenant Lush became the vet's courageous new assistant. He helped veterinarian Dutch anaesthetise men for surgery. Doug's qualification? Perform at your best whatever the track. Doug used the packing of a Red Cross parcel as a mask, soaking it in ether to anaesthetise one soldier who had fallen and dislocated his shoulder. The assisting group around the sick soldier were amateurs. No soldier had any more medical experience than holding down men in pain.

The vet gave instructions to his new anaesthetist. 'Don't give him too much after he goes off. Ease the mask off and look to make sure he is still breathing. Watch his chest move while I put the shoulder back in its socket.'

Doug held the ether mask tightly over the patient's nose and mouth. Violent struggling occurred when the soldier, going under, could not breathe air. As he tried to gulp air, his wildly flailing arms and legs were dangerous. Doug knew big doses of ether can be fatal but kept the patient unconscious while the vet, using his fingers to feel his way in strange territory, replaced the dislocated shoulder.

## Tooth extractions by a vet and untrained dental assistant

The vet extracted teeth, too—some with big roots wedged into the gums and bony jaw. Tooth removal is a difficult art, and most doctors refer extractions to dentists. Before the war, Dutch had removed many big roots of a dog's large bone-crushing molar teeth. He had also extracted equine teeth. These are special teeth which are anchored deeply into the horse's jawbone, designed for grinding tough grass. In his veterinary surgery, his dental patients were either asleep or with a gag in place to make sure strong jaws did not bite his hands. In prison Dutch had no such equipment. He just had Doug.

Dutch's dental tools in the prison camp were not as good as the forceps he had in Holland. People like to say they have their teeth 'pulled', but teeth anchored firmly in the jawbone are extracted with more push than pull. Back home, the curved blades of traditional dental forceps were pushed with force into a tooth socket to squeeze out a conical root. But in prison blunt-ended automotive pliers were boiled in the camp kitchen and used as Dutch's crude forceps.

Dutch had large arms and used all his veterinary strength. The trouble was that car pliers did not hold a tooth crown well and did not fit into a tooth socket beside a root to wedge it out. With the awkward design of the car pliers, the strong Dutchman did what dentists try to avoid—he crushed the crowns of many aching teeth with his pliers, at the same time failing to extract the tooth roots. The vet, however, was lucky—he could call on Doug, who had a more gentle touch, to do the more difficult part. Doug finished the job and removed shattered tooth fragments hidden in the gums, telling soldiers all the while, "Hold this on your gum to stop the bleeding." 'This' was not a wrapped gauze pad which had been sterilised in an autoclave, but a small folded piece of torn-up shirt.

After months as a POW with 500 Dutch and 500 Australians, Doug was moved from Changi to Kobe, Japan. The men hoped for more food but found poor rations in their new camp. They soon discovered Americans did not just bomb the Japanese capital, but many miles away from Tokyo, American incendiary bombs were falling near Doug's camp. Luckily, the American bombs missed Doug in his Japanese quarters. Who knows what would have happened if the bomber crew had been Australian?

But the tide of war was turning. Mick Armstrong, a cartoonist for Melbourne newspaper *The Argus*, depicted a traveler asking his readers, "Excuse prease, how far to Tokyo?" Australia began to think of VP Day—Victory in the Pacific.

Doug did not know how the war was going. He thought of home, marrying his girlfriend and owning a poodle.

Poodles have a long history of service to people. Recognised in Russia and Germany since the early 16th century as a friend and efficient retriever of waterfowl, the name 'poodle' comes from the German puddeln, meaning 'to splash in water'. The stylish hair trim made popular in France was originally for protection of joints and chest from the cold when the dog took to the water. It was a working style haircut long before it was in fashion parading under the Eiffel Tower.

## Poodle bumping into things

Years after I heard Doug's song about being glad he was not young, he came to me in Melbourne with his much-loved Louis, a black six-year-old miniature poodle. No-one had noticed any trouble at first or had warned Doug that poodles were one of the breeds that can develop PRA. This was in spite of the disease being recorded in another breed, a Gordon setter, in 1911, which should have served as a warning to all other dog breeders.

PRA was first recorded in Australian poodles in the 1950s. Vets in Australia were onto it quickly. In 1953, HB Parry, who was an innovative teacher of veterinary medicine at Sydney University, wrote about PRA in Irish Setters, not in a veterinary journal but in the *British Medical Journal*. Nine years later PRA was recorded in British and Australian poodles in the esteemed UK journal, the *Veterinary Record*. A veterinary ophthalmologist well known to breeders, Keith Barnett, wrote about PRA in the UK. In Australia one of my teachers, John Keep, recorded poodle PRA. All this Australian information was available to poodle breeders.

The disease was hailed as a canine equivalent of a human inherited disease causing night blindness. In people, *retinitis pigmentosa*, or 'Ret Pig' as it is commonly known, shows up in people during teenage years or early twenties. Retinal receptors degenerate until most disappear, leaving those affected severely disabled.

## Dog stands waiting to be helped

Louis stood in the waiting room with his head up expectantly, and moved very slowly on the floor of my waiting room. Mostly he just stood there, waiting for Doug to guide him with the tone of his voice. Doug told me Louis seemed unwilling to leave the back porch at night and had begun to stumble going down stairs. This was not a sign obvious enough to go to a vet immediately, but a few weeks later when he was in strange surroundings during the day, Louis had started to bump into things. This alarmed Doug enough to ask my advice about his gentle little dog. He came to see me years too late. Although an earlier consultation might have done little to save sight, it would have been best to talk to Doug before he bought Louis.

## What we learn from the soldier's dog

*If we allow any eye disease to be bred into 90 and more breeds, at least we should learn as much as we can to avoid being landed with pain and expense. All animal lovers should know what happens in the breeding world for us to be sold a pup.*

Owners get confused about pupil response to light. Pupil response is one test owners learn about because they can do it at home, but it is NOT a reliable home test of vision. The pupils control how much light is reaching the retina. Pupil closure is vital for sharp vision and avoiding glare, but pupil response can be tricky to interpret. Watching a dog hesitate in strange surroundings in the dark offers a clue.

## Diagnosis for Louis

I shone a penlight into Louis' eyes to check pupil response to light. The pupils got smaller, but too slowly for me to be happy about the little dog's eye health. This led to a teaching point I made to students about pupil response in the dark using a small torch—"Do not look for *yes* or *no* but whether it is *fast* or *slow*". Slow pupil movement can indicate retinas not taking in light photons efficiently. The pupils were slow to get smaller because they were not getting brain messages to close down. Small pupils in normal eyes protect light receptors at the back of the eye.

## What we should have done for the returned soldier

Before Doug bought his dog, we should have suggested he contact the Victorian Canine Association, to consult breed lists of inherited diseases. He needed veterinary advice with his breeder selection. The Poodle Club could have provided him with a list of studs free of PRA. *True dog scholars don't breed for dollars.*

When I looked into the back of Louis' eyes, would I be able to detect the thinning of his retinas? PRA in poodles starts with loss of night vision and is not curable. Would the retinas get better? Would they get worse?

The eye, originally a piece of brain in the embryo, is displaced to the front of the head to pick up light. The retina is delicate and can be damaged by too much solar radiation. Eyes work best if the amount of illumination coming in is controlled, hence pupil closure in bright light.

## Large pupils in poodles

For sharpest vision, we need small pupils. Too much light confuses, blurring vision. Large pupils are seen in some latter day poodles because we have unwittingly bred in another disease of pupil muscles, or rather lack of them. Modern poodles have iris muscles too thin and weak to create a small pupil. Although handicapped by pupils which are too large, dogs can see well enough to get around inside. The dog pays a price outside in bright light when pupils cannot close up. Animals with weak iris muscles are uncomfortable for life.

You can easily be misled with a pupil response when the retinal light receptors are ailing. In spite of severe disease, the eye behaves as though it does not want to let on something is wrong. At first glance, pupils seem to respond 'normally'. It is as though it tries to conceal dysfunction, somewhat akin to animals in the jungle concealing an illness. Looked at more carefully, I noted pupils in front of the suspect retinas constricted but did so too slowly.

## Pupil size and speed of getting smaller

Checking pupils is something owners/carers can do, and indeed must do when looking for inflammation in their animal's eye. *Don't leave all eye exams to your vet; owners are the examiner at the front line.* Talking to clinical groups around the exam table, I say, "When looking for the pupil reaction to a penlight shone into the eye, *remember this about pupil response.*" I paused, and said it again, waiting for the class to give me their full attention as I shone the small light onto the most sensitive part of the retina. Talking of pupil closure, I continued, "Judge not closing yes or no, but if they're closing fast or slow."

## Eye shine is too bright—a veterinary diagnostic aid not available for the human eye

Louis' pupils were slow, and when I looked at the back of his eyes I saw the answer for his bumping into things. Parts of his eyeshine—tapetums, or more accurately tapeta—were too shiny. I could see retinas too thin in areas of brighter reflection. The disease, retinal atrophy, had been there for many months before Doug had noticed vision loss.

> Eyeshine: Tapetal fluorescence from behind the retina reflects light back to the light receptors. Looking at an animal's eyes from the front, we see eyeshine as a disc of light coming to us through the retina. As it reflects it gives rods and cones a second exposure to photons, a second bite of the cherry. Retinal cells pick up photons coming into the eye and then from tapetal fluorescence pick up more photons reflecting back through retina.

## Blood layer disease in human eyes—macular degeneration

We are aware of our own choroid, the blood filled layer behind the retina, in disease. If it should lose its blood supply, we lose vision. Many people lose vision because their choroids become unhealthy. Macular degeneration involves an ailing choroid and retina—Age Related Macular Degeneration, or AMD. It is now a common cause of human vision loss. Antioxidant therapy may help. Ask the eye specialist.

The macula is a small yellowish spot in the middle of a human retina that provides the greatest visual acuity and colour perception. Degeneration of the human macula is emerging in epidemic proportions. In 1960, at the Royal Victorian Eye and Ear Hospital, 1,500 people from 60 to 90 years were examined for AMD. Not one was found. At last report, the hospital was seeing 10,000 new cases each year (Brennan pers. comm. 2005).

Animal choroids are noticed in healthy animals because of eyeshine, shown as circles of bright light in a kangaroo looking at our torch from among the eucalypts in the night bush. The tapetum is a unique layer of vivid beauty in the choroid giving rise to brilliant fluorescence. Depending on coat colour and breed, the tapetum gives dogs a brilliant yellow-green to red-orange reflection most easily noticed in the dark. A puppy's developing tapetum is blue.

The name 'tapetum' comes from the Latin for tapestry. Eyeshine helps animals on sea and land. Whales, seals, possums and kangaroos have improved night vision from eyeshine. When I look at the back of an animal eye, the colour of the tapetum is due to interference of light like a film of oil on water. I continue to be full of joy seeing tapetal colours. This joy is denied medico ophthalmologists, as it is not present in people.

Poor Louis, his choroids were diseased as well as his retinas. It was not by chance, it was bred into him with his retinal disease. Foolishly, we like 'pretty' dogs, which look so because they have less melanin pigment. Different, yes, but it is unwise to have less melanin, as the dog needs pigment as protection from UV light. Moreover, poorly pigmented parents don't create enough melanin in the embryo, and the eyeball does not develop properly, nor does the visual cortex. Albino beings have poor vision.

Do not buy pretty dogs which look different or, the latest fashion. Avoid breeding with animals with markedly less skin pigment. Albinos (all white coat with pink or blue eyes) and part albinos (mostly white coat) are bad news. Melanin pigment is needed for development in the embryo. Some albinos are deaf. Pink eyes and some blue eyes mean there is too little pigment in each iris around the pupil allowing us to see pink or red iris blood vessels to be seen. Lack of pigment in the iris means too much light gets into the eyes resulting in less protection of the retinas from bright light. Most uncomfortable.

## We don't need to breed blind dogs any more

Today, DNA testing has equipped us with a new tool to prevent PRA in some breeds. When one parent is shown to be free by genetic profile, the genetically free dogs can mate with carriers. Carriers, safely bred to genetically free dogs, do not produce blind animals. No PRA dogs are produced.

Elimination of PRA was successful because breeders were honest that their stud dogs included carriers and these were not used for breeding. Remember, carrier mated to carrier produced blind dogs. A breeder would say, "I won't breed from that dog because his family is suspicious. No, you can't have his pup, he might go blind. Do not buy this pup for breeding, he might be a carrier."

The gene causing PRA does not always show up until later years, and in American and English cocker spaniels, the first signs may not appear until as late as eight years (Aguirre and Acland 1998). Vets using an ophthalmoscope do not detect signs until three-to-five years in miniature and toy poodles. In earlier times, when ethical thoughts were in vogue, PRA was controlled by dedicated breeders, testing mated dogs to find which were carriers. Their dedication limited the number of breeds affected. Breeders avoided using suspect dogs, carriers or dogs from PRA affected families. Breeding only dogs genetically free of PRA reduced the disease.

## Triumph of Irish setter breeders between 1960 and 1975

All breed clubs have to be aware of the Irish Setter Club's successful disease control. Similar to PRA in poodles, Irish setter retinal rods also degenerated first, causing night blindness. Breeder discipline freed the Irish setters and showed the way to control inherited disorders to the dog world.

Early PRA was easy to breed out because blind pups are easy to exclude from breeding. Late onset inherited disorders, and there are many of them in dogs, are much more of a challenge. In spite of this, due to dedicated Irish setter breeders who wanted to get rid of inherited blindness, PRA was eliminated between 1960 and 1975 without the modern procedure of genetic profiling.

These fifteen years of landmark action showed the world how we can look after a breed in trouble. Had all breeds with inherited diseases copied the Irish setter campaign, tens of thousands of dogs, and Doug Lush, could have been saved from much heartache.

## Did we follow a good example?

The Irish setter campaign did not inspire breeders of other affected breeds. I listed these breeds in *Everydog* in 1990. But other breed clubs could not stop breeding dogs which went blind. I had to say, in 1983, that any breed could develop PRA. I became disappointed to find out how correct this statement was.

Dogs are there for us. Are we there for them? How are the breeders of Doug's poodle feeling, breeding a dog developing a well-known blindness? Why no action so that no more affected poodles would be sold?

Whatever success the original group of Irish setter breeders had during the fifteen 'PRA control years', it was short-lived. The disease reappeared in 1977 (Rubin 1989). Vision once more is at risk.

## The blind dog at home

What would I say to Doug about his friend Louis becoming blind? Here was an ex-POW survivor of starvation and ill treatment imprisoned for years, a defender of my way of life. Could I help his later years—*his* way of life—by offering reasonable sight for his pet?

"Will Louis go completely blind?" Doug's question was softly spoken.

"It looks like it, Doug."

He touched my arm as if to say it can't be helped. I did not tell him we had known enough to avoid this blindness in dogs for fifty years. And I told him nothing about blind eyes which could become painful later. If a PRA-affected dog's lens works loose inside the eye and flops about causing severe damage, glaucoma could eventually result. Perhaps Doug did not need to know about this impending pain, but breeders should.

"What can I do to help Louis?" Doug spoke sadly.

"Limited treatment, Doug. The cells of the thin retinas are too jumbled to give Louis any vision. You cannot bring back the ten healthy layers of retina once they have degenerated."

Retinal atrophy is incurable, but some dogs retrieve sight following low energy laser therapy. Not high energy, but *low* energy laser moved over the retina. It seems to help photo-receptors get rid of cell debris and let the ailing retina work well. Some afflicted dogs can even catch a frisbee again after low energy laser. I could not do much for Doug; did I want him to pay for therapy which helped for only a short time?

Many human degenerative diseases, including senile dementia and macular degeneration, have their origin in free radical damage (Florence 1995). Free radicals are of interest to people as they contribute to aging. The free radicals are molecular sharks damaging all cell membranes, energy centres (such as mitochondria) and cell intelligence such as DNA. Vertebrate retina has higher oxygen consumption than any other tissue by a factor of at least seven (Handelman & Dratz 1986). Blood going into the retina needs to have high levels of anti-oxidants to give retinal cells a better chance to pick up photons of light.

"Avoid cutting hair on his nose. The poodle-style close hair trim on his nose is a no-no. Leave those strong black whiskers on either side of his nose. Louis needs those as antennae to help find his way around."

Whiskers are called *vibrissae* because the thick black strands of hair vibrate when touched. Cats' whiskers are sensitive to delicate air currents, and protect the eyes. Louis' would too.

When vibrissae are touched the eye blinks, and the vibrissae stop the animal going through narrow spaces.

"Is that all I can do?" I sensed his disappointment.

"Don't move the furniture. He will respond to your voice when your tone goes up as a warning. And he will need all his hearing. Make sure his ears are clean and healthy. And you can try a natural anti-oxidant fruit juice twice daily." I liked the concept of trying oral therapy to help brain and body towards better vision.

War veteran Doug had a blind dog because not enough people took up the cause and changed breeding practices when mature dogs lost vision. We all let Doug down. The pups were adorable, but by the time adult dogs went blind breeders forgot it was because gene carriers had been bred together. I wish I'd had a group of breeders in the consulting room to see Doug's grief. Doug's son Stewart described how his elderly father felt: "When Louis went blind it was like a death in the family."

# 23 AVOID A MORAL HANGOVER—SAY NO TO TIGER WINE

The tiger may be 'king of the beasts' in Asia—the stripes on its forehead proclaim it so—but there is no evidence that products from tigers have any benefit that cannot be derived from herbs. How well do we control products harvested from the big carnivore? Tiger bones are no different to those of other mammals. In spite of this, tiger-bone wine sales are booming.

Tiger parts have been used in traditional Chinese medicine for more than a thousand years, pushing three remaining species close to extinction. There are only 5,000 Bengal tigers and between 300 to 500 Sumatran tigers alive in the wild (King 2006). Professor Sheng Holin, a mammal expert and co-author of *The Mammalia Of China*, tried the wine. From Sheng's personal account, the wine didn't work. Are you sure? It made a lot of money, and 'anyone who drank the wine felt that it was special'. Nevertheless, tigers and all conservationists are in agreement that the striped carnivores are more special when alive and well. Tiger wine does you doubtful good but definitely harms the tiger population. When will we learn to leave animal products alone?

In the past, to hunt down the tiger, landed gentry riding high on elephants used honking horns and thrashing sticks at ground level. Things are somewhat better today. Some of the once private reserves are now havens for the tigers to live and breed in peace. And in 1983 there was a domestic ban on tiger wine—sales of which had been booming up until this point. One concerned supplier of Traditional Chinese Medicines (TCM) made a substitute bone wine from moles and herbs, marketing it as 'Rodent Wine'. Funnily enough, with this inviting title, it didn't sell.

The Xiongsen Bear and Tiger Farm at Guillin is China's biggest, holding 1,300 tigers. Dozens of sleek tigers laze on the grass in the sun. The farm sells its six-year-old wine as 'bone restoring wine' in 500ml tiger-striped bottles. The guide explains: *The wine is made from tigers which have died fighting or from old age.* Fatal fights in the park? When wine demand goes up, so do the fights. Sounds suspicious.

Tough restrictions on tiger products were put in place in 1993; and this was lauded by the one hundred and seventy one nations of the Convention on International Trade in Endangered Species. But after a decade of animal protection and heavy suppression, tiger bone wine is on the market again. Traffic International and the World Wildlife Fund say the Chinese Government is worried about the farms closing. Who will look after all those tigers? What about the tiger farm being hit for compensation? Could the Chinese consider a free-range tiger zoo, more restorative to the soul than a bottle of tiger-bone wine? At least everyone can share a park.

The tiger itself reveals the sad consequences of incarceration. The ticket price at the farm includes watching the feeding of a live water buffalo to a tiger. A revealing spectacle follows when the live meal is served. As the water buffalo hunches in fear, the captive-bred carnivore cannot complete the kill. He lacks the skills. Murderers come out of jail and kill again, informing us that people do not forget how to kill. In confinement, tigers sometimes do. The buffalo wants to be able to run with the herd and die quickly with dignity. But, as a captive slave, the buffalo cannot do this, and has to be finished off with a rifle by human attendants. Dying well is denied the herbivore.

However, a more alarming business than denying natural death emerges. At an upmarket local restaurant, customers can eat 500 grams of tiger steak, stewed or fried (fried tiger—do you want French fries with that?). With enough notice, meat is served fresh rather than frozen. Someone has it wrong. *Man is not an obligate meat-eater.* He eats meat by choice. It's the tiger that is equipped to eat meat. He has teeth to rip flesh from the carcass. To keep the earth in true balance, the local restaurant will have to change its menu. We should offer meat *to* the tiger, not *from* the tiger.

Everybody in the jungle reserve can look at, admire, and take in the animal's strength. Morally, people drawn to the big carnivore are told by the tiger spirit to face their issues head on (King 2006). If we want tigers to survive for our grandchildren to marvel at, keep them in large jungle reserves. If you want a glass of wine, drink it from the vineyard. No tiger wine, thanks.

# 24 UNDER THE SEA TO EIGHT DAYS A WEEK

*Veterinarians are industrious and so dedicated to their job that their family can be disadvantaged. They are caring, kind and sympathetic in spirit to a point of self sacrifice. They underestimate their strengths. It could be said vets are self effacing to a fault.*
*—David Hendle, retired long-time supplier of instruments and pharmaceutical drugs to the veterinary profession.*

Most veterinary students, like myself, had lived a sheltered pre-veterinary life before starting their course at the University of Sydney. While we were wet behind the ears, Howard 'Dusty' Rhodes was a direct contrast. Although not much older than us, in his early twenties he had been a volunteer in the British Fleet Air Arm during the Second World War. He had seen mankind at its worst, and he brought a worldliness to his studies that we didn't have. We looked up to him as a war hero. He was several years ahead of me at university, and I knew him more by reputation than acquaintance. Dusty knew who he was and where he was headed. We did not.

Dusty told me his life story years later in front of a blazing fire in his living room. His eyes shone with the memory as he looked at a photograph of a group of men in his squadron who had been lost in the war. Typically, Dusty had his crossbred dog called Runty nestling into his lap.

Dusty Rhodes, born on 25 September 1922, was one of ten survivors out of two squadrons, or twenty men, who served in the British Fleet Air Arm. The Corsair fighter planes were vital for the war and took part in strikes on the German battleship *Tirpitz*, lying at Norway in the Trondheim fjord.

Hitting your target was one thing. Landing safely was another. Landing on the deck was not easy. One commander showed consistently poor ability to land his Corsair on deck. "You'll bloody well get killed," his men pleaded. He had lost two brothers in this war, and his father died in World War One. His comrades urged him to give his mother a break and resign his commission. Reluctantly the pilot went to other duties.

One commander was shot down into the sea and managed to escape the wreck of his plane. Unfortunately, he could not swim. Dusty flew around him like a mother bird wanting to protect an injured chick, but to no avail. When the Japanese planes arrived, Dusty had to fly off. Enemy guns shot the commander in the water. The Admiralty in London did not let the commander's family know, and when Dusty told them later, it was the first they had heard of his death.

Morale was low. It was not just the loss of this particular commander that shook the young volunteers—the squadron had lost four commanders within a few months. Not only was the pitching, tossing deck of the aircraft carrier a threat to the pilots in training, two aircraft had collided in mid-air, killing both pilots. The skipper of the aircraft carrier had acted quickly to avoid the Corsairs in the water, but the massive ship cut through one of the downed planes.

On another occasion, following routine maintenance, one aircraft mechanic incorrectly wired Dusty's plane so the joystick worked the opposite to what was intended. Dusty moved controls to go right and the plane went left. This was disconcerting at speed, and Dusty had to adjust to the new responses mid-flight. Teaching himself an opposite set of joystick controls, in spite of the ocean swell, Dusty got the disabled plane back on the deck of the aircraft carrier. It was called at the time a most remarkable effort of flying skill. The pilot took it all in his stride.

One day—12 September to be exact—in an attempt to escort bombers making a raid, there was a call to action. Dusty's Corsair fighter was to take off from the aircraft carrier. He knew the bombers needed protection, but did not know he would have trouble getting into the air. A Barracuda bomber from the aircraft carrier suddenly had no power on take-off. It went down with all three crew immediately. The fighter crews learned later that the Barracuda crew all drowned. Next Dusty faced his Corsair down the carrier deck towards the ocean. When he was halfway along the carrier deck, he realised he also did not have enough power for take-off. His aircraft failed to reach the sky and immediately plunged deeply into the ocean. He could not get out of the plane because of water pressure on the transparent cover of the cockpit. The trapped pilot had to wait for the space around him to fill with water before he could move the canopy and get out.

Why had the planes started to fall off the carrier? The answer, which came later, was in the fuel. Someone was trying to make money by adding seawater to the aeroplane fuel. The chief petty officer had not supervised plane re-fuelling as he should have. He was severely dealt with, but the person responsible for doctoring the aviation fuel before selling it to the Navy was never caught.

"It was really black down there," Dusty told me.

Just black? I could imagine much more than a feeling of black. Deep in the sea where no light could reach, how would you know whether you could take a big enough breath to make it to the surface? Dusty had no such fear. Make sure the Mae West was in place, take in a lungful of air, push the canopy back, and up to the sunshine. When Dusty reached the surface he found the carrier was out of sight.

It seemed to Dusty that he had been abandoned. Lucky for him, he had a good Kiwi friend, Van, in his squadron. Dark-haired and handsome, Van looked rather like Tyrone Power. He had wanted to find the downed pilot and asked for his Corsair to be placed on the catapult so he could get in the air as quickly as possible. Van was flung into the sky and immediately began to search for a streak of yellow in the vast blue of the ocean. A cake of yellow dye in a pocket of Dusty's Mae West life jacket would help Van trace the lost pilot. Floating in the deep waters of the ocean, with the terror of a potential shark attack, changes a man. There was the very real possibility that Dusty would perish alone. It was a different, older man Van rescued some hours later.

By the time Dusty, aged twenty-three, joined us at Sydney University, he had been a Lieutenant Commander awarded the Distinguished Service Cross twice. He had spent four years flying fighter aircraft, and ditched into the sea three times. He took away the ability to think positively and make the best of any situation.

Considering his vast contribution to the practice of veterinary medicine, it is strange to think that Dusty almost didn't become a vet. After he left the Fleet Air Arm and returned to New Zealand, he had actually been accepted to study medicine at Otago. One day he was sitting on the tractor of the family farm, deep in thought. The New Zealand countryside gave him time to think. He was about to begin studying medicine, when he suddenly wondered why. His recent experience with the human race in the war had left him with the impression that humans were really a bunch of bloody madmen. It was a kill or be killed kind of world.

Pondering this, Dusty decided that the animal kingdom was the opposite. While animals might kill to survive, they would never do it for power or greed or political ideals. Animals do not grab something they do not need. They respect other beings.

Dusty had been talking to an old friend who was depressed because his application to study medicine at Otago had been rejected. Dusty had a sudden brainwave. He offered his friend his own place at the university, deciding to become a vet instead. His friend went on to become one of New Zealand's top paediatricians, while Dusty went on to become a legendary vet.

After some enquiry around the world, Dusty decided to come to Australia to study because there was no vet school in New Zealand at that time. In Sydney he met his wife, Maudie, a local beauty who became the key to Dusty being able to manage family life and that of an eight-day-a-week practitioner.

After graduating from Sydney University, Dusty went to Singleton, northern NSW, and joined a dairy company as a salaried vet. One night when Dusty was on call, a dairy farmer called Harry rang him at 10:30 pm. Harry had a cow called Daisy in difficulty calving in a paddock. When Dusty got there, he found Daisy staggering about suffering very severe milk fever. The so-called 'milk fever' is a common condition brought on in cows producing more milk than their bodies were designed to do. Producing a high milk yield decreases blood calcium to dangerously low levels, and without an intravenous drip-feed calcium injection, the acutely affected cow dies.

With great difficulty in the dark, Dusty and Harry managed to catch the staggering animal, put a halter on her head and inject the calcium solution into her jugular vein. Dusty then delivered a live calf, picked up his tools and headed off to his car in the pitch dark.

"Wrong direction, Dusty!" called Harry as the vet disappeared into the night, but he did not realise that, as a pilot, Dusty had learnt to navigate by the stars. He got to his car with no problems.

A week later, Harry again called Dusty at 10.30 pm, and again with the same problem—milk fever. When Dusty arrived, Harry was limping badly.

"What's with the limp?" asked Dusty. "Looks bad."

In spite of his obvious pain, Harry was dismissive. "'I've got a nail in my boot that's sticking into my big toe," he explained.

Dusty watched as Harry painfully tried to move about. "Why on earth haven't you had it fixed?"

"Haven't been into town lately."

The two men set off in the dark winter's night—Dusty walking and Harry hobbling—into the paddock to find the sick cow. As soon as Dusty saw the cow in question, he realised that not only was she sick, she was also calving. Harry hadn't said anything about a calving on the phone, and Dusty had no chains to pull the calf's legs through the pelvic passage. Dusty left Harry with the cow and returned to his car to get the necessary equipment.

Half an hour passed with no sign of the vet. Nearly an hour later, Dusty loomed up in the darkness. For once, his Captain Cook skills had let him down. There was a bit of cloud about and he had ended up walking in circles.

Despite this blip on his navigational radar, Dusty was nevertheless unrivalled in his district for delivering calves. It took a lot of skill and patience to stumble in the dark through a wet paddock without a torch, avoiding the cowpats, and catch the patient. Then—mostly singlehandedly—came what could be the hard part. Without much more than a bucket of soapy water, he would deliver the calf. And for his efforts, he was often chased away by the mother—an indignity obstetricians never experience in hospitals after delivering a baby.

And payment wasn't guaranteed. One farmer, who used Dusty's services, would put all the bills in a hat at the end of each month and then pull out some bills from lucky local traders. These bills were considered for payment. If Dusty complained about slow imbursement, the farmer would say, "Ah, you'll not be in the draw next month, son."

As part of clinical experience in final year, Dusty worked in a cattle practice in New Zealand in the 1950s. He worked with a vet called George McDonald, who was an exceptional vet despite being a renowned boozer. George would be called to a cow down with milk fever.

"A bit of brandy would be a good idea," he would say to each farmer's wife. The obliging spouse would go to the liquor cabinet and return with a bottle of brandy. George would usually take four or five large swallows and wipe his mouth with the back of his hand. "Ah," he would say, smiling, "she looks much better now."

From that point, it was all too simple to get the cow back on her feet. Something by mouth for George and an intravenous injection for the cow, and everybody was happy.

Late one night, Dusty was driving in an old Vauxhall on a winding country track at his usual 100 kph and slammed right into a very large Aberdeen Angus bull standing in the middle of the road. The bull returned the compliment by shitting all over the front of the car before toddling off into the bush. Bullshit was the only evidence Dusty could show as the cause of his badly damaged Vauxhall to the dairy company paying his salary.

In the district late one afternoon and after a hard day's work, Dusty was out of his overalls and gumboots, showered, shaved and all dressed ready for a rare social event. It was the local ball, and everybody would be there. Then the phone rang. It was a farmer called Joe on the line. He was worried about a sick Friesian cow called Florence. Dusty took off all his fine gear and drove the ten kilometres to look at Florence. The cow was sick indeed. A severe infection had made the toxins build up in her blood to the point where she was effectively poisoned. Fluids were needed for the toxic shock, and Dusty gave sulphonamides—which were the best anti-bacterial treatment available at that time.

"Keep her in. She'll need to have more tomorrow," Dusty instructed.

Next day Dusty phoned to find out how she was. Joe told him not to bother coming out. According to Joe, Florence had rallied a little after the treatment and then she went outside the barn for a drink in a deep trough between paddocks. While doing this, she had got her head stuck under a wire across the trough and drowned.

Dusty could have left it at that, but the dairy company had an arrangement with the local knackery for any cow which died after being treated by a vet to be brought to the knackery for a post-mortem examination. It was a way for vets to get immediate information about why animals had died and perhaps utilise it in the future.

Joe agreed to the procedure although he wondered if it would be worthwhile. He had his doubts. He'd lost a good cow and her milk he could sell. This post-mortem was not going to bring her back.

The knackery soon had the big Friesian skinned and laid out. Dusty took up his big curved post-mortem knives. Joe agreed to help. They sharpened the blades on stone and steel. Joe did not like opening up one of his cows. It was bad enough to lose a good cow. What small businessman was asked to look inside a departed staff member? Or perform an inner examination of yesterday's faithful servant?

The cow opened up like a book. Intestines were inflamed. The heart showed many small haemorrhages; the lungs showed a few but the spleen was huge.

"Jesus Christ! It's fucking anthrax!" Dusty exploded.

The knackery staff was stunned. And Joe, a bit fuzzy from little sleep looking after his cow, was suddenly alert. Anthrax was serious. It was a nasty organism called a bacillus that not only killed animals but was dangerous for people too. Joe had kids to think of as well as his cows and the ones on neighbouring properties. If the bug could not be seen with a microscope on the spot, samples would have to be sent to a lab so the bacillus could be identified.

The University of Sydney, the nearest authority at the time, believed that there was no anthrax in the district. Joe and Dusty raced blood and tissue to the local doctor, the nearest place from which they could send a sample for a laboratory diagnosis. Both men knew that the causative anthrax organisms form spores. And spores can live for years in the soil. What they did not know was that in the previous century a soil deficiency in calcium was diagnosed on the farm. Because of this, a thick layer of blood and bone was spread over the pastures. The blood and bone had come from India where anthrax was endemic.

The passing days left Dusty and Joe in limbo.

"Ring the lab," pleaded Joe, and so Dusty picked up the phone.

"Yes . . . yes." Dusty nodded vigorously before slamming down the phone. "Bloody hell, it's anthrax!"

Anthrax in the district! The shit hit the fan. Phones ran hot across the country. It was like a bomb had gone off. Police cordoned off the area. The army was on the alert to help isolate affected cattle. Cattle were vaccinated. The crisis passed.

After some years practising in Singleton, Dusty decided to make Colac, in the western district of Victoria, his home. There he established a cattle practice, and over the years had four children with his wife, Maudie.

By that time I was working in my first job in a veterinary practice in Warrnambool, about an hour's drive from Colac. Dusty and I were reacquainted when he was confined to bed with mumps and needed someone to look after his practice. He gave me daily instruction from his swollen face across the bedroom. Well aware that mumps could make a man sterile, I kept my distance and stood in the doorway. He wrote instructions and drew maps for me on pieces of paper. I took them gingerly, wondering if I could get mumps from a piece of paper.

"You'd better hurry to Murphy's choking bull. It could be a hunk of turnip. If you drive too slowly, he might swallow it before you get there."

I drove Dusty's car, hoping that some of his vast experience would rub off on me. I hoped that the farmers wouldn't compare me unfavourably to their treasured local vet. While nervous, I looked forward to the opportunity to pass a probang—a semi-flexible rubber tube—down the bull's oesophagus to push any obstruction into the stomach.

Veterinary work relies a lot on confidence. If people knew that Dusty was ill, they might call in a different vet and Dusty would lose business. To create the illusion Dusty was still on duty, I drove his blue Ford Fairlane at flying speed, being careful to leave my foot on the accelerator and skid in the gravel going around the country corners. No-one would question it was Dusty doing a wheelie on the job. I was not as tall as Dusty, but I decided not to use a cushion on the driver's seat. It was safer to be low down behind the wheel at the pace I was travelling, given that seatbelts hadn't yet been invented.

I noted a sign saying 'Cape Clear' miles from the coast as I flew past. I suddenly wondered how you could have a cape in the middle of a forest. I found out later that the name came from Irish lumberjacks calling out just before a large tree was ready to fall to the forest floor. "Keep clear," they would cry out, though in their thick Irish brogue it sounded like 'Cape Claire'. The cry was heard so often in the forest that the name Cape Clear stuck.

I was so crafty with my flying approach to corners of the road that when Dusty recovered I was sure the secret of my impersonation would remain largely intact.

"Saw your car on the Apollo Bay road, Dusty," said a local pig farmer, a couple of days later. "But there was no-one driving."

Dusty roared laughing. I was less amused. I knew I was short, but that was a bit rich.

Dusty could never spend much time at home due to the demands of country practice. The phone started to ring when the cows came in for their morning milking. His wife, Maude, would start the day padding softly in her slippers on the lino down the passage of their weatherboard cottage to answer the phone.

"Good morning," she would answer in her soft voice, surprisingly articulate for the early hour. "Oh, at Carlisle River, next to Danny's turn-off at the store and then four miles . . . Oh, you have to take Mary to the doctor . . . in Geelong . . . Sorry to hear that . . . If you're not there, the cow will be in the yard . . ."

The day's work would be listed in a simple exercise book tied to the phone in the kitchen with string. Maude would write down the jobs in a fluent hand and then tear out the page for her husband. Dairy farmers scribbled notes and stuck them to the big aluminium milk cans sitting on a wooden stand at Dusty's front gates.

On this typical day, Dusty spent many hours on the road. He wound his way down to Carlisle River for a cow calving, then back to Colac for a 'cow down'—prostrate and only just conscious due to a disease like milk fever. Calcium was injected intravenously and the cow sat up. As soon as she was looking better, Dusty got back in his car and was on his way.

There was never any time to lose if he was to get through Maude's list. Through the Otway Mountains to Apollo Bay, and after winding through tall eucalypts, he caught a splendid view of the glorious sweep of the southern Victorian coast.

At Apollo Bay there was a horse with colic, and he had to be sure and tell Nancy O'Brien that her kelpie bitch, Red, was pregnant. And then back again to Simpson for another cow in trouble. All this without the benefit of a mobile phone. At home, Maude was dispensing common sense advice to worried farmers while looking after their offspring. When Dusty returned home to Maude and the family, there could be a bitch whelping, or a dog with a broken leg.

Dusty had to be able to drive hard and be relaxed. One Sunday Dusty drove 400 kilometres on his rounds. And it was not easy driving. The roads were winding, and you were never sure what was coming round the sharp curves. He swore that it was his piloting skills from WWII which helped to keep him driving safely even when he was weary. Negotiating the winding Wild Dog Creek Road through rain beating on his windscreen was especially difficult.

There was no time for golf, or any other recreation. The pressures of caring for animals in his huge district sapped away interest from other parts of life. Regular attendance at something like Rotary was not possible. There was also too little time spent at home, and this was one reason Dusty took his four kids in turn on his calls. His eldest son, Christopher, was shown the art of relieving a difficult bovine birth.

"Pull calf out, pull calf out," sang three-year-old Chris as Dusty drove at great speed through the Otways. As Chris got older, he would report to his mother when the two got home: "I don't know how the calf got in there, but Dad had a helluva job getting it out."

Dusty worked seven days a week because livestock do not take weekends off. One weekend he had a call from a man called Jackson, who used to be a dairy farmer but was now building up a very fine beef cattle stud of Charolais. The Charolais breed of cattle originated in central France, and the cows were so big that Dusty had to stand on fence rails almost a metre up from the ground when delivering their calves.

The stud cow in trouble was called Petite Chou, a handsome off-white giant with a pink mouth. She was expecting a calf sired by an imported bull, and Jackson eagerly anticipated this birth. He was very keen on the sire. When Dusty had a feel inside the uterus—and he could only just reach up there—he found the calf was back to front. It would be a difficult breech birth. Dusty could not feel where the back legs of the calf were—which was a problem, since he had to get a hold of the back legs to pull the calf out. The hind legs of the large calf were tucked up, its feet out of position, near the calf's head instead of pointing towards the exit passage. It was a vigorous half hour of reaching and pulling, reaching and turning, for Dusty to get the legs out before the magical delivery. Then out she came. Joy of all joys, another new life. It was a heifer, and Jackson and Dusty hung up the big beauty by her hind legs on the fence to drain fluid from the chest. Both men were pleased.

When Dusty lectured veterinary students, he always told them: "When you've pulled the calf out, come down from your high and have another look—there might be a second one in there." It was a golden rule of calving.

The Charolais calf weighed nearly sixty kilograms. It was so big that Dusty never imagined there could possibly be a second calf. As he washed his arms, chest, face, head, and anywhere soiled by the back end of a cow, he was on a high, and getting mentally ready for another job twenty kilometres away.

That night, Jackson's wife called Dusty. "We did appreciate your good work this morning," she said, obviously happy. Dusty smiled to himself—it was nice to get positive feedback. The farmer's wife then explained that the cow had the second calf herself. Dusty felt like an idiot that at such a late stage in his clinical life he would leave a calf behind in the uterus. He did not think so much about the fact that without his help the cow could not have been delivered at all. Furthermore, Dusty gave little thought that for Petite Chou he had intuitively followed a most sound rule of therapy—do not interfere if you do not have to. The second calf came out on her own. Unwittingly, Dusty had followed the non-interference rule to the letter.

Shortly after this incident, Charlie the dairy farmer called Dusty to look at one of his Jersey cows who was having trouble calving. Dusty swore he would check for two calves. So after the first had been delivered, Dusty then had a feel in the uterus. With a smile on his face, he delivered a second calf. Charlie's two little daughters, Sarah and Lucy, looked on, engrossed.

Starting his rounds the next day, Dusty saw the two girls walking to school because the school bus had broken down. Dusty offered the two happy bright-eyed girls a lift.

"Great job yesterday, Dusty," enthused Sarah.

Dusty beamed. The girls were obviously impressed with his skill.

Lucy joined in. "And you were sooo cool!"

It was moments like this that Dusty thought that being a country vet in calving season was surely the best job on God's green earth.

And then Lucy dropped the bombshell. "The third calf was born one hour later," she said.

Seven days a week, morning, noon and midnight, Dusty was always there for the animals and their owners. He went the extra distance in animal care. A foal with tetanus was given the first blood transfusion in the district and fed through a nasal tube into the stomach.

Not everyone appreciated Dusty's long working day. One Gellibrand dairy farmer seemed anxious about his stock horse and asked Dusty if he could look at him next time he was passing? When Dusty called in, the farmer seemed less passionate, almost sleepy, about his animal's diagnosis. Dusty felt the limb up and down, found where the leg was sore, and when he looked at his watch, discovered why the farmer showed heavy-lidded enthusiasm about what Dusty was telling him. The vet's watch told him the time was 1 am.

When formal moves were taken to reopen the vet school in the University of Melbourne, Dusty was President of the Australian Veterinary Association in Victoria during this vital time for the profession. This meant driving far and wide across the state of Victoria to draw together support while also running his very busy practice.

On the university wall at Parkville there is a life-size painting of a professor appointed because of Dusty's fundraising. There is, however, no picture of the practitioner who made it possible.

Dusty asked the question often repeated by other vets. How did my wife put up with it? Vets in country practice are taken away from those who need them most. Although he spent so much time in the car, his family life, under stress, did better than survive. Today he and Maude enjoy the company of thirteen adoring grandchildren.

Western district farmers didn't think of him as just their vet. He was their larger than life fighter pilot legend who happily worked eight days each week.

*Acknowledgement:* Vikki Petraitis helped write this story

# 25 YOUR FRIEND CAN KILL

*Irresponsible breeders are the first culprits for creating bad dogs. The second culprits are irresponsible owners. If your dog savages somebody, you may face time in jail. So should irresponsible breeders. Don't let's focus first on breed but who is in charge. All owners, if you can't offer strict discipline especially for vigorous dogs give the dog away*

More than 13,000 Australians need medical attention for dog bites each year, mostly by family or neighbours' dogs (Wood 2007, Working Dog Club newsletter). In the US, eighteen people die each year from dog attacks. The most famous death was that of thirty-three-year-old lacrosse coach Diane Whipple in 2001. Two dogs with separate owners were responsible for the death, and neither of the owners took any notice of the warning signs of aggression.

Locals who had seen the dogs urging each other on—dogs in packs do that—had warned of danger. Their veterinary surgeon had sent them a warning letter that their powerful undisciplined dogs were 'ticking time bombs' of danger. This failure to realise your happy dog at home dog can be a killer is a common owner blind spot.

The two mastiffs broke away from their leashes and charged, out of control, at Diane, who was terrified because she had already been bitten previously. The owners, who had failed to listen to both expert and common sense advice, were sentenced to four years in prison for manslaughter (Millan and Peltier, 2006).

Children, particularly boys, who are often more impulsive, and the elderly are the most at risk of attack from violent dogs, and bites on the face are the most common area of injury. Here are a few ways of preventing dog attack:

- ❖ Training children and pups when young helps to prevent dog bites, and so do muzzles.
- ❖ When you approach strange dogs or when they approach you, safety rules apply to all breeds
- ❖ Avoid eye contact with the dog
- ❖ Let the dog come to you rather than you go to the dog
- ❖ Once in close proximity, approach the dog from the side with fingers bunched—folded fingers are more protected than extended fingers
- ❖ Allow the dog to sniff your hands if approaching with tail wagging and no aggression.

*It is the owner's responsibility to prevent their dog from biting, not the dog's.* This especially applies to breeds derived from ancestors of canine gladiators and carrying a reputation today as fierce guard dogs.

Dogs in front of theirs homes can be aggressive. *Lack of strong fencing and poor discipline off the leash can mean the danger of biting and tragedy.* If your dog shows enthusiasm for biting passers by, lock him in the back yard. You cannot do that safely? Rehome to a strict owner.

Lack of discipline leads to aggression and the danger of biting. If your dog pulls on the lead, takes you for a walk instead of being at your heels, he has too much energy for you to control, and this heralds trouble. Bear in mind the poorly controlled dog who does not readily obey and acts aggressively to people can become a biter, and indeed a killer in bad canine company. *Powerful breeds need special owners* (Millan & Peltier, 2006). If you observe uncontrolled aggression in your dog, seek advice *immediately* from a professional dog trainer. If the dog has too much energy for you, be prepared, as a matter of urgency, to rehome him to a sterner disciplinarian with safe fencing at once or send him to a professional trainer.

# 26 BITING THE HAND THAT EXAMINES YOU

Valma, my receptionist, came in to the consulting room to announce my next patient. "There's a huge dog to see you next. This has to be the biggest dog I've ever seen." Val isn't one to exaggerate, so I immediately expected a giant. "He's got one eye closed."

I hoped the owner had brought this dog in as soon as the condition presented itself, as I knew from experience that owners would often wait for several days before seeking medical advice.

A debonair man called Wally walked into my office pulling beside him an Irish wolfhound who, standing on all four legs, came up to my chest. Dogs are usually reluctant to enter my consulting rooms—it must be information from their secret world of smelling that we can only guess at. The dogs who have traversed my rooms are often at their worst or sickest, and we can only imagine the scent messages they leave behind for future visitors. It's like a time capsule of odours.

"What's his name?" I asked of the owner.

"Bruno," he replied.

My attention was drawn first to the dog's eye. I could see that Bruno's left eye was swollen and half-closed.

"How long has the eye been sore?" I asked.

"He was running in the bush two days ago, and when he came in, his eye was half-closed," said Wally the owner, not overly concerned. Wally looked like a bit of a man-about-town, with his thin moustache. Sometimes men buy huge dogs to prove their masculinity, much like today's four-wheel drive owners. On first appearances, Wally was that type of man.

A vet's first examination takes place from across the room—I was looking for symmetry from a distance. The left upper eyelid was drooping. This could mean a number of things, most of them serious. I moved in closer to the huge dog and, as Bruno opened his sore eye, managed to glimpse a very small brown spot in the middle of his eyeball before the lid closed over it again. I also noticed that the lower lid of Bruno's good eye was a bit slack and didn't sit snugly against the cornea like it should. Many breeds have this fault, with the result that some lids don't fit eyeballs. While racing through the bush with a lid that didn't close snugly, Bruno had obviously got something in his eye.

It was time for a close-up examination of the eyeball itself, to see what damage had been done. Val could see what was coming and had prepared a sedative for Bruno. From the short time Wally and Bruno had been in the surgery, it was obvious that Bruno was not a well-trained hound and wouldn't cooperate with any attempt on my part to look more closely at his eye.

"I need to look at his eye through a microscope. He'll need to be sedated and then anaesthetised to knock him out completely," I told Wally. Over the years, a vet gets a sense about owners. I certainly didn't feel a wave of compassion from Wally for his poor dog. Wally was as cavalier about the anaesthetic as he had been at the beginning of the visit.

I asked Wally to hold Bruno's head while I approached his rear to give him the shot of sedative. The Irish wolfhound is the world's largest breed. In pre-Christian Irish legends, he was the hunter of the wolf, the Irish elk and the wild boar. The breed almost disappeared when wolf numbers dwindled, but was resurrected when a Scottish officer in the British army made it his life's work to restore the breed to its former glory. Not only is the Irish wolfhound the tallest of all dog breeds, it also has the biggest jaws—and it was these very jaws that I hoped to avoid.

Wally did his job awkwardly, holding on to Bruno's head while I administered the shot that made the giant flinch momentarily then relax. Taking advantage of this relaxed state, Val compressed the cephalic vein on one of Bruno's front legs. As soon as the vein stood up, I quickly injected a dose of Pentothal anaesthetic, which acted immediately. Bruno was out like a light.

Between the three of us, we managed to lift the enormous dog, which was full-sized and would have easily weighed in at over 50 kilograms. Once Bruno was safely on the table, Wally retreated to the waiting room.

Val held Bruno's wide jaws open while I slipped a cuffed tube down his trachea to help him breath while he was unconscious. On the surgery table, I positioned the wall-mounted microscope over Bruno's sore eye and had a close look. I could see that the brown spot I'd caught a glimpse of earlier was in fact a tiny thorn that had pierced the cornea. The thorn was firmly wedged into the eyeball. This was a really dangerous threat to the dog's eye. When the cornea is penetrated by a foreign body, it tends to soften, which unfortunately allows the foreign body to move further into the eye.

I put a retractor on the eyelids to keep them open. Seeing the thorn dug into Bruno's eyeball made me furious. This had happened two days ago and Wally hadn't bothered to bring him in when the condition first presented itself. Every hour Wally had waited, the thorn had slowly worked its way into his dog's eyeball. And if I couldn't get it out, Wally could at best lose sight, and at worst lose the eyeball completely.

"Pass me two 25-guage hypodermic needles, Val." I took one in each hand and delicately pushed the needles into the cornea on either side of the thorn, watching the progress of my steady hands through the microscope. With gentle manipulation and lifting, the thorn finally came out. I sighed with relief. If Wally had left it any longer, the thorn would have totally penetrated into the eyeball and it would have taken major surgery to get it out.

Bruno would have to stay at the surgery for a couple of hours to recover from his anaesthetic and his ordeal. I placed the thorn on a piece of white gauze and took it out to show Wally. I wanted to say, *You stupid idiot. Next time your dog's eye is half closed, bring him in immediately. If it was your eye, I bet you'd be at the doctor's whinging and whining straight away, so why the hell didn't you give your dog the same courtesy?* But instead I said, in a calm voice, "Wally, a half-closed eye can indicate serious injury. If it happens again, bring him in straight away."

Wally grunted and left the building, returning two hours later to collect his dog. Val showed Wally how to apply drops to Bruno's sore eye without touching the eyeball, and organised a follow-up appointment for me to check the result of the surgery.

That night I had a glass of wine with an old friend of mine called Ben. I told him about Bruno and explained to him how huge Irish wolfhounds are.

"Have you ever been bitten?" asked Ben, perhaps working under the assumption that vets have a magic way with animals.

"Well, Ben," I pontificated, leaning back into my armchair and taking a contemplative sip of red, "you have to read the animal, keep a safe distance until you are sure of the temperament, and keep all situations well in hand. So, Ben, a dog would have to get up pretty early in the morning to get the better of me."

Pride goeth before a fall.

Not surprisingly, Wally didn't turn up at the appointed time for the check-up, but did show up two days later—the second time he'd been *two days late* that week. Val ushered him and Bruno into my surgery and followed them in to assist if I needed her. I was pleased to note that Bruno's eyelid was back to normal, indicating that the danger had passed. There were no signs of any infection and, from a distance, the cornea looked good. However, I needed to have a closer look to make sure that the iris behind the cornea hadn't become inflamed. I picked up the hand-held slit lamp, a handy device incorporating a microscope and a slit of light that can be shone into the eye from different angles.

I instructed Wally to hold Bruno still so that his head couldn't move and I could take a good look.

"Good Bruno, good boy," I said to the dog in a soothing voice, moving within reach of his eye.

Without any warning at all, Bruno lunged at me and clamped his full set of teeth around my left hand. Crunch! Luckily, Bruno chomped once and then released my poor crushed hand. Wally might have been a debonair man-about-town, but he was sure no Errol Flynn in a crisis. He let go of Bruno's neck and did nothing to try and control his dog.

Within an instant I felt a wave of nausea and staggered over to the sink to run cold water over my bleeding and damaged hand, leaning against the sink to stop myself from fainting. I barely registered Wally's voice saying something to Bruno, but noted through the haze that he didn't ask me if I was okay, didn't apologise, didn't rebuke his dog, and certainly didn't come to my aid.

Despite my dissertation to Ben a few days earlier, I had received the occasional nip in my career, but nothing like this. Irish wolfhounds were bred to kill wolves and wild boar. The strength in their jaws is incredible—something I now had first-hand experience of, literally!

Val rushed to my side and poured iodine on my wounded hand. She ushered Wally and his dog out of the room and tended to me with aspirin and a glass of water.

"Go home and keep warm, or you'll go into shock," she told me.

I must have looked as white as a sheet because Val, who's normally unflappable, looked concerned. She wrapped a towel around my hand and phoned my wife, Sue. Val explained what had happened and told Sue to expect me home shortly. By this time I was shaking. Strange things were going on in my body. Luckily I didn't live far away and made it home driving with my right hand while holding my left hand under my armpit like a newborn baby.

Sue was horrified by the size of my injured hand. She had carefully unwrapped it to assess the damage, and by now it had swollen to twice the normal size. She rang our local doctor to find out if my tetanus immunisation was still current. It was. I took to my bed and nursed my injured hand.

The following day, I felt terrible. My immune system had suffered a severe shock, which had taken twelve hours to become fully evident. I felt sicker than I had ever felt before—and that included the time I was recovering from major cancer surgery. With my body fight-back under challenge, my mouth was full of post-trauma thrush, which felt as if I had a mouth full of rotten carpet.

Sue was in her 'don't-argue-with-me' mode. "You'd better not even think about getting out of bed," she said sternly; and for once I agreed with her. While she was on this winning streak, she added, "And I'm asking the doctor to call in and see you." Again, no argument from me.

My injured hand was just as swollen, and it throbbed with a rhythm that would rival a metronome. My mouth was as swollen as my hand, and I could hardly swallow. At this stage, on top of everything else, I was in danger of becoming dehydrated. When the doctor visited, he examined my hand and prescribed antibiotics. In his opinion, it was probably badly bruised rather than broken, and I was suffering from shock.

By this stage, Val had spoken to Sue and both women agreed that all my appointments for the next week would have to be cancelled. The doctor amended this to two weeks. The bite had challenged my body's entire immune system, and my physical reaction was severe. Over the many hours that I spent restlessly in bed for the next fortnight, I started thinking about soldiers wounded in battle and the so-called 'collateral damage' when civilians were wounded as well—not that I was comparing my relatively measly dog-bite to the horrific injuries suffered by many in war, but I realised that there was a lot more to injury than just the initial wound. If I could react the way I did to a single bone-crunching bite, then how much worse would it have been for injured people in the aftermath of the initial shrapnel wounds?

While I was recovering, Ben called around to see me. We both had a cup of tea, and I had a slice of humble pie. Ben couldn't believe that I had been bitten after the way I'd carried on the week before. He asked why I hadn't put a muzzle on the Irish wolfhound. I explained that vets don't automatically muzzle all dogs prior to treatment, and the procedure had supposed to have been very quick. Furthermore, I told Ben, I had trusted the owner to control the dog—foolish, in hindsight.

Since Wally had hurried out of the waiting room with his dog—both with their tails between their legs—he would never have known that his failure to control Bruno cost me a lot of pain and two weeks away from work. Not to mention that Wally never received the follow-up information about taking care of Bruno's eye. I must mention that when he telephones me to ask how my recovery is going. Not surprisingly, I have not heard from Wally or Bruno again.

*Acknowledgement:* Vikki Petraitis

# 27 MAKE HASTE WHEN THE WIND BLOWS

When horses are carried as deck cargo from the UK to New Zealand, it might be considered a sure thing that the horses arrive safely. But if the horses are confronted by a hurricane on deck, then this is by no means a certainty. In 1967, eight mares, a filly with a crooked neck (called 'wry neck' in horse circles) and a handsome stallion, 'Make Haste', sailed from Liverpool on the *MV Hinakura*, a merchant vessel of 10,500 gross tonnage, under the command of Captain George McCathie.

Insurance companies like to know the condition of the animals before they leave home. Veterinary surgeons acting for the shipping agents had a good look at the horses on shore and classed them as 'fit for the journey'. The filly's wry neck was noted by the vet, but dismissed as 'nothing we can do about the filly's neck'.

The voyage started quietly enough on Sunday 22 January 1967, but the forecast was for stormy weather. Two and a half days out, the *Hinakura* was well into the Atlantic. The gale was mild at first, and it seemed it wouldn't be too bad. The crew did not realise how ferocious the weather would quickly become. All too soon, the first big wave hit the ship. It washed aboard and knocked the horsebox from its tough cable moorings. The crew moved the horsebox back, again secured the cables holding it and prayed the weather would settle.

Alas, the crew started to see massive seas from force 9 winds (speeds of between 75-88 kph). Waves 10-15 metres in height crashed against the ship and smashed the wooden horseboxes. It was chaos on deck, for the horses and the crew. But it was only the start of it.

During the night the sea rose and the gale freshened. The ocean came aboard in huge rolling foaming green mountains 15 metres high. The swell became larger. Wave crests on top of the swell tumbled and rolled over. Dense strands of foam were in the air. Angry spray blocked visibility. Nothing could be seen beyond the ship. Fifteen metres up, on the bridge, Captain George McCathie could barely see the top of the swell right around the ship. The captain would later relate: "The seas were uncomfortably high, but not as bad or as lonely as Cape Horn, where the sea and swell arrives from right around the world unhindered by any land mass."

Relying on his nerves, Captain George stayed on the bridge, where he was to remain for five days and nights. When he thought it safe to do so, he catnapped in the chair in the wheelhouse, having scheduled a team of officers to alternate four-hourly watches with him.

By 2 am the loose horsebox, which had been secured again, was still in place but was no longer intact. It had been reduced to a large pile of oversized matchwood. But where were the horses? In between swirling waves on the deck, the crew found Make Haste under the pile of timber. The stallion was lying on his side, rigid, wide-eyed, and not fully conscious. With each new wave the horse was submerged beneath the cold, turbulent Atlantic Sea.

A former Yorkshire farmer, Brian Palmer, aged 29 years, came to the stallion's rescue. He had signed up with the crew and was acting as the horses' groom. He had heard tales of horses thrown overboard in rough weather when a crisis came to a ship at sea. His mind conjured vivid images of a line of whinnying horses swimming hard after the men who had been their friends but had discarded them when trouble set in. Swimming desperately, equine heads held above the waves, calling out to human friends. Whinnying again, high-octave horse-screaming lifted above the sound of the sea, loud agony trying to reach the ship.

But the ship was moving away. "Wait for us. Wait for us," the horses called. Waves swept over heads held high. The ship sailed on. The trumpeting screams of the horses grew more difficult for the crew to hear, and the sea spray made the horses harder to see. The sounds of the wind and sea took its victims into silence.

Brian had seen many veterinary surgeons at work. Now, as well as he could, he had to be friend and nurse-attendant to the threatened horses, as well as a veterinarian—especially to the half conscious stallion. He held Make Haste's head above water as each wave swept in. It was no easy task. The heavy horse's head weighed down tired arms. While Brian struggled to lift the poor creature's head, at the same time he tried to prevent the foamy water from entering the stallion's nostrils. He was speaking with soothing words. Make Haste, through his fuddled brain, seemed to know Brian was helping him. Animals depend on the psychic strength of people nearby, just as we depend on animals near us. The stallion took in what the young farmer was giving out, his thoughts spoken and unspoken. Even without knowing it, the crew reinforced the energy of the horses in their care.

Flooding of the deck, and with it a near drowning, went on through the night. Brian had trouble enough with Make Haste, but George McCathie had greater trouble. As the winds persisted, the seas got bigger. The ship rolled and pitched more violently. At each big wave Captain McCathie, even 15 metres up on the bridge, was knee-deep in cold Atlantic Sea. He waited for each huge wave to darken the wheelhouse windows with green foam before water plunged with the power of Niagara Falls onto the ship's deck.

In the horsebox next to the stallion, the filly seemed very uneasy. She was indicating it was time for her to move, knowing she had to escape from where she was. She acted as though she knew something big would shortly happen. So did the crew, so they decided to let her out of her box. She could not get out of her quarters quickly enough. Snorting and prancing, the filly jumped out with a rush, free.

The reason for her restlessness was evident minutes later. A slow, giant wave slid silently over the rail and crushed her box into splinters. At one moment it was her strong horsebox and haven, the next it was potential flotsam destined for the surface of the sea. Lucky the filly had an innate warning system.

As the giant wave receded, Captain George now had two horses on board without a home—one semi-conscious and nursed by his devoted farmer, and one free filly. The next task was to move the semi-conscious stallion. He fortunately had a dedicated, albeit brine-soaked, crew; but they needed rest and thinking time. George understood that if the stallion was seriously injured or presented any kind of danger to the crew, he would have to be pushed over the side. On his knees, Brian pleaded with the captain not to do this. "I will look after him. Save him! Save him! I beg you!" It was so much more than an exchange of words. Most of Brian's communication was non-verbal. His gestures, the look on his face, the way he was moving his body and his hands expressed to all those around him the level of his passion.

But where could the big horse go? The crew rallied to Make Haste's cause, and many hands rolled the partly awake stallion onto a coir carpet. With some difficulty they slid him towards the seamens' quarters, where Brian, in the best veterinary tradition, ran his hands over the horse to feel if he had any breaks. As Make Haste moved into the protected alleyway leading to the seaman's quarters, he woke up and realised what was going on. He bit the nearest seaman on the stomach. Powerful jaw muscles and sharp teeth, together strong enough to convince a rival stallion to keep his distance, inflicted a vicious fighting wound. It was a painful payback for restricting the stallion's liberty. It was testosterone protesting at his space having been invaded. Thick sea-weather gear did little to stop extensive bruising of the seaman's stomach.

The stallion had to be held safe in a pitching ship while allowing his legs to bear most of his weight. He was held so that his feet were touching the deck with each roll of the ship. Eventually, in the entrance to the alleyway, Make Haste was held suspended partly in mid-air by bands of canvas, with more straps under his belly and chest and behind and under the tail. He moved like a drunken puppet when the ship rolled, supporting straps under his belly.

The filly had new quarters too, and went into an alcove by the crew recreation room. She peeped coyly at crew members from beneath a tarpaulin. Not bad for a filly with a crooked neck as the ship rolled, pitched and lurched. Or was it a crooked neck? She seemed to be moving her head normally. The wry neck had gone. There is nothing like a sea voyage and manipulation by tons of swirling water to improve your health.

The crew were too busy to notice the whine of the wind was lessening, the sea not as mountainous. The *MV Hinakura* had weathered the storm. Sailing flatter seas, Panama Canal was the next destination.

In Curacao, and later in Panama, the weather was warm, the sea calm. The horses needed a new home. Building new horseboxes was an unusual request for that part of the world. In the town of Horta, locals opened the timber mill, and carpenters made new horseboxes of the only timber available—dressed mahogany. Working overtime, the locals created horseboxes that were more elegant than the captain's table. Insurance companies talked for years about the expensive claim of the mahogany timber for the horses' comfort.

While still in Horta, vets came aboard and wrote their reports, using local veterinary jargon of *abrasions to the hock, contusions to the orbit*. It was written in Latin, the international medical language. George did not appreciate information in unusual lingo. He used words he heard at the captain's table. In his cable to New Zealand, the captain added one vital sentence to the veterinary report. He wanted to be sure the New Zealander shipping agents, and hence the owners, could understand whether the journey had been worthwhile. He cabled: *In spite of all the hurricane dramas, Make Haste's marriage tackle appears to be intact.*

This message was picked up by all the ships' radios within the wide reception area of the *MV Hinakura*. The world beyond the oceans soon knew Make Haste was entire and ready for a season's stud duties. George could also have told the world that the filly's neck was now working normally. He did not need veterinary jargon to say a Force 9 gale was helpful chiropractic for a crooked neck.

Brian left the ship in Auckland with the stallion. You could see they were strongly bonded together. They had formed a connection forged by crisis and the fury of the seas.

*Acknowledgement:* Captain McCathie

# 28 OVERBOARD FOR ROSIE

The captain of the container vessel called for help. The ship, near Singapore, was travelling four weeks out from Italy to Japan via Korea. Elephants from the Hungarian Zoo were on board. These elephants were born in the Terai Forest regions of Uttar Pradesh, along the foothills of the Himalayas. The crew was not happy with one of the elephants, Rosie, living in a custom-built box on the deck of the big ship. Rosie's attendant had noticed she had very swollen legs and feet, and he was very concerned.

The captain telegraphed his agent in Singapore: *Urgent. I need a vet for an elephant with swollen legs and swelling under the belly.* The shipping line agent's secretary translated this as *thick ankles.* She was suffering from that herself, and it stopped her from looking sexy. Her doctor kept checking her kidneys. The situation looked serious—What could it be in the elephant? Elephantiasis had found its way into our lexicon to describe swollen 'elephant legs' caused by parasites. Elephantiasis, however, is not just think ankles and lessened sex appeal. The secretary thought thick legs a real inconvenience until she saw a picture of elephantiasis of the scrotum. The patient needed a wheelbarrow to carry his testicles about. Nobody wanted that. It could certainly be the cause of much embarrassment and awkwardness on the Singapore cocktail party scene. She hoped the vet could help.

The Singapore Zoo asked Shane Ryan, an Australian vet working in Singapore, to answer the call, but he didn't know anything about elephants. Treatment of Indian pachyderm from the deep forests was not covered in his Sydney University veterinary course. But at 27 years of age, he was at that stage of life where he was willing to give any challenge a go and every clinical task his best shot.

There was some difficulty involved in being able to examine the elephant. For quarantine reasons, the authorities did not want the ship to be near Singapore. The consultation would have to be undertaken in international waters. So the agent's launch took Shane out to the container ship in the South China Sea.

The launch met the container ship moving at five knots, and drew close to the pilot ladder hanging loose down the side of the huge vessel. The ship's officer clambered up the swinging ladder with some of Shane's veterinary equipment. Shane began to follow. He was just three rungs up the ladder when something very unusual happened. The ladder broke. Shane fell down heavily, backwards into the water. So did some of his gear. As he fell he caught his thigh in the ladder side rope and was dragged under by the big ship heading non-stop for Korea. Korea was a long way underwater.

These were dangerous moments below the big ship. Shane was quickly running out of air as he was hauled along underwater, unable to pull free. He kicked with his free leg and fought the ladder with his hands. Alas, he was being dragged along a metre below the surface. He tried to wrench his leg free. The waters of the South China Seas pressed upon him. He became desperate. He was starved for air, dying to take a breath. His lungs hurt; he was fast running out of oxygen. Fear of no oxygen gripped every fibre of his being as he tried again. He twisted his trapped leg this way, that way. There was an overwhelming weight of water. He had no strength left as his hands wrenched at the ropes one more time. Another twist, it could only be his last, and somehow he managed to free his leg. Bursting for breath, he reached the surface.

But his troubles were not over. Twenty metres away, he could see a lifebuoy someone had thrown him. He started swimming. But could he make it? The launch was a hundred metres away. Would that be a safer haven? The container ship, in spite of the fact the propellers were now in reverse, was powering further away every minute. His instinct told him to swim for the launch.

Shane swam hard. Relief and joy at being above water fuelled his efforts. He made it, although not easily, to the launch, its harbour crew in white leaning over to help. It was a great joy to be hauled on board. The air that he breathed was sweet now that he was out of the water. Look at the sky. So blue. Someone gave him a large towel.

The launch took him around behind the container ship, in time to see an interesting sight. The powerful whirlpool created from a full propeller reversal was sucking the buoy to murky ocean depths. Shane had a few moments to feel glad he was not holding onto it. Those on deck watched the buoy go down. It was not to be seen again.

Shane was taken up the other side of the container ship in a bosun's chair. Crew members, towels, and a swollen elephant awaited him. The legs were indeed large, the belly distended with fluid under the skin. The contents of his veterinary bag did not offer much in treatment. It was full of water but not much else. His drugs were ruined except for the diuretic drug Lasix. A diuretic was something, but precious little to work with. Shane was dismayed to have so little but hoped increasing Rosie's urine flow would help her.

The big trunk of the mammal nudged Shane in greeting as the vet moved closer. Animals know their friends. Rosie's Indian attendant made sure she did not nudge her vet too hard. She seemed to know the vet was her saviour. He had come to help. She did not care that her vet looked bedraggled and not as well groomed as the men in white.

Shane wanted to put an injection under her tough skin. "Hold your ear still, Rosie. This is going to help you. Now stop that flapping."

The attendant held the massive ear still.

Shane decided the swelling was due simply to lack of exercise rather than anything more sinister. A syringe full of Lasix with a small needle went into an ear vein. Would the injection dose be high enough to take away the swelling? It had to work. Oedema like this must be relieved. Pooling of body fluids can so upset body chemistry as to be fatal. Shane had just enough a supply of Lasix to offer as follow up therapy for the next week. He had to guess what dose an elephant needed from a tablet pack designed for people.

"Let's know how she goes." Shane patted Rosie on the trunk as he spoke to the captain. "Remember to walk the elephants out of their boxes twice every day!"

He looked into Rosie's eyes—well, one of her eyes, as he was standing at her side—as he picked up his almost empty wet bag.

"And be sure to see the vet at the next port," he advised, hoping the Lasix would work.

With a final pat for Rosie, it was time for Shane to get back to Singapore. New problems had been created. The vet was pleased to have been able to help Rosie, but his passport and green Singapore work permit were lost. Shane would need a good story to get back into the country. Customs officers can be suspicious. What sort of believable yarn would the immigration desk listen to? No-one swims with the big ships.

"Looking at an elephant in the South China Sea? Tell us another. What have you been drinking?"

They could see in his pocket one large bottle of double malt whisky the captain had given him. The bottle was there to make up for Shane losing $1,000 worth of gear from his clinical bag. The gift worked against his credibility. Would he have to return to the sea and look for the bag contents on the ocean floor? Luckily, someone vouched for him and saved him a second underwater adventure.

Two weeks later the circus wrote a card to Shane from Japan: Rosie is performing well. We had her checked again with the vet like you recommended. But he didn't know all about elephants as you did.

*Acknowledgement:* Dr Shane Ryan

# 29 THE GIRL IN THE PURPLE DRESS

Before the advent of modern drugs to control uncooperative small animals, ether was widely used as a general anaesthetic. For a short time it was the anaesthetic of choice for small animals. It was hazardous, difficult to administer, and best used with extreme caution. Being explosive, it was also potentially very dangerous. In fact, it was used as fuel in model aeroplanes.

The freethinking physician Paracelsus of Basel, Switzerland, did not accept what others did and looked for new approaches. He first prepared ether in the 1500s. At that time medicine and veterinary medicine were considered as one discipline. A human doctor, he also treated animals. It was Paracelsus who first uttered the famous aphorism 'Dose alone makes the poison'. And so it was with ether—you could kill a cat or dog if your mind was not on the job. A fact many vets discovered for themselves.

Paracelsus was a firm believer in gaining knowledge from experience, not from reading books or ancient manuscripts. He noticed ether made chickens sleep for a long time and then wake up unharmed. However, the full significance of his incredible discovery did not register. Paracelsus was not looking for a clinical anaesthetic. In spite of his enquiring mind, he missed a commercial goldmine.

In addition to anaesthesia, in the 1950s ether had a wider veterinary use than in human medicine. It played a role repairing broken limbs. One big challenge for vets was dogs chewing off their plaster casts. Plaster of Paris casts on dogs invited chewing, and plaster had to be as near to chew-proof as possible. Replacing a chewed up Plaster of Paris cast on a dog's broken leg was tiresome.

Elastoplast was widely used either as the sole material holding small broken limbs in place or for covering all too easily chewed Plaster Of Paris. A layer of Elastoplast, wrapped around the dried plaster sticky side out, could save a cast from tooth attack, as the sticky surface was hard for dogs to chew. It could at least slow down canine teeth assaulting the cast while owners were away at work. Elastoplast that went on, however, had to come off again before the plaster could be removed.

Plaster cast and Elastoplast bandage removal took time; but in a busy evening of consultations, cast removal had to be done quickly, while the owners of the animal waited. The considerable downside of Elastoplast was it was very hard for vets to remove, especially when stuck to the thick hair of the animal's coat. Ether was an excellent solvent for removing sticky tape like Elastoplast.

One evening, the volatile qualities of ether not so well described by Paracelsus were revealed to a Sydney vet, John Holt, who when not in his surgery was President of the World Small Animal Veterinary Association. John discovered unusual things could happen with an Elastoplast bandage after it had been removed with ether. The patient was an Australian Cattle Dog, 'Bradman', recovering from a broken leg. The cast came off quickly, as the waiting room was full. The discarded cast and Elastoplast bandage was placed in a flip-top bin.

Twenty-five minutes later three clients, two men and one blonde woman in a purple miniskirt, came in with their long-haired spaniel, which had irritated skin and was shedding large patches of hair. With areas of dermatitis the size of dinner plates, the dog looked strange. John made him look stranger when he clipped off more hair around the irritated skin.

The men in the exam room were macho Aussie-outdoor types, but John, in between sweeps of the clippers, was more interested in the woman, Cheryl, wearing the miniskirt and pantyhose. The miniskirt would have been more compelling if it hadn't been upstaged by the woman wearing it. She carried a Marilyn Monroe look with her blonde hair, come-hither eyes and pouting lips. Yet she was full of mystery. Nothing mysterious about her hair, though. "It's out of a bottle", was the verdict of one old woman. Cheryl was too cool to worry about what others said. She took a lazy drag from her cigarette, which was allowed in the consultation rooms of the 1950s. Cheryl was holding the cigarette languidly, her hand casually held out like Marilyn used to do.

The skin was well clipped away from the messy diseased area, and it was time for John to make a diagnosis. He opened his mouth to say the spaniel would need long-term skin care. *Sounds boring,* thought Cheryl as she quietly and with studied grace flipped up the lid of the flip-top bin to dispose of her cigarette.

*WHOOF!!!* There was a loud explosion. Cheryl's pantyhose was blown completely off. The miniskirt survived the blast but was blown upwards, as high as Marilyn Monroe's skirt in the press photo taken when a sudden updraft through the street grid showed her famous legs. The dog was not harmed, and no-one was hurt. The crowd in the waiting room had a moment of silence, then everybody laughed. The skirt returned near enough to its original position to keep Cheryl, clinic towel in place, modestly covered as she was escorted out through the waiting room.

It was not yet an era of lawyers looking to sue for things like mental stress and psychological damage. No-one had thoughts of making big bucks. The onlookers heard a big bang and had a big laugh. Simple as that. John saw the episode differently. He already knew enough about inflamed skin in dogs to clip off hair around dermatitis. Glamorous women, however, were still a mystery for the young vet. Today had been a day of learning. The vet found out something he did not expect to discover in the middle of a busy afternoon. Cheryl was a true blonde.

## Grigory does it his way

Not everyone wanted to gamble with ether. Vets do not like explosions near animals they are operating on, so injectable anaesthesia was soon favoured. Even the relaxed Grigory, the old-time veterinary surgeon from Yugoslavia, was a bit of a surgical Frank Sinatra. He liked surgery 'My Way', and took to injectable anaesthetics as soon as they came in. No ether for him—he enjoyed tobacco while he was operating.

He smoked Balkan Sobrani tobacco and could not have used ether anyway, for safety reasons. In spite of protests from staff who tried to put a surgical mask on his face, he used to operate with a cigarette in his mouth. Inject anaesthetic, drape the dog, make the incision, and ask the nurse to light the cigarette. Then in 'My Way' mode, he'd sing Frank's signature tune through his partly closed mouth.

In spite of this very poor and unacceptable tobacco habit, Grigory was a caring surgeon. Of course he was caring. He 'did what he had to do'—kept smoking. When cigarette ash got too long and fell into the incisions, he meticulously wiped it out of the wound. Well, most of it out. As much as he could with one or two sweeps of his hand. He 'saw it through without exemption'. Some ash may have gone into the abdomen, it is true, but Grigory was at pains to keep cigarette ash deep in the wound to a minimum. The ash must have been sterile, as no trouble to the ash-contaminated animals was recorded.

A disciplinary veterinary board would not have appreciated the Yugoslav doing it 'his way'. Authorities did not appreciate pioneer Paracelsus, either, who 'travelled each and every byway' to find ether worked on chooks. Defying convention with cigarettes, Grigory would 'have faced his final curtain' if he had used ether at the same time. Forget convention, that's the part Paracelsus would have approved of. Some of his thinking in the 1500s proved to be explosive. Surgery was supposed to be fun. He would have enjoyed the laughter when a pretty woman had her pants blown off. Bottle blonde indeed!

# 30 LIAR LIAR, CAT ON FIRE

**Learn what to do for burns when no vet is within reach**

One Sunday morning Bernie, a big eight-kilogram black, battle-scarred male cat with pieces missing from his ears, was asleep. Cats sleep a lot, and Bernie was no exception. Well, he was a bit of an exception. Up all night and sleep all day was his preferred life style.

"Where is Bernie?" someone asked. Nobody took much notice. You can't be worried every time a tom-cat is out of sight. Bernie had his hobbies and kept late hours. While old soldiers had ribbons on their chests, indigenous people wore paint for dance and conflict, Bernie was happy with his campaign-torn ears. They were a true record of his conquests. Cats do not kill for sex, but they do fight off rivals with loud voice and loss of fur. Bernie's night activities could be tiring; hence his sleeping through much of the day.

He had chosen a pile of pine logs for a Sabbath slumber. Sweet smelling logs were a great place for a morning nap. This Sunday, however, it was not to be so great. Someone lit the pile of logs without looking inside the pile for something like a black cat. Who looks for a cat under a woodpile?

"Here, Bernie!! Puss puss!!"

But there was no sign of Bernie. "He's definitely not around," said his neighbor Digger, who thought midday was too early for Bernie.

*Crackle crackle* went the fire. Smoke began to billow. Suddenly Bernie emerged from the flames. Not only from the fire, he was *on* fire. The cat was terribly burned. The owners were horrified. They rushed him to the local vet, arriving within 20 minutes.

The vet, Tonia, was more than dismayed at the damage. She could imagine the intense pain the cat was experiencing. Some burns were especially deep, and the footpads were badly charred. Where exposed skin and muscle were burned, the damage was very serious, even down to tendon and bone. Much of Bernie's fur felt hard and brittle, like velvet which has been wet then dried. The skin was an ugly sight. First the vet cooled the skin with saline. It was something she had advised all owners not only to know about, but to do as the first aid for burns. Everyone must have Rescue Remedy as well, for people and animals.

Next she put Bernie on an intravenous saline and electrolytes drip because she knew fluid loss and shock could kill the patient. She applied copious layers of the clear gel from *Aloe vera bardadensis* to all burned parts. The aloe was growing in the surgery garden. After the application of the aloe, Bernie seemed in much less pain and allowed the vet to treat sensitive burned areas like between the toes, edges of the ears, the face and nose.

While he was being assessed, each 10 minutes Tonia gave Bernie repeat doses of Rescue Remedy, the emergency flower essence created by Dr Edward Bach. This essence helped to moderate shock. Bach had a passion for immunology, but he also believed recovery would be improved if anxieties and fears were treated. There was no lasting happiness or true healing without peace of mind. Intuitively, he harvested wildflowers from bushes and trees at the height of their energetic power, when flowers were fresh and wet with dew.

There was another serious threat to Bernie's life—absent owners. The owners were going to Indonesia for six weeks to visit relatives. To overcome this challenge, the vet took the patient into her own home. With so much tissue destroyed she thought it was probable that Bernie would die. She explained that burn patients often die from shock, organ failure, or later from infection. "Even if he survives, he may be too badly damaged if his whiskers do not regrow or his footpads do not heal," she warned. The owners gave permission for euthanasia if there was too much pain or disability for their pet.

Bernie was put in a cage with a tray lined with newspaper so nothing would stick when he had a pee. Even on the first evening after the fire, Bernie ate with enthusiasm. He was as happy as a burned cat could be. Each day, with no infection of the burned parts, he was comfortable enough to allow the vet to wash the wounds, using calendula tincture in the water. Fresh aloe gel was taken from the vet's garden and then reapplied.

In a few days the burned flesh began to granulate. Healing appeared to be on the way.

However, it was not without disfigurement. Bernie's severely damaged nose, in a dramatic sequel to the burning, fell off one day while he ate his dinner. With no black pad on the end of his nostrils, you could see naked cartilage inside the nose through a huge hole. More herbal therapy was applied. Calendula ointment replaced the aloe treatment. Calendula is renowned for its ability to promote healing. It is bacteriostatic and anti-inflammatory, without destroying tissue like some antiseptics. Later, as the area improved, comfrey ointment was put over the top of the calendula. Comfrey ointment, also known as symphytum, should only be used when the danger of infection has passed. It promotes more rapid healing, often without scar tissue. Because cats lick, care must be taken in choosing herbs to be applied to their skin. Aloe, calendula and comfrey are all safe to be eaten in small amounts.

Somewhat like a miracle, the entire damaged nose regrew. Lost nostril, cartilage, button on the end of the nose were all completely replaced. Ear recovery was similar. The ears regrew with straight edges. So much so that one family member rejected the healed tom-cat.

"That's not my cat," said the youngest daughter when she first saw Bernie again. "His ears were not like that, they had bits out of them."

It was true. The notched irregular ears had healed over! They looked better than before. His footpads looked normal—no scarring at all except for the loss of pigment. This was extraordinary, particularly as in some places the damage had been third-degree. His whiskers also regrew, somewhat distorted but adequate to be safe detectors of narrow spaces.

"All he needed was good nursing," explained the vet, with some understatement, delighted the treatment had been successful with no need for antibiotics.

*Endnote: As Tonia explained to the owners, only the clear inside gel from the aloe should be applied to the skin. The green sap which exudes from the skin of the aloe is irritant.*

**Acknowledgment:** Dr Tonia Werchon

# 31 CORKS IN THE HEAD

### Have a look, have a tap-tap, have a go

The phone rang at 6:30 in the morning. It was a woman's voice and she was agitated.

"The stable door swung shut on my dog's tail. It's so sore! He won't let me touch it!"

Jim could almost feel the pain from the first injury call of the day.

In his early career as a veterinary practitioner, Jim had plenty of early calls to fill his day. He treated domestic pets each morning and, after two large cups of tea, completed a few operations before lunch. He then conducted home visits in the afternoon. It was no good phoning him at 3 pm.

"You can't see Dr Jim, he's on his rounds," his loyal receptionist would tell impatient owners. What she did not say was, as often as not, Jim was on his *golf* rounds at three in the afternoon. Because "golf clears my head", he would tell his staff. "You need a clear head or you can miss a diagnosis.

One of these home visits saw Jim treating a dog two miles from his clinic. The dog had a strange kink in its tail. It was easy to find the kink in the Australian cattle dog. Alfie was a watchdog for a thoroughbred racing stable, and the tail had been caught in the stable door when it was suddenly closed. One of the horses had assisted with the door closure, bumping its feisty rump against the door as she backed into the stable.

It looked easy. Alfie's tail was at a crazy angle and had to be set straight. Dr Jim had no plaster in his bag so he improvised and applied splints in the form of two wooden tongue depressors, held firmly with gauze and Elastoplast bandages. Alfie would have less pain immediately and the tail would heal in three weeks. Jim pointed out the breed used to be called Blue Heelers. At least he wanted this dog to be a healer.

Alfie belonged to a horse trainer Jim had not met before. Jim was cautious. He did not get on well with all horse trainers; they moved in a different world. After wrapping the tail in a splint, he mentioned that he would return next day to be sure that the dressings were still firmly in place. Some owners do not notice when their dog has chewed and chewed so the splint no longer holds broken bones together. Jim had an intuitive feeling the trainer, deeply immersed in caring for his horses, could neglect his ailing dog.

As Jim packed his bag, the horse trainer had his own burst of inspiration. Could Jim look at the stable pet?

The pet was a kid's pony. Bessie and the request was almost an afterthought. The trainer vaguely wondered if he would look after her. Jim only needed a glance to tell what was wrong. The pony looked wretched, suffering from thick green-yellow pus coming out both nostrils. The trainer was forthright and told Jim that "two proper horse vets have already treated the pony with more antibiotics than you could wave a stick at, but there was no improvement at all. Surely a dog vet could do no worse. Even a vet concentrating on a dog's rear end must know something about what goes on in a horse's head."

Jim looked at the very miserable pony with a dry coat and head hanging down. The pony's ribs were easily seen. There was an obvious weight loss easy to explain—loss of the sense of smell from the pus meant the fresh smell of lucerne hay was no longer tempting. No sense of smell and taste causes loss of appetite.

Poison from pus affected the blood, and a horse, like us, doesn't eat when it feels lousy. When Jim and Alfred entered the stable they noticed the pony had her head pressed against the wall. A sign of headache in the equine world. A nose full of pus must have been most uncomfortable.

Horses have a broad flat forehead extending across from eye to eye and roughly up to the ears. Jim was no horse vet but he had to have a good look at an animal in pain. His father taught him that. With his ears as close as possible to the horse's head he gently tapped on each side of the pony's forehead. The trainer was not impressed and reminded Jim that the pus was coming from the nostrils. Why had he asked the dog doctor to look at a horse. Maybe Jim should look where the problem was—in the nose.

"Put your head close to the pony's forehead and listen," Jim asked the horseman.

He once again gently tapped on both sides between each eye and in the centreline of the bony forehead. Grudgingly, the trainer admitted that each side sounded different.

"It sounds a bit duller on one side."

Jim explained that the head of a horse is not solid bone. If it were, the pony would not be able to lift her head up, so horses, like humans, have sinuses, which are hollow spaces. To lighten the load, so to speak, again as in humans, there are two sinuses in the forehead. Jim was warming up. He had a class in front of him.

"It is in this sinus that the infection and pus are located, and that is the reason for the difficult sound or levels of dullness when I tap my finger on each sinus.

What Jim did not reveal to the trainer was that he came from a farming background, which gave him a good understanding of horses and their troubles.

Then came Jim's bombshell. And Jim was ever the showman. Jim offered to fix the discharging nose surgically by drilling holes in the pony's forehead. He wanted to do it when he came over the next day to inspect the dog's tail.

The trainer was taken aback. How could this young dog vet clear up the pus discharging when previous treatment from horse vets had failed. What about the contents of the horse's head? Would brains and blood fall out of the holes in the skull?

"Leave it to me. There is nothing to lose."

The horseman gave a sigh, indicating that he was resigned to the demise of the pony.

Next day, Jim arrived to find the trainer had two mates present to help him move the carcass "after you have finished". This was a most encouraging confidence booster to the young professional.

Jim injected local anaesthetic solution into areas between the skin and bone of the forehead, each about the size of a fifty cent coin between the eye and the midline of the forehead on each side. Then he cut through the skin with his scalpel. The incision was long enough to apply a tubular saw with teeth at one end to cut the bone. The instrument used for making circular holes in the bone were called a trephine. Jim rotated the saw clockwise and anti-clockwise until he cut through the sinus. Surely the pony was about to leave this life.

The task was simple, and a circle of bone was removed in a matter of minutes. Then came a gasp of surprise. Greeny-yellow pus poured out of the pony's forehead. The smell was putrid.

"It is not Bessies' brains," Jim was quick to assure the onlookers. Jim performed the same procedure on the opposite side with similar result.

Jim then took a hypodermic syringe attached to a piece of hollow tubing. "I'll suck out the remaining pus from each

228

sinus," he told the enthralled throng. The dog doctor took up yet another syringe, and flushed out each sinus several times with an antiseptic solution. "No more pus there now," Jim said, hoping all possible infection had been removed. Finally, Jim put antibiotic solution into each sinus.

At that point the audience realised the pony was not going to collapse and die on the spot. "How can you keep all that antiseptic fluid in the sinus when Bessie puts her head down to eat and drink?" The horsemen were definitely smarter than Jim. "What happens when the pony shakes her head?" There were murmuring words of support from the audience for this outspoken wisdom. They all knew vets don't think of everything. But Jim was not worried. He wanted what antiseptic went into the sinuses to come out again.

Now it was Jim's turn. He reached into his large black bag and drew out a glass jar of antiseptic with two corks floating in it. "You see, as part of the preparation back at my clinic, I have selected corks just the right size to neatly plug those two holes in the bone. We have to do this to give access to the sinuses over the next two weeks." Jim loved holding the stage. The audience was enchanted.

"When we flush out pus again, the corks will stop straw and flies getting into the sinuses through the holes.

The pony liked what Jim had done and already looked happier at the end of the operation.

Jim told the trainer, "Take it easy with exercise for the pony. We only want regular breathing and a few snorts to help clean out the nasal passages."

The trainer took this advice literally and rode the pony quietly around the local exercise tracks, visiting his local mates. He was an overnight expert in equine sinus infections and their surgical correction and proved it with his horse with two corks in the middle of the forehead. "Look at my corker horse," he would announce.

As arranged, Jim arrived next afternoon to redress the dog's tail splints, and to inspect the pony's sinuses. "I must flush some more." Jim has warned that more flushing and antibiotic solution would be needed. To Jim's surprise, the place was packed with cars and spectators—more like a carnival than a horse stable, all those present wanting to see the corks come out and look inside the horses's head.

The trainer, whose horses had not been winning for the past months, now had a claim to fame—a prize exhibit. He made sure that all in attendance inspected and smelt "them sinuses", so everyone was able to enjoy the surgery and offer their two bob's worth. The trainer had kept the locals up to date at the pub, and was repaid with large glasses of beer. The final outcome was most successful, the discharge disappearing by the tenth day, and the corks discarded by the fourteenth day when the wound was stitched close.

"Bone healing is slower," said Jim. But the forehead was fully restored after six weeks, leaving only a slight skin scar and a small bony callous where the corks had been.

Alfred was delighted with the recovery and still keeps those corks in a bottle in the stable as recognition of the dog doctor. They were not as good an advertisement as corks in Bessie's head. However, as Jim says, "How many trainers have a corker horse to brag about?"

Incidentally, the tail fracture healed well too, although close inspection did show a bit of a kink. No one complained, however. Jim was king.

Acknowledgement and in memory of a great vet Dr Jim Gannon

# 32 SOME STICK WITH MEAT

Early one morning in 2002, Dr Emma Mason, a young vet gaining clinical experience as a staff member at the Werribee clinic of the University of Melbourne, was presented with a kelpie cross male dog, Hoges.

"Hoges has been a bit off colour since early yesterday," the worried owners explained.

The owners, Connie and Phillip, were thin, and so was Hoges.

"Has he been doing anything unusual?" Emma asked.

"We're not sure. We went away at the weekend, on the spur of the moment. We never do that," Connie replied. "We left Simon, our seventeen-year-old son, at home to look after things."

"But what was the dog doing? Anything out of the ordinary?"

"We left him at home with Simon to keep him company. It was his first time at home alone."

Emma continued her search for information, and examined Hoges all over, feeling carefully, thoroughly looking in his mouth. "How's his appetite?"

"He didn't eat this morning."

Emma repeated the examination from all sides and looked down his throat. At last she found a small, soft lump at the back of the rib cage on the left side. It looked innocuous. Her next move was to X-ray the area. But the X-ray gave no indication of the cause of the lump.

"That's strange." Emma realised she had no option but to examine the area more closely. "Must get to the bottom of this," she said as she injected anaesthetic into the skin. Was it an infection? She picked up a scalpel and gently cut over what seemed to be a point in the lump. It was a time-honoured way to open a possible abscess. No pus appeared, however.

It was getting curiouser and curiouser.

With a little probing, Emma found a very small fragment of wood with the point of her scalpel. She managed to grab hold of the small end firmly enough to pull at it.

She pulled, and a small section of a narrow wooden stick appeared. A wooden stick! Emma very slowly and carefully pulled and pulled and pulled, finally retrieving a twenty-five centimetre kebab stick. Must have got into Hoges' stomach, all twenty-five centimetres of it. What an appetite! Try swallowing a stick as long as that!

The kebab stick was whole, without any bends or splinters. In fact it could be said it was as good as new.

When one foreign body is discovered, further exploration is always required, so Emma gave a general anaesthetic so that a thorough investigation of Hoges' insides could be made. She opened up the dog. Lo and behold, a second kebab stick was found in almost as pristine condition.

Everyone was immensely surprised—particularly the owners.

"We didn't know that Simon was planning a barbeque party," Connie said.

"It takes a visit to the vet to catch up on what family are up to!"

Hoges recovered after two hours. In the surgery's recovery room, he immediately asserted his authority by chewing through the IV tube in his front foreleg. Emma, now an authority in charge of Hoges' life, administered a very firm rebuke to the dog for his unhelpful behaviour. She was not pleased.

"Wait a minute, Hoges! The tubing has been put there to help your quick recovery. Leave it alone!"

And for good measure she later turned to his owners with helpful dietary instruction meant to be overheard by the cavalier canine.

"Meat is OK, but there is very little nutritional value in the wood of a kebab stick. Kebabs do not make a complete diet, *so do not stick with meat*. Furthermore, avoid meat on a stick. And no gulping your food, Hoges. Bad manners got you into trouble. Did you wait until the food was on the plate, or steal it from the barbeque? Where are your party manners?"

Admonishing Hoges for his eating habits, Emma couldn't help thinking she sounded like her grandmother scolding her grandchildren for wolfing down their food.

Phillip and Connie demurred a little. "Table manners. I don't think Simon listens," Connie said. "His table manners need attention; it has rubbed off on his dog."

"Well, look on the bright side," said Emma, who felt protective of the naughty Hoges, a lover of kelpie dogs as she was, "not only is your dog alive and back with you as the family pet, but the barbeque skewers are re-useable."

*Acknowledgement:* Dr Emma Mason

# 33 CHARGE A FEE FOR THREE VISITS, THEN REVISIT EVERY DAY FOR SIXTY DAYS

### Farm vet counts his piglets

Jack Auty chose a different car to many vets, who typically used utilities or larger sedans. His fellow vets would say, "You can't use a Beetle, there won't be enough room to fit all your gear for treating cattle." Bunkum. Jack was not your usual kind of vet, so he wouldn't drive the usual kind of vehicle.

He managed with his smaller car by following a well-tried technique. Jack packed his new VW Beetle very carefully, and everything fitted fine. "I had a place for everything in my car, and everything was put in its place." He even had a spare scalpel, $20 cash and dry socks in the glove box. The scalpel blade was well covered by a piece of folded cardboard taped around it, so no-one was injured looking for money in his glove box. Jack was feeling he could become his own best source of knowledge.

To get to the sick animals beyond the front gate of each farm, Jack drove 100,000 kilometres each year in his carefully packed VW Beetle.

Jack had graduated from Queensland University in 1954, aged twenty-eight, believing he was well equipped to tackle the world of veterinary challenges. There was no problem he could not alleviate. Life as a vet was meant to be easy. At least Jack thought a young vet's life was going to be easy. George Bernard Shaw offered a different view—"Life is not meant to be easy, my child; but take courage; it can be delightful". GBS was often closer to the truth in describing Jack's early days. This philosophy fuelled his dedication and stood him in good stead for all his ten years of veterinary practice. He was always ready to have a go, and established several firsts. He made the first heartworm diagnosis in a dog, which had not been identified out of Victoria before, and offered the first diagnosis of ulceration of the abomasum, a disease of one of the cattle stomachs.

Doctors Jack Auty and Bill Gee created the first two-man dairy cattle practice in Victoria. It was a 'Three P' practice: Prompt, Penicillin and Piss off. Farmers quickly got used to the skill and dedication of the two-man team. If a Shorthorn cow came in with her tail up—starting to calve—or looking not quite normal, the farmer called out from the milking shed to the house, "Hey Mum, get the vet!"

Bill Gee was a brilliant diagnostician at every level. Before Jack Auty joined him, he could finish his day of thirty farm visits at 3 am.

Bill was called to an unconscious cow at the end of a very busy day. Geraldo's cow was ill from low minerals in the bloodstream. It was a potentially fatal metabolic disease induced because the community placed high milk production above the welfare of the cow. The cow was valued for her butterfat, but her body could not easily handle her highly productive life. A vet was needed immediately to treat her low blood calcium.

"When did you first notice this cow was sick?" Bill asked.

"Yesterday morning".

Bill exploded. His dark eyes flashed, his large mouth opened wide. "Why did you not call me yesterday?"

"Wait a minute," the farmer protested. "It's your job."

"Be buggered! Not my job to let a cow get close to death when she does not have to. I have been called too late! Much too late!" yelled Bill, making no effort to keep Geraldo as a client.

In spite of Jack's self-assurance, Queensland University had given him no instruction about the first three cases he was asked to manage. Jack had been taught very little regarding his first case, a huge Large White sow farrowing (in labor) a veritable mountain of difficult patient. Charles, the owner, greeted the new vet, but he was not the only one who had decided to watch. The locals had gathered to see what the young animal doctor could do. Jack anticipated an expectant sow, but surrounding the pigpen was more of a crowd than he anticipated. He had an expectant audience of neighbours, all in battered hats, leaning on the pen and muttering to each other. But the new vet was not intimidated by the audience. His time at vet school had at least given him a love of a crowd to perform in front of.

Jack knew little about delivering a fresh batch of piglets, and didn't have the confidence to feel inside the giant patient. Yet he was aware he had to produce piglets for the farmer and entertainment for the audience.

"What do you know?" asked Charles.

Jack could have answered, "Not much." Instead he gave a grunt—a grunt which said, "I'm in charge. Don't ask me any more questions." He knew, or thought he knew, to expect, on average, eight piglets. There were three sturdy white piglets beside the pigging sow, each pushing their mother's udder for their first meal. John gave the sow an injection to help the uterus contract. Two more piglets appeared.

The audience shuffled their feet and murmured approval. "Seems to know what day it is," observed one of the more articulate pig farmers.

Jack had five piglets for the audience. Another injection produced one more piglet. The audience leaned forward. Another piglet was squeezed out. The happy muttering became louder.

Seven piglets. Jack was getting there. The battered hats seemed happy. What was he to do now? Audience interest was threatening to wane. Jack thought it was time to leave.

"She's got another one in her." Jack might have been God himself. "Expect one more piglet!" was his final and forceful verdict as he packed his bag and swept away in his VW Beetle. It was a wild guess, of course. His teacher had explained that, after the boar served the female, the gestation period of a gilt (a pig who has never given birth before) or sow (an older female) was 'three 3s': three months, three weeks, and three days. Little squealers therefore arrived in 115 days. His university pig lecturer was obviously not aware that some sows could have many more than eight in a litter. Top Chinese pig farmers produced 30 or more piglets per sow per year. Jack's university lecturer may have given him confidence, but he had given him incorrect information. But in this case Jack's wild guess turned out to be accurate.

"You were right," pig farmer Charles told Jack when he saw him in Main Street four days later. "Another piglet was born thirty minutes after you had to leave. She had eight!"

The young vet's first performance on the veterinary stage was a success. Jack might have had little knowledge of pig obstetrics, but he did know how to count.

Jack's next case was at Harry's, to examine a sixteen hands' high stock horse with an injured joint. After struggling through a barbwire fence, the big bay gelding, Bundy, was left with deep gaping cuts over the stifle joint. You could see deep inside the joint, as it was exposed to the open air. During Jack's veterinary course this injury had been called incurable. Luckily Jack had paid very limited attention to his lecturer.

He advised Harry to thoroughly clean Bundy's injury with an iodine-derived solution. The joint got better. Another treatment triumph was just what he needed to gain local approval.

But something more important was happening. Jack was learning not to take too much notice of the experts. He began to be convinced of the wisdom in the ancient saying, 'You are your own guru'.

## Listen to wisdom but above all else trust your own judgement

Jack was on his way in dairy cattle practice to a caseload which would later often peak at 40 cases per day. At his peak, Jack opened fourteen gates each day for 365 days—a total of five thousand gates each year. He fussed over any sick animal until it was better. On any animals that died unexpectedly Jack did a post-mortem himself. Local doctors envied this opportunity for follow-up. His approach meant he learned much quicker than the local medico.

The third case Jack was called to after graduating involved a big obstacle to professional joy—a lying client. No-one at vet school had told him about that either. Vets work best with owners who tell the whole truth. Guisseppe did not want to do that; he had sprayed arsenic as an herbicide on the tomato bush weed. Big Guisseppe with-a big-a side-a boards-a all the way down his cheeks went to church every Sunday and was embarrassed when his cows got really sick. But he did not tell Jack the truth. He left that 'tell the truth' maxim in church.

Jack was firm. "Tell me the truth if you want me to be your vet."

Guisseppe paid a big price for deceit—he was about to lose his whole source of income. Within the next weeks, forty-four of his forty-five milking cows died from a most painful death, arsenic poisoning.

Jack did so well because farmers knew he cared. One high butterfat-producing cow caught her foot in the sickle mower and pulled her toe off. Jack visited daily for sixty days. No professional charge was made after the third visit, only for the drugs used. Another cow was caught under the feeder. The farmer Constanto was on his way to the pig sale and became restless when Jack took so long to remove the bolts from the metal bar holding the trapped cow. Constanto, acting too impatiently, received Jack's straight talk. The cattle vet was in charge.

"If you want me to be your vet, don't go to the pig sale."

Constanto stayed home and became a loyal client.

# 34 A SHOT FOR TETANUS

Tetanus is a highly fatal and painful disease, which causes muscle spasms and lockjaw in people and animals. Tetanus is caused by the contamination of a wound by the organism *Clostridium tetani*. A common, long-lasting inhabitant of soil, the bug thrives in human and horse intestines, producing spores and damaging toxins. A horse with tetanus is severely distressed, moaning continuously and unable to swallow.

Due to a bacterial toxin destroying nerve function, more than eighty percent of horses affected by acute tetanus die. When a horse is in spasm, the third eyelid is seen as what looks like a skin flickering across the eye, a typical symptom of tetanus. The clinical picture otherwise resembles strychnine poisoning. Out in the paddock, a horse can be spiked in the foot or cut by wire, with no-one knowing about it until it's too late, missing the signs of stiff muscles which usually start appearing in the head.

Consult your vet. For unvaccinated horses or those whose tenanus shots are not current, horse vets will give an injection of tetanus antitoxin whenever a horse suffers a wound. Vaccinate your horse and follow with a booster one year later. Repeat the vaccination every five years

So difficult and unrewarding to treat, tetanus is best prevented by vaccination. This advice is directed at all your family. "Face up to it, everybody, get your shot," the local health authority firmly advises.

Septimus Flattery wore his tattered hat on the back of his head of unruly curls, and called Decker Khads to his sixteen hands' high gelding, Windsor. The horse had recently been injured and now could not lift one leg in front of the other.

"Do you have your horses vaccinated?" Decker asked, though it was not the best time to ask such a thing when the horse was so obviously suffering.

"Naah." Septimus knew best, and was following a family tradition. His father never gave the horses tetanus shots; though he was beginning to doubt his father's wisdom on that score.

The sick horse seemed totally paralysed, standing like a sawhorse, legs apart, unable to move at all. Windsor looked very distressed indeed, snorting noisily, unable to understand how this affliction could have taken away his leg movement. What had done this? He had only been getting stiff in the legs twenty-four hours ago.

"T'be sure, t'be sure, it's tetanus," said Septimus, rather proud of his inspired diagnosis, but nevertheless upset about how much his horse was suffering.

"Uh-huh," Decker agreed, tapping under the gelding's chin and seeing the third eyelids blink across both eyes.

"He's hurtin' bad. Ya gotta shoot 'im, Decker, ya gotta shoot 'im."

Septimus was hurting too, sad at the thought of losing an old friend due to his own neglect. (Why didn't I call the vet when the gelding started to get stiff?)

The vet moved back towards his car and opened the boot. Decker knew about the pain, and was resigned to end the horse's suffering. He had no option but to take up his rifle. He stood three metres in front of the horse. Decker aimed at a point to go through the gelding's brain; not low between the eyes but high on the forehead, so the bullet would go between the eyes and straight through Windsor's brain. To hit the correct spot was essential.

He fired one bullet. It produced a loud bang but the horse did not move.

"Begorra, ya missed," cried Septimus. (These bloody vets, they don't know much; they talk about vaccination, but this one can't even shoot a horse.)

Decker was silent. He was always quiet when he knew he was right. He walked up to the side of the horse and pushed hard with all his weight. The big gelding toppled over, legs outstretched in tetanic spasm.

Septimus began to think the vet knew something after all, especially about shooting a horse in pain using one bullet. The horse had his shot, but a much different shot to that recommended by the Health Department for people. Tetanus is so common, the death rate so high and the disease so agonizing, it is a pity so many owners do not bother to prevent it through simple vaccination. Such a waste, which could have been avoided if Septimus had only listened to the vet's advice about prevention. Nevertheless, both men were glad Windsor's suffering was over.

# 35 JOY TO THE WORLD— THE VET PREVENTS HUMAN DISEASE

## TB disappears because of the vet, but so does the car

The Polish composer Fryderyk Chopin, gifted beyond measure, was infected with TB. As one friend put it Chopin played not the piano, but the soul. Veterinary Science was 200 years too late to prevent his death. In his fortieth year he choked on his own bodily fluid.

Country vet practice depends on the ability to travel between farm jobs quickly enough to get the day's work done. More visits means more income. Bruce MacLean, a pioneer large animal vet, started cattle practice at Corryong, a town in the northeastern uplands of Victoria. As a vet, he served farmers near Australia's highest mountain, Mount Kosciusko (2,000 metres in height). Bad roads and mountain rain did not combine well for an easy day.

The local butter factory helped Bruce by paying him a small retainer. The factory also collected his veterinary fees from the dairy farmers. He was grateful for the butter factory support, but alarmed at how the soft roads down into the valleys and winding up the steep hills did not support the tyres of his

Holden utility. Mountain air uplifted him but his car had a sinking feeling.

Vets need their cars. It is their on-the-road service, with their mobile store of calving gear, which is vital for the treatment of cows that, among many other things, become unconscious from blood mineral deficiency. Getting to sick cows in time is one challenge. Bruce found farm-to-farm mountain travel another. The uplands country was glorious to work in but the roads were terrible. Night and day the road edges were soft and hazardous. No-one told him that after heavy rains the middle of the road was just as bad. When there was heavy rain in the uplands, mountain roads swallowed cars, and the Royal Auto Club of Victoria offered no help. When he tried keeping his car out of trouble, Bruce was on his own. Mobile phones were not yet invented.

His sturdy car had to run well seven days a week. Bruce did some calls in adjoining New South Wales, across the river, and often crossed the Upper Murray River by boat. It was easier than driving a car full of gear over the border on the treacherous roads.

To get through dense forest and over a steep mountain, roads were often cut in rock. Following heavy rains, water flowed through a natural watercourse downhill and fell freely over the rock face which formed the high side of the road cut into the mountain. In a storm you could see the rain tumbling down the rock face beside the road. You could not see rain going *under* the road, but that's where it was flowing. The rain disappeared from sight to emerge in the middle of the road as mud. Mud, mud, deep sloppy mud. The stream of water tumbling down the mountain had travelled underground to become a soft mound in the middle of the road. A deep soft mound, it looked so innocent as to deceive unwary drivers.

Bruce warned vets working for him, "You need to be careful. You can suddenly come across a swelling on a mountain road. Beware, it's where mountain water is trying to surface. If you stop on the soft spot, your car will disappear. It will get swallowed, just like in quick-sand. Be careful, you can lose your drugs and two-way radio. More important, if the road takes your car it will be more difficult to complete your farm calls. There could be a horse with colic waiting for you at your next farm call. If you sink deep enough it will be much worse for you than failing to get to the sick horse—you'll be late for dinner." His assistants were used to his attempts at humour.

"If it looks like your car is a goner, try to avoid going down with your ship. You are not a captain. Vets leap free, they have more work to do. If you get trapped under mud, there is no oxygen down there and you are a cert to be worse than late for dinner."

"A *dead* cert, Bruce?" The cattle doctor's new assistant liked to swim under water but was not sure about swimming under mud. He was also a budding comedian. Both vets agreed mud over your head is inclined to get in the way of a good life.

Deep mud hazards weren't just a threat for your own car sinking. Bruce had to take care when he drove round a bend. You could be met unexpectedly with the sight of someone else's car—or perhaps half a car—submerged in the soft middle of the road. (What a place to park! Where are the parking attendants when you need them?) When driving fast to get through the day's workload, sweeping round the bend into a car parked in the middle of the road was not helpful.

Soft road centres were a worse hazard at night. When moonlight was obscured by tall eucalypts, all was pitch black in the forest. Focused concentration was needed to see the back end of a car suddenly in front of you. Bruce's eyes had to be alert even when he was weary. After struggling to deliver an oversized calf in a heifer through a small pelvis, he was driving fast and could not allow fatigue to slow his reflexes. Was that mud ahead in the middle of the soft road or not? Hard to tell until you were on top of it. What about the next bend? Make sure you have your mind on the road. Put aside thoughts of the next animal you are hurrying to. What was it? Cow choking on a turnip stuck in her throat? Bruce was not going to be much help; he hoped the cow had managed to swallow it before he arrived.

In his more relaxed moments he asked himself why he was there. An important community health job was helping to control cattle TB. Cow tuberculosis can spread to people through milk. When Bruce reached the yards to TB test, say, two hundred cows and two bulls, he injected test antigen into the cattle.

Deep mud roads were hazard enough, but not the only barrier getting to the animals. Once off the main road, farm tracks on grass went through many paddocks to lead Bruce to where the cattle were. Many paddocks meant many gates. Get out of the car, open the gate, get in the car, drive through the gate, get out of the car, and close the gate. On one farm Bruce had to go through seventeen gates to reach the cow yards. Then he had to go through the same seventeen gates to come out again. After he closed the last gate he had no time to lose to make it to his next job.

Four days later, Bruce had to return to the same farm to read the TB tests. He had to feel for a small swelling in the fold of skin under the tail where he had injected the antigen. No worries. He opened the seventeen gates again to go in, and the same number driving out. Gate opening can lose its novelty even when a vet is on a vital mission to prevent a disease fatal to humans.

In an effort to stop the road devouring cars, Corryong Shire tried tipping loads of monster stones into the mounds.

The result was that thousands of stones left the tip-truck and disappeared in the mud. As stones were lost, moving towards the centre of the earth, the Shire tried using trucks carrying sand. Loads of sand disappeared from sight. Not only that, trucks disappeared as well. The truck drivers noted, when they arrived at the mound, that it was different from delivering bricks at a building site. In the town you could just sit there until the foreman came to talk to you. This was different. Deliver the load and get the truck the hell out of there.

The Shire did not like losing their trucks into the soft road. So their next project was to place a layer of eucalyptus saplings cut exactly to fit across the road to make what was called a corduroy road—eucalyptus corduroy, not the coarse cotton pants you might see at the Corryong art show.

It was hard driving over road bumps. Hang onto the steering wheel. Hold hard, sometimes making your knuckles white. Bruce was talking to himself. "Slowly does it." He would have to have that loose muffler fixed. He'd better check that front tyre which looked a bit flat at 6 am. He had been in too much of a hurry to check it by the foggy light of morning. Now it was 6 pm. Can the flat tyre get him to the next farm? He was going to be late, and it was getting dark. It was dangerous changing a tyre on a dark, winding road.

The radio reception was poor in the mountains, so he couldn't call base to ask for help. If he could have contacted the butter factory he would have heard, "Hurry back, you've got work to do." *Work to do* meant more mud mounds tomorrow.

Joy to the world, vets controlled a human disease. Joy to the farmer, Bruce found few TB positive cows, so the cattle man would lose few of the herd to the abattoir. It was a bonus the bulls tested negative and were not affected. Joy to the vet. Bruce looked at his list stuck to the dashboard of his car. Getting to the next farm was going to be easy. He knew the road. No soft mountain mud, and only seven gates to open on the farm track into the cow-yards. Oh, the many joys of mountain cattle practice.

Bruce opened many gates to stop people getting TB and died at 62 years of a heart attack.

If only he'd had the chance to save Fryderyk Chopin.

*Acknowledgement:* Andrew Turner

# 36 GO AND DANCE WITH THE STARS

Dr Rodney Syme, a medical opinion leader, is one who believes euthanasia is necessary for those we love who suffer incurable and terminal pain; but for many, 'mercy killing' is hard to accept. While each of us would prefer an easy and painless death, nothing, it seems, can stir the emotions more than thinking about euthanasia for humans. From a veterinary point of view, it is hard to understand why we should recoil from offering a suffering person or animal an easy death.

Euthanasia is a significant part of veterinary care. The word comes from two Greek words—*eu*, meaning well; and *thanatos*, meaning death. As we want a gentle life and an easy death for our friends and all animals, we need to think about euthanasia to avoid extreme suffering before it sets in. Animals are aware of impending death. The consciousness within animals is as valid and eternal as our own (Roberts 1994).

I was grateful when, at a low ebb of his life, caring people gently eased my 68-year-old close relative to his final rest. He had cancer in his left eye socket, pushing his eye forward. Six months earlier, extensive surgery included eye removal and chasing the cancer in his sinus. There is nothing more ugly than an empty eye socket. In spite of the dedicated skills of plastic surgeons moving muscle from his temple, he had an ugly deformity after surgery. Unhappily, the cancer came back.

Animals are aware of how we feel when it is the end of the road for them. Before my brother became sick, a handsome German short-haired pointer, Rudy, aged nine years, had been visiting me for some months with cancer of his left eye socket. It was a nasty neoplasm slowly invading the skull. One morning Rudy came in and I saw the affected eye was threatening to become dry because the prominent eyeball was pushed so far forwards that the lids could no longer sweep over the cornea.

With my fingers in his mouth, past his molar teeth, I could feel the cancer growing at the back of the mouth. I had warned his dedicated owner, Celia, weeks ago this day would come. Wisely, she chose not to have surgery or chemotherapy. Rudy was now facing pain as the cancer continued to grow into his skull. Pre-arranged with his owners, Celia came into my exam room for her dog's euthanasia. I sat on my chair soon after the dog walked in. Rudy walked straight up to me and put his head on my lap, his eyes locking into mine. I felt strongly the dog knew he was about to leave this life. Dogs seem to have a more sensible approach to death than we do. They can tell when their owner is shortly to die (Sheldrake 2000), and know when their own time is up.

After sedation, in a gentle way, an overdose of barbiturate anaesthetic was given intravenously. It was a painless demise. Gentle death came for Rudy without fuss. He was sent to go dancing with the stars. The dignity of dog and owner made Rudy's euthanasia a moving experience. I know Celia felt deeply about saying goodbye to her dog. The emotion was masked in part by a most sensible owner, and I hope by my professional manner. All vets are sad at the euthanasia of an owner's beloved pet. Many shed tears. One of my colleagues remarked that the day he stops feeling the owner's emotion during loss is the day he stops being a vet. I wrote *PTS* on the case history, which in veterinary practice is short for 'Put To Sleep'. PTS describes this final act of owner love.

The no-fuss procedure was in stark contrast to the ritual of executing serious criminals by injection in North America, where insensitive government protocol has pushed aside common sense. Spectators see it all through a large window. A compassionate veterinary approach could make the US Government-sanctioned lethal injection procedure much less barbaric. Execution could be as gentle as the tiny intravenous needle vets place in an animal's leg. If we need to kill criminals, do we need to dehumanise their families, officials, and humanity?

I was able to provide the same compassionate service for the three owners of Moshe, a very old dog who shuffled into my surgery one day, visibly suffering, disabled by the last stages of a failing heart. Her abdomen was distended with fluid. It was time to go to God. It is one of the blessings of the veterinary clinic that we can help choose the time. Moshe's family of owners did not tell me, however, one detail which disturbed the morning's tranquility. An eccentric family member, Anastasia, had not been consulted about ending Moshe's earthly life. She was not warned but told after the event. Bear in mind the death of a companion animal causes as much grief as the loss of a close human friend—sometimes more. Many people become closer to their dog than to the people around them.

Anastasia was a person who needed to be well-informed, professionally, weeks before such bereavement. Anastasia arrived at my surgery—and it was some arrival. I quickly learned why the family had kept her in the dark. She was beside herself with grief, her face contorted with anger. She came into the waiting room and screamed "Murderer!" into my face "Murderer, murderer!" To make sure she had my attention, she was standing right in front of me, and with each word advanced large strides towards where I was standing. Although we were separated by a few centimetres, she kept advancing. I like close communication with owners, but I thought she was overdoing it. I was not keen to tangle either with her emotions or her large flailing limbs. Not as nimble as Sugar Ray Robinson, I backed away three paces. Or rather, I tried to. The room was too small for effective retreat.

Escape? Anastasia had other ideas and advanced to stand even closer, eyes bulging, slobbering at each insult, her canine teeth more prominent than her pet Moshe's. Dogs had occasionally fear-bitten me. It seemed I was about to have a new experience. In contrast to her saliva flow, my body was pouring out adrenalin. Her screaming voice convinced my receptionist, Valma, to come into the waiting room. She tried to stand between the owner's vigorous desire for intimacy and me. Anastasia's arms looked so strong and well muscled. At that time I thought Valma saved my life.

"Phone the police," I mumbled. They were not very inspiring words. Last words? I had hoped for something else as my epitaph.

When Valma judged I was out of imminent danger of death by shouting, she left the waiting room and phoned triple 0. Would Valma suggest the police be so kind as to send several strong policeman, and a strait-jacket?

Now, I knew human teeth to be painful even without their flesh tearing potential, but there was this threat of bodily harm from an owner to the upper, albeit less vulnerable, part of my body. The Malvern constabulary, however, was not accustomed to saving vets' lives in their clinic waiting rooms and did not seem very interested in my predicament. I appreciated how calm the police were. Would they be too calm to leave the police station and rush to my aid? Their front desk was helpful—I should let them know when Anastasia's hands were around my neck and I was having difficulty breathing. What colour was my face, white or blue? Perhaps they would need me to stop breathing before they climbed into their squad cars. I admire police who are so trained they don't show emotion. Or better still, on some occasions they just don't show. They received my episode of loud owner grief by staying at their desks. Before taking action, Homicide Squads need a homicide.

After what seemed half an hour, Anastasia's family arrived. Val had phoned them. By then The Angry Grieving One had run out of energy. And so had I.

Little wonder new graduates recoil from the task of PTS. Many young vets find their most stressful task is ending life in front of a grieving owner, even when there is no extra family drama. Some owners come in for PTS of a beloved pet as the last port of call before committing suicide. Fortunately a home phone number in the case record can save a life.

They call euthanasia easy death. And it is—as long as the entire household is pre-warned. Should there be no pre-death warning, euthanasia is less stressful if you have plenty of room to soft shoe shuffle away from flailing arms of grief.

On occasions it seems more sensible for the animal to be put down at its home. Owners like this, for their pets to live their final moments in familiar, comfortable surroundings. It seems more compassionate. From the kindness of his heart, Dr Nev was happy to house-call for euthanasia. There was one owner, Carl, however, who did not reveal the animal was a very large and savage German shepherd, Himmler—'Himm' for short. Himm was savage when the owner was not there to restrain him. Moreover, late in the afternoon, Nev did not notice the bottle of green PTS barbiturate in his visiting bag was running low.

The vicious Himm was fortunately calm at home in the presence of his owner. Carl held him restrained with little trouble, using his thumb to raise the cephalic vein for an intravenous injection. The injection into the vein went well. Nev injected all the PTS solution he had and the dog sagged to the floor. Breathing was slower and slower, and Himm's eyes closed as he was heaving the last big sigh. It was a successful and peaceful demise. Nev offered to dispose of the body, to save Carl the unhappy task of burial. With the owner's help, he carried the dog's body to the boot of his car.

The day was drawing to a close. Nev had a busy round of visits and hurried on his way. Night was falling when, back at the surgery, the vet opened the boot of his car. He was greeted by a deep, vigorous growl coming from the dark depths of his car boot. The vet did not wait to look more closely. A glimpse of canine lips pulled back to show Himm's bared teeth was enough. He slammed the boot lid shut. He needed time to think, preferably when his life was not being threatened. He would need a loop of rope threaded through the end of a long broom handle. This would act as a noose to hold the dog so he could be given a massive dose of sedative. Easy death would follow, sending Himm on his way dancing with the stars.

Euthanasia is easy for the dog when, after sedation, you inject into the vein of the front or back leg. And easier if you check your visiting bag for a bottle of 'green dream' barbiturate before you leave the surgery . . .

# 37 CRUELTY OF THE FUR TRADE

*Animals are not our property or possessions but our peers
and fellow travelers* (Kowalski 1999).

*Some 15 million big-cat pelts are bought and sold
worldwide every year*
**(Reader's Digest Assoc 1997).**

In just a few years, China has become the world's largest
exporter of fur garments. According to a 2005 report by Swiss
Animal Protection (SAP) (http://www.animal-protection.net/
furtrade/beijing_news.pdf), raccoon dogs are skinned alive for
their dense, long brown fur. But the stripping of the sensitive
outer layers from an animal without anaesthetic is not just an
exercise in rural China.

In 1994, veterinarian Murray Grant photographed a vendor
in the market of a coastal Chinese town called Haimen, about
600 km south of Shanghai. There he saw a member of the human
race peeling the skin off a bucket of live mottled-green frogs.

According to Humane Society International, over 8 million
animals are trapped yearly for their fur, while more than 30
million are raised in fur farms. Ancient wisdom suggests
*there's more than one way to skin a cat*, but fur traders claim
it is easier to take the skin off an animal who's alive and warm
than one dead and cold.

The large eyes of the frogs looked up at Murray but the frogs were mute. Caught in the act on film, the vendor moved menacingly towards the tall Australian. With greater speed than the vendor, Murray carried his camera aloft. Still the frog-man cometh. As he pedaled away on his bicycle, the vet sensed he was not going to be asked about frog pain relief. Neither was he waiting to study the size of the vendor's meat axe. Murray had a scheduled day of veterinary tasks ahead. As did the frogs, he needed his own skin firmly in place.

Prehistoric people looked at animal skins for clothing against the cold night air. Early churchmen saw human skin as something which could be stripped off to loosen a heretic's tongue. The early Catholic Church learned a human being, when skinned alive, could live until the skin was peeled down to the waist. Man has removed skin from living innocent and criminal people throughout history. The Rawhide Valley in Wyoming is said to have been named after a white settler flayed alive for murdering an Indian woman. Today the Myanmar (Burmese) Government has been accused of massive human rights abuses. In 2000, government troops in Myanmar reportedly flayed all the male inhabitants of a Karenni (Kayah) village.

Once worn for human warmth, fur is now used for fashion. Although there is no difference between humans and animals in being able to feel pain, today we continue animal skin harvesting. And people continue wearing fur.

Early human interest in seal fur was stirred when Captain James Cook's crew cast eyes on the many seal colonies as the explorer sailed in the South Atlantic and discovered the South Sandwich Islands, west of the inhospitable Antarctic Peninsula. The slow moving mammals were easy targets for the sealers, who could kill and remove a pelt in 60 seconds (Mc Ewin 2008). Elephant seals were a source of oil, and fur seals supplied warm brown velvety slippers. Cook found more than seals, and, unlike other explorers, discovered how to keep his crew healthy, surveying many lands with the loss of only one crew member. In 1779, the natives of Hawaii clubbed the distinguished explorer on the beach. Someone in the killing party noted he was breathing after the clubbing and finished off the famous life by stabbing Cook to death. It was a senseless death of a kind man.

By the 1820s, in line with the culture of the day, seal mothers and their fluffy black pups were among seals slaughtered indiscriminately. As far as we know, the animals were dead before their pelts were stripped away, although it seems unlikely. At a time when there were no steam ships, more than 200 ships took part in wiping out entire colonies in southern oceans.

Humankind progressed slowly towards humanely ending animal life. It could be said a sixty second death by skinning on the ice at a seal's home is as humane as transport to a modern noisy slaughterhouse. Cruel killing of seals lingered until 2001, when five eminent veterinarians—two British, two American and one Canadian—established that thousands of animals suffered a long, painful death in Canada's annual seal hunt (Millar 2001). The vets found the seals were alive after clubbing prior to skinning. They also found more than 40% of trapped seals were likely to have been conscious when they were skinned.

The fur industry is currently experiencing an unhealthy resurgence, as seen on the catwalks of Paris and the pages of glossy fashion magazines. Dr Plavisc, a former President of the Serbian half of Bosnia, was the Iron Lady, aged 79, who pleaded guilty to crimes against humanity and was given six years' jail. She arrived home smiling and wearing a full-length fur. A former biologist with no remorse about supporting genocide, she is waiting for the end of her life in freedom.

We have as little control of genocide as animal killings. In spite of seal product imports being banned in the US since 1972, China supplies more than half the fur garments imported for sale in the United States. Import bans have been in place in South Africa since 1990, and in the EU from 2009. The Chinese would like to retain world respect, if not world leadership, and to do this will turn back to traditional values and phase out its fur trade. They will do this because Buddhism tells them so.

What happens to wildlife sets a pattern for humankind. As the Chinese are well aware, when we listen to nature and become kinder to animals, we become kinder to people. Kinder to people? China's one-child policy has caused people to steal boys for money, as parents need a son to look after them and carry the family name. According to Britain's *Guardian* newspaper (http://www.guardian.co.uk/theobserver/2007/sep/23/features. magazine77), nearly 200 children are stolen in China each day. And this is considered to be a conservative estimate. If the Chinese government is worried, it is keeping a firm lid on its concerns.

The Buddha would be worried, because seals aren't the only animals to suffer for fashion. In China, there are no standards of care for animals and wildlife bred for fur. People for the Ethical Treatment of Animals (PETA) have investigated China's dog and cat fur trade. Undercover investigators from Swiss Animal Protection (SAP) toured fur farms in China's Hebei Province, and it quickly became clear why outsiders were banned from visiting fur farms. There are no regulations governing these farms in China—fur farmers house and slaughter animals as they see fit, causing miserable lives and agonizing animal deaths. The Swiss investigators found horrors beyond their worst imagination, and concluded, 'Conditions on Chinese fur farms make a mockery of the most elementary animal welfare standards. In their lives and their unspeakable deaths, these animals have been denied even the simplest acts of kindness'.

We quote further from the Swiss team who visited China:

> On these farms, foxes, minks, rabbits, and other animals pace and shiver in outdoor wire cages, exposed to driving rain, freezing nights, and, at other times, scorching sun. Mother animals, who are driven crazy from rough handling and intense confinement and have nowhere to hide while giving birth, often kill their babies after delivering litters. Disease and injuries are widespread, and animals suffering from anxiety-induced psychosis chew on their own limbs and throw themselves repeatedly against the cage bars (Humane Society International).

Footage taken from undercover investigators from PETA shows that, to skin the mammals, farm workers put them onto their backs or hang them up by their legs or tail. The conscious animals kick their free limbs and fight to free themselves as the workers cut into their flesh and rip the skin from their bodies. The workers stop frequently in an attempt to stop the movement, stamping on the animal's head or picking it up by the back legs and swinging its body against the ground. When fur traders strip off the pelt of the animals, their naked bodies are red. The only hair remaining on their bloodied bodies is their eyelashes, which blink slowly as the animals fight to stand on their now skinless limbs. Not a gentle approach to living beings relying on our care and compassion.

When skin is finally freed from the animal and peeled off over its head, the underlying muscles and tendons are left exposed. These bodies are then thrown into a pile of already skinned animals. Some of the bodies clearly show signs of life— breathing in gasps and blinking slowly, with some animals' hearts still beating up to 10 minutes after they were skinned. On top of a heap of carcasses, a skinned North American raccoon caught the attention of one investigator. The raccoon had just enough strength to lift his bloodied head. The former forest dweller had to do it—he wanted to stare into the eyes of a cruel human criminal.

Are we aware of the pain we are inflicting? These are potentially sobering thoughts for humans who inflict such cruelty in the name of profit. Early Buddhist teaching told that people are affected by karma, similar to the Bible saying *we reap what we sow*. Cruel people today come from thoughts of yesterday, and their present builds their tomorrow—*what goes around comes around*. But all is not lost. We are not infinitely tied to our mistakes—new actions create new karma, and this is the impetus for change. Human beings are basically good, but quests for power and profit get in the way. Cruelty is damaging to the human spirit, but skinning animals alive is convenient. From an anatomical point of view, there is negligible difference between the millions of nerve receptors in a human's skin and an animal's skin. When a living being is skinned alive, receptors are activated and the brain interprets this as pain.

All animals, including *Homo sapiens*, need to feel pain in order to survive. Pain tells us to withdraw from the stimulus that caused it, to prevent further damage to the body. One of the challenges of veterinary medicine is that whilst animals feel pain as we do, they do not display it as readily as humans. There is an evolutionary reason for this difference. An animal in the wild displaying pain appears weaker, and risks predation or abandonment from the group. In the wild, the ability to hide pain and fear can aid survival. Human beings may be too self-absorbed to acknowledge this difference.

We need to know the root causes of cruelty. What insight can China draw on to look after all beings? Can they open the cages, allow fur animals to benefit from an ancient regimen of care? For four thousand years Traditional Chinese Medicine (TCM) has given the planet healing wisdom, treating the whole body and its environment. This contrasts with Western thinking and the fur trade. When we in the West are unwell, we attend to that part of the body which appears most sick. Moreover, many Western drugs have side-effects. TCM offers gentle therapy for recalcitrant disease.

TCM takes into account not just the body and emotional status, but weather conditions and the animal's environment. Chinese herbal medicine occupies more than 90% of TCM, and offers a natural follow-on from acupuncture. TCM set a standard of care which Western medicine and fur-animal farmers had difficulty following.

Helping our minds to break patterns of brutality bring us to Hindu and Buddhist philosophy, and the concept of karma. A basic precept of these beliefs is that of no-harm. In Buddhist thought, animals are regarded as able to feel suffering. Although different to humans in terms of their intellectual ability, animals are no less capable of feeling.

The Buddha, 'the enlightened one', son of an Indian king, was born on the slopes of the Himalayas near the border of Nepal about 568 BC. One day, when he was almost thirty years old, Buddha left his comfortable life, beautiful wife and son to begin an austere life of self-denial. Once he was far enough away, he cut off his long black hair, exchanged his fine garments for simple clothes, and sent his servant and horse back home. Gentle thoughts, his karma, stayed with him.

In the middle of the first century AD, a Han Chinese Emperor became interested in Buddhism and sent envoys to India. In 67AD, the envoys returned to China with Buddhist writings. Currently, surveys put the total number of Chinese Buddhists between 660 million (50% of the total population) and over 1 billion (80% of the population) making China the country with the most Buddhist adherents in the world (Smith 2003). Could the Buddha have known that, years after his preaching, Hippocrates, the Greek physician born in 460 BC and called the 'father of medicine', would set the clinical path of 'above all, do no harm'?

Although the Emperor asked for Buddhist texts to be translated into Chinese, the philosophy of 'do-no-harm' did not reverberate with neighbouring leaders and their peoples. Many in China, Burma, Pakistan and Afghanistan were caught up in their own conflicts. The Buddha's teachings did not reach the brutal minds of warlords. Nor did it change self-centered desires for fashionable furs when humankind had access to modern clothes.

Animal brutality occurs beyond China's neighbors. Namibia, a country in southwest Africa, wrestles with managing their seal colonies, carrying out seal culls similar to those formerly undertaken in Canada and Greenland. Fur-trading sealers remove skins from the live animals while they are still fully conscious. The seals feel as we would with all our skin removed, eyes blinking in mute pain while they bleed all over from blood vessels normally hidden beneath the skin.

What can we do to stop this cruelty, to teach young children to absorb kindness as they learn to talk? It is a challenge to stop fur being perceived as fashionable. But through the work of organisations like PETA, we can reduce the number of people wearing fur. Human and animal violence go together. Photographers trying to document the skinning horror need support. Club-wielding sealers were just as violent towards people as they were towards seals. It started with punches in the journalists' faces, and was followed by Namibian legal charges of 'trespassing in a marine reserve' against anti-fur trade protestors. A maximum sentence of 20 years in jail might follow conviction.

Some in Namibia respect animals, and it is the only country in the world to specifically address conservation and protection of natural resources in its constitution. Moreover, the Namibian government declared as protected species penguins, most seabirds and 36 species of marine mammals (including dolphins, whales and great white sharks). Unfortunately, Namibian protection law did not reach the sealers.

The barbaric and cruel practices of fur traders and sealers must be stopped. Like all violence, there must be a better way to have a life.

Written with Dr Melissa Meehan

# 38 FARM ANIMALS ONCE WERE NOMADS

When did I realize how animals need each other's company? It was probably when at ten years I took one of two horses out of the paddock and watched the other whinnying loudly, pace up and down the fence until I had brought the equine friend home again. Seventy years later I wonder how chickens and mother hen who have been separated feel. A mother hen scratches at the earth talking to her chicks then a few days later she no longer has them near.

Do we feel enough about breaking the strongest mothering, family and tribal bonds of farmed animals? We stop their natural life as they serve us loyally. Researchers who have studied how chickens relate naturally to their friends rate them highly as planet dwellers. Must we commercially so overcrowd them? We owe animals more respect and need to update our definitions of kindness and cruelty.

Originally nomadic in an open space, animals do not need to live and die cruelly to feed us meat. If we can't legislate to look after animals well, we can at least legislate for compliance with codes of animal welfare. *We need unannounced random audits by veterinary officers or paraveterinary staff to enforce compliance of big business.*

Do we think enough about the half a billion animals—yes, that's *billion* with a 'b'—raised for food each year in Australia?

*No animals suffer as much as farm animals and none as much as the humble chicken. A lot of this suffering is unnecessary, because people can live without meat.*

Early earth dwellers watched animals move across the planet peacefully in herds. It was humankind's simple idea to confine selected beasts for later access to food and skins. Prehistoric people could not have foreshadowed that shutting up livestock would lead, years later, to the animal abuse which is intensive livestock production. At present there is no active auditing of farmer compliance with welfare codes. In much the same way we audit compliance with speeding and drink driving laws, we need random audits for what occurs on the farm and during livestock transport.

There are three times more domestic animals as there are people on the planet (Singer 1993). Year after year we confine millions of food animals, imprisoning them in artificial habitats far removed—much too far—from their surroundings and way of life. Once we confine animals to a paddock or shed, we are responsible for their welfare. Just as we need booze buses to deter drinking driving, so we must consider random audits to ensure compliance of welfare codes. Many people need random checks to keep on the straight and narrow. Not only some farmers, but anyone who musters, owns, manages, drives or handles livestock being transported. Saleyard agents, railway officials, abattoir managers and butcher staff also have a legal duty of care. Animal welfare is relevant to all they do.

Once a part of the factory farming process, the fate of these once nomadic dwellers is confinement in a small living space. No longer moving across the land in herds, the livestock is now transported, in cramped conditions, by unsympathetic truckies. We have also discovered that we must use cattle sparingly. Methane gas from the rumen stomach is the most potent of greenhouse gases.

Over the last 10,000 years, whether ploughing the farm or in sport, in war and peace, humankind has gained much from animals. In return, have we gained wisdom in their natural care? Under pressure from multinational corporations to make profit, more and more livestock is raised with little or no outdoor access to open fields of grass, fresh air and sunlight. When laws are not in place to protect them, farm animals are raised in conditions of legalised cruelty. Deliberately causing animals pain and distress is similar to war. It is immoral. If companion animals are treated cruelly, people are prosecuted. Why the difference? Farm animals also have feelings and souls.

It was heartening that one young person who was upset by a dramatic and fatal horse fall during a 2009 steeplechase at Warrnambool decided that the sport was cruel. Sometimes it is, as is much of what we do. Her photograph showed a horse breaking its neck. In a country we like to call a land of fair go and sport-loving, we can do so much better for our animals.

Over ninety-five percent of Australia's pork, ham and bacon comes from factory farms. Australia's largest pig meat producer sends about 950,000 pigs to slaughter annually. Mankind has had centuries to realise the pig is a good friend. In medieval England, commoners were forbidden to keep hunting dogs, so pigs were trained for the hunt. In the Second World War, pigs were excellent at detecting land mines and easier to train than dogs (Gardiner 2006). Pigs, as pets, are as sociable as dogs, tuning in to how we feel. They are noisy in groups at the best of times. When their senses tell them death is nigh in the slaughterhouse, as their mildest protest, pigs squeal. If not stunned, they scream before the knife is plunged deep in their throats. Some abattoirs stun pigs with a massive dose of electricity to the head or kill them with carbon dioxide gas. The mentality is apparent in this telling quote from within the pig farming industry: 'Forget the pig is an animal. Treat him just like a machine in a factory'. John

Byrnes, quoted in the industry journal *Hog Farm Management* in 1976.

Many people speak out against the cruelty of sow stalls. What is more troubling is that they were created in the first place. To compensate for their piglet brood being born on a concrete floor, sows want to spend time mothering their litter outside on the grass. Can they? No way. Sows cannot turn around in their farrowing crates, and can do little more than eat, drink, shit and offer their teats to their young. Mother-love is the best start for a good life. Really? One of humankind's cruelties is to deprive a mother of her newborn. It is a common practice in dairy farming to take the newborn calves away because we want the cow's milk. To lessen separation stress, can cows at least be close to their calves seeing them through a fence? Well, no. Big business sees it differently. Don't consider animal stress— animals can't talk. Some wildlife young stay with mum for years when nature decrees their young need parenting. Piglets bred for pork may be harshly weaned as early as three weeks of age!

Lambs are so cute gamboling in the paddock, but there is cruelty around this happy scene. Calves and lambs can be born onto freezing pastures. Later, at weaning, without their mothers, thirty percent of newly weaned lambs can die. Newly shorn sheep must endure blizzards in the paddock. Humans in a warm room, not the sheep, schedule the time of lambing and shearing.

Vets prefer to use anaesthetic any time they carry out a painful or stressful procedure. Pig raisers watch costs and use technicians for routine surgery. Technicians cost the multinational company less, but a price is paid—paid by the pig. Without anaesthetic, after castration, tail docking and teeth clipping, pigs tremble, have shaky legs and vomit for several days.

Is the chicken industry finger-lickin' good? The Colonel suggests it is, but many do not think so. The chicken industry has exploded in the last few decades, but our compassion for crowded farm animals has not. Although chickens raised for meat may spend their lives cage-free, Professor John Webster of the University of Bristol says *chicken meat production is 'the single most severe example of man's inhumanity to another sentient animal'* (Sharman 2009). The Bristol professor must have had difficulty choosing the species to which we are most cruel—poultry or pigs.

One of three big poultry corporations now slaughters over 2.4 million chickens each week. Sometimes the machine which cuts off their heads misses the target and the chicken remains trussed, legs up, head down on the conveyor belt, alive for the next painful procedure.

It is certainly frightening for the birds held on the conveyor belt. To keep up with Australian demand, 407 million chickens were slaughtered in 2005/2006. *Worldwide slaughter in 2009 was 52 billion (National Geographic May 2011.).* This represents 90% of all farm animals used for food. To save costs, chickens were crowded in large artificially lit sheds for their entire lives. Past the cute little chick stage and growing fast, it was 20 birds per square metre. Egg-laying birds were stacked layer upon layer in batteries. The floor size of their living space was only three quarters the size of a sheet of A4 paper, and a long way from the natural space needed.

Poultry in battery cages cannot stretch their wings or scratch at Mother Earth. Hens cannot do other natural acts, such as nest building, nurturing young, dust bathing or socialising in the sunshine. Confined hens suffer many diseases. Lack of space to stretch causes leg cramps in larger chickens. Crowded chicks peck each other. Industry can't have that, so at eight to twelve weeks of age, chicken beaks are trimmed with a hot blade. Continued pecking indicated even larger cages were needed. But the multinational had an easier answer. Another beak trim was scheduled. According to the March 2005 issue of *Agricultural Research* magazine, 'Farmers trim from a third to a half of the beaks off chickens, turkeys, and ducks to cut losses from poultry pecking each other'.

Some people at the fast-food counter can still recall when poultry was special. Chickens hatched from hens in a quiet nest were raised with their mother. Wheat was scattered in a grassy backyard in the sun and fresh air. It was a life in stark contrast to that of the many animals currently enduring brutal confinement in large commercial operations. Does the girl in the crisp red coat serving behind the fast-food counter know these chickens have their beaks cruelly cut off? You open your mouth to ask for that big chicken, but you suddenly decide you would like your snack to be cruelty-free. "Just chips, please," you say, because growing spuds involves no violation of nature.

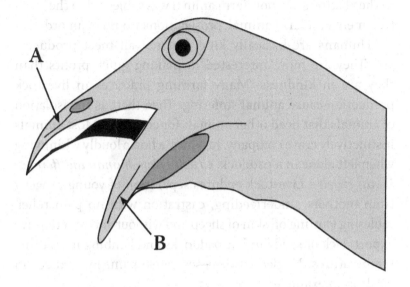

Courtesy Luke Harris

*Cutting off the nose in spite of the pain. Some chickens deprived of space and sunlight, have one third to half their beaks cut off. Nerves of the beaks (A and B) are many. The effects on the brain and chicken well-being are not shown here. What do we tell our children about this atrocity? World wide in 2009 52 billion chickens were killed for food (National Geographic, May 2011). Not just a million but a **billion** each week. Some chicken crowding. Some beak chopping.*

We undervalue vegetables as food. Potatoes contain large amounts of Vitamin C, as well as calcium, iron and phosphorus. Spuds are rich in potassium, the concentration being higher in the potato skin and just beneath it. As a primary production vet, Graham knew it was not only the pig and poultry industries which were a target. Other farm animals suffered just as badly, or worse. Life was tough but the manner of death was tougher.

In the abattoirs, if a non-farm animal was subjected to the same treatment as a farm animal, prosecutions would be in order.

Humans are basically kind, but not all meat producers are. They are more interested in making quick profits than they are in kindness. Many farming practices in livestock production cause animal suffering. Then there is the isolation of animals that need other animals for company. Most animals instinctively crave company. Just hear a horse loudly whinnying when left alone in a paddock. *Cruelty from human indifference is still cruelty.* Livestock endures separation of young progeny from mothers, underfeeding, castration with no pain relief, mulesing (cutting off skin of sheep and without anaesthetic), live export, lack of shade in hot paddocks and lambing in freezing temperatures. Neglected diseases cause pain. Eye cancer in cattle is an example.

We are horrified to hear of a pup whose ears were chopped off, but we do not target farmers, truckies and the meat industry about cruelty. On a planet shattered by violence, inflicting pain and distress on animals sets a poor example for young people. How many people shoulder the responsibility of being kind to all beings? What Western example do terrorists look at?

Isabel Allende reminds us that *'ignorance and apathy are just as reprehensible as the acts of brutality'* (Allende 1987). Fortunately, there are wise heads on young shoulders pushing for radical change. Visiting an intensive piggery in South Australia, Rachel Westcott, after a couple of hours with her fellow veterinary students among the pigs, was sickened by what she came face to face with and sat silently outside. Other students felt the same way. Her ethical standards were again compromised when she saw heifers tied up for bull testing. One of them was bleeding from the vagina. Supposedly wiser elders in the food production industry provided limited or no leadership against welfare abuses (Westcott 2009). As Rachel remarks, "Because we are on the well-worn path, it doesn't mean we are on the right track." These words could have been offered to the young students from the farm community and the pig raisers.

It is the emerging adults who can save us. A young person protesting at the racecourse realised that, on and off the racetrack, animals feel pain as humans do. We need a young, sensitive person photographing horses jumping at speed to keep protesting about cruelty until all animals, fast and slow, have a natural life and an easy death.

*Dedicated to the memory of Professor Bede Morris, John Curtin School of Medical Research, Canberra, who reminded us 'You can't legislate for compassion'.*

# 39 TURTLE SLAUGHTER IN QUEENSLAND

*"Slaughter On The Beach"*

*Four Corners film from the ABC on May 30, 2011 re-vealed shocking evidence of animal cruelty in Indonesian abattoirs. Mediaeval methods included blunt slashes at throats of terrified cattle, eyes gouged, heads partly severed, cows falling onto slippery floors, one breaking a leg, being bea-ten. It has been going on for decades and occurs in many slaughterhouses in the world. The film from Lyn White of Animals Australia was too graphic for most viewers.*

*Animal killing styles come from ancient times and reach well beyond today's slaughterhouse walls. What methods do we see today in what is by most people called the lucky country? Is it always lucky for the animals?*

*An Australian Broadcasting Corporation 7.30 reporter Rupert Imhoff filmed indigenous routine killing of turtles on Green Island off the coast of Queensland. Limbs were removed from live and conscious animals. It was legal butchery of turtles lying on their backs on the sand. The meat was sold through non-indigenous traders for drug money.*

> *In no way was killing necessary or in the spirit of being respectful and gentle to another species. Where do cultures meet and greet in the modern world? Australia, the kind and lucky country does not need meat from wildlife and can end barbaric habits.*

Because of some cruel slaughterers, watching cameras are need at all abattoirs from the unloading truck to slaughter. *Temple Grandin a famous livestock-handling consultant, documented a saving of $500 to $1,000 per day at one slaughterhouse after she trained employees to handle cattle quietly (Grandin and Johnson 2009). To reduce cruelty, pre—slaughter stunning and years of education are essential.* Money is saved simply when there is no shouting and yelling. *Stock people need to recognize an animals—even robust livestock—has feelings. Careful selection of staff, financial incentives for no noise and lack of livestock injury pays off. Supervisors must be accountable for the actions of all slaughterhouse workers. People who enjoy abusing animals should not be working with them.*

*Reference: Grandin, Temple and Johnson, Catherine (2009) Making Animals Happy How to Create the Best Life for Pets and Other Animals*, Bloomsbury, London

Humankind has yet to discover how to transport and slaughter animals *en masse* humanely. If we continue to insist on killing animals to feed us meat, at the very least we can do it without cruelty. Every year around five million pigs are slaughtered in Australia. Cooped together in cramped conditions before their slaughter, it is the ideal setting for the spread of diseases such as foot and mouth, as seen in the European outbreak of the disease in 2001, caused from pigs held together in saleyards. If the virus gets past Australian security and enters the country, innocent pigs will become a serious threat to the whole livestock industry. The spread of the foot and mouth virus hurts not just cloven-hoofed animals but us all.

'The ramp's too steep!' Livestock veterinarian Graham was definite. 'That sow won't go down from the truck because it's too steep.' The vet spoke in a loud voice to carry to the top of the multi-layered transport and be heard above the noise of livestock.

Graham was trying to explain to the truck driver why a poor exit design meant the bulky sow of some 200 kilograms was not moving down the narrow ramp onto the ground. The truckie had his own answer to stop her blocking the unloading of 70 pigs for slaughter. He applied the electric prodder to the sow's rump. *Zap zap zap.* Australian truckies are not properly trained for the use of such equipment and therefore tend to lack emotional restraint. The use of electric shock is not contained in the truckies' guidelines, but nevertheless the sow must be moved. *Zap zap zap.*

Grunting loudly, the sow lifted her head, taking the hint from the shock of electricity, but still there was no forward step. It wasn't just that the ramp was too steep. After a 150-kilometre journey in temperatures of 4 degrees Celsius, with no cover on the truck, the pigs were cold. In the US, exposing animals to such extreme weather conditions risks prosecution for lack of livestock care. The truck could have been pulled over and the driver asked for his competence certificate. Just as well the pigs were transported in Australia, where the regulations are more lax.

Better than 20 years ago, if an animal could be dragged onto a truck it was fit for slaughter. Now a beast must walk on all four feet to enter the abattoir. The big sow almost did not make it into the killing room. One leg got caught in a gap at the top of the ramp, tearing skin off her hock, but there was not enough damage to make her lame—she could still walk down the poorly maintained ramp. So the big sow moved, and 70 other pigs hesitantly made their way to the ground.

That ramp needs attention, thought Graham, before the next truckload.

The pigs would have done more than hesitate if they had known what was going to happen within the hour in the slaughterhouse. Moving closer and closer to the carbon dioxide chamber, the pigs were squealing noisily. Did they know death was imminent, or was it just the general racket of a group of pigs crammed tightly together? Noise reverberated from the stainless steel fittings and the stark white butcher-shop walls. It was hard not to speculate that the stressed pigs knew something serious was about to happen.

The pigs were pushed into a small race leading to the carbon dioxide gas chamber installed for sedation. Amid the shouting of staff, six more zaps from the electric prodder were inflicted to jam one pig against the one in front. The unconscious pigs rolled out from the gas chamber and were quickly strung upside down and hooked onto a conveyor belt, their heads almost two metres from the floor. Slaughterhouse workers placed a chain around one back leg prior to each pig being strung upside down for slaughter. The clanging of metal gates made sure it was not a quiet death.

Level with the pig's head, a tall, strong butcher was dressed in white overalls and gumboots. The blood sprayed across his overalls showed his task in the assembly line of the long knives. The pig's head hung down. The big butcher plunged his long, sharp knife deep in the pig's neck, into the large blood vessel near the heart—the *anterior vena cava*. The butcher was proud of his skill with the blade but there was little perfection in the methods of killing in the slaughterhouse. Most pigs, but not all, were unconscious as the blade found its mark deep in the neck. The huge sow bled quickly. For most, death was painless.

One suspended pig was recovering from gas sedation, and was beginning to feel pain and stress. How often were they waking up? It was a quick demise for all the pigs, well before expert knife slashes eviscerated each, allowing lungs and stomach to fall into a stainless steel tray below the suspended carcass. Graham looked carefully for disease in the organs in the tray. There was a strong smell of faeces, blood, viscera and death. For all it was stressful. As much as feeling the knife in the throat, the pain was in the strange and the unknown, the terror and hours of separation from the natural life the pigs knew.

If we continue to raise and slaughter, as humane and compassionate beings we need to minimise stress and suffering, improving transport, livestock loading and movement in the last yards of the animals' life on earth. At present there is no system of checking farmer compliance with welfare codes, no easy pass or fail test to be applied. Unannounced random audits by government inspectors are needed. Penalties for non-compliance must be immediate, costly and harsh. What we need is a system of auditing of animal welfare similar to the methods used to check compliance of speeding and drink driving laws. We need auditing of animal welfare to be as successful as the work carried out by booze buses. An ethic of 'give the animals a fair go' will help us pass compassionate laws. These laws must also ensure better abattoir design and staff training, for the more humane handling of animals.

Sometimes the law helps in protecting animal rights, but the first line of defense is usually public vigilance. There was a call to arms in Animals Australia. This animal protection organisation exposed animal abuse, promoting cruelty-free handling of livestock. Some 40-member societies supporting Animals Australia believed that we could create a better world through promoting kindness to animals.

Customers, moreover, can choose where they buy. In 2009 two major Woolworths suppliers fronted courts in Tasmania, charged with animal cruelty. A battery hen operator of Sun Valley Poultry was found to have confined hens in cages on top of the rotting carcasses of their cage mates. As a result, Sun Valley was charged and convicted of 'failing to provide veterinary treatment to a sick and injured animal', and received a $3,000 fine. The second case involved a commercial piggery operator charged with serious breaches of the Tasmanian Animal Welfare Act, including aggravated cruelty. Desperately sick and injured pigs were discovered at Longerong piggery, with no attempt made to provide them with veterinary assistance. One moribund pig had maggots crawling out of a wound.

Dedicated as she is to wildlife, Jane Goodall asks what does it take to melt the ice in the human heart? There is no answer in the slaughterhouse.

# 40 FOR HEAVEN'S SAKE, SKIP THE STEAK AND DON'T BRING HOME THE BACON

Meat eating is entrenched from when we lived in caves and is now a multi billion dollar industry. People can live without eating meat. We must offer food produced without violence and then we do away with slaughterhouses. *Slaughter before and after stunning may still be brutal.*

Our silent acceptance of brutal killing can extend to other forms of violence: workplace bullying, cruelty and abuse of children. Does genocide have its origin in the license we give ourselves to murder another species?

With their matching physiology, pigs are more similar to people than other animals raised for food production. Pet pigs moreover are much loved by their owners but in 2009, worldwide 1.3 billion pigs (which is equivalent to the population of China) were killed for food (*National Geographic* May 2011).

Politicians are not all forward thinking people and we lack information on so many challenges which impact on the animals of the planet. Overpopulation is the greatest. Fortunately people are omnivores—they can eat all food and do not need to eat meat.

We do need to be more kind. Spain has led the way in eliminating bullfighting from the province of Catalonia. The veterinary profession has the challenge of eliminating all cruelty in the production, transport and slaughter of animals.

University researchers state that an overpopulated planet is the biggest problem that we face today, followed by climate change and a need for renewable energy resources.

According to the State University of New York College of Environmental Science and Forestry (ESF), overpopulation is the world's top environmental issue, followed closely by climate change and the need to develop renewable energy resources to replace fossil fuels.

## A no-meat climate solution

Cattle are bad news for the planet. Meat is a luxury food compared to what most of the world's population can afford to eat. Meat eaters must now consider reducing their consumption of meat to one meal a week. Better still, no meat at all. With the world's second highest population, India's Environment Minister told the world *"the single most important measure to reduce greenhouse gas is to stop eating beef"* (Wade 2009). Furthermore, trying to supply meat for so many hungry people in the world encourages food animal cruelty.

## Greenhouse gases worse than from transport

According to the UN's 2006 report on the food and agriculture industries, 'the international meat industry creates about eighteen percent of the world's greenhouse gas emissions—more than transportation. ('Global warming, fifty-one things we can do, skip the steak', *Time Magazine* 5/4/07). *Methane is produced from bovine digestion, and is 23 times as warming as carbon.* Nitrous oxide in cow manure is 296 times as great in its warming effect.

## Too much water used

Water conservation is one aspect of reverence for the earth. Australia's annual water footprint per person is more than the global average, half as much again as Bangladesh, and more than Britain. *Growing crops rather than beef saves water.* One hamburger takes 2,400 litres to produce; a pair of leather shoes 8,000 litres; an egg 135 litres; and a tomato 13 litres. ('World's worst at water use', *The Age* 20/5/07).

With limited world resources, meat on the table means other people go hungry, hand in hand with more animal cruelty. Many farmers are dedicated animal people, but livestock must be transported to the slaughterhouse in crowded trucks in all weather conditions, from freezing cold to baking hot, suddenly separated from food, water and all life they know. Even tight-lipped terrorists talk if you isolate one from life as he knows it. Some Gippsland beef farmers keep their cattle groups together, so cattle live together, travel together and die together.

Animal protein is not the gentlest way the planet can nourish and sustain the growing masses of people. Vegetable protein crops are not as thirsty as steers. *Time* magazine asks which is responsible for more global warming, your BMW or your Big Mac? Believe it or not, it's the burger. The scourge of climate change means we cannot eat so much meat any more.

Animal protein is an inefficient way to feed the world's exploding population. We simply do not have enough water to sustain animal production. Activists ask:

❖ What does production of all that meat cost the planet?

❖ Are there enough shady trees in the paddock?

- ❖ Can the animals walk in the sun, see the sky?
- ❖ How comfortable are the animals during transport? Are they too hot, too cold, and is there ample water?

# 41 ELEPHANT LIFE AND MASSACRES

My first encounter with an elephant was at age ten watching a circus keeper in High Street, Glen Iris, belting his charge with a metal hook behind the ear while trying to go downhill from Malvern Road. The elephant lorry, with shafts wide enough for the largest of land animals, had no brakes. Pulled downhill, the lorry was banging on the elephant's hocks at every step. The elephant would not continue down the steep road in spite of the beatings. A High Street tram conductor raised his voice in protest at the cruelty. His voice won the day and the elephant was unhitched from the truck to walk freely down the steep and busy road.

Cruelty to the giants is legendary. Hundreds fell to death trekking over the Alps by a poorly informed and ego-driven Hannibal, full of hate for Rome. The elephants struggled with tough terrain while the troops cared little. The narrow alpine paths were no place for huge herbivores who every day ground up a quarter tonne of tough vegetation and drink between 80-180 litres of water. Tusks are special front teeth, but 24 molar teeth are used as grinders for the big mammal. Elephants live to an average of 81 years in Asia, but molar teeth can be so worn at 60 or 70 years that, in the wild, the animal can starve to death.

The story of elephant conservation is a story of strong women following Gandhi's principle. One is Daphne Sheldrick, widow of

David, founder of Kenya's Tsavo National Park. Daphne, Kenyan born, found out how to rear milk-dependent orphan elephants and rhinos. Another is Belinda Wright, born in Calcutta in 1953, from a family of conservationists and also a pioneer in protecting wildlife. Her love for animals began when she was a child brought up in a house full of unusual animals, including a tiger cub and a leopard. She is now one of India's leading wildlife conservationists. It was she, disguising her blonde hair and blue eyes, who discovered the illegal trade in animal parts in India.

I met a third woman, Dr Catherine Tschanen, in Switzerland. She is a vet who teaches children to love animals. To this end, Catherine visited 36 villages in Togo, Africa, to present to them an aspect of wildlife they had not considered before. "We need to explain to the village children that elephants are not just beasts which destroy village crops." Catherine tells the children, *"Elephants have many of our human feelings—a sense of humor, sense of caring, of loving, mischief and of jealousy."* She asks the villagers to "try to understand animals that appear destructive also have a right to live. When we destroy their forests, put farms and crops on their migratory paths, we are asking for trouble."

The elephant is threatened daily by the ivory trade. Their tusks are more than 3 m in length and weigh up to 90 kg each. The tusks are irresistible to poachers, but human greed and thoughtlessness is threatening the animal's long-term survival. Catherine told me about elephant massacres in Africa for ivory tusks, the modified long teeth the animal uses for digging up roots and tubers. The ivory harvest occurred during the 1970s and 1980s, when locals slaughtered nine million elephants. Walking through the savanna during that time, more than 10,000 elephant carcasses could be found lying in the hot sun, their tusks removed by poachers. To elephant lovers, it was desecration.

Wild elephants treat their dead with respect, covering the bodies with leaves and twigs, akin to burial. When an elephant dies naturally, the herd removes the tusks and throws the ivory away, out of the reach of man. Elephants are browsing animals, feeding on fruits, leaves, shoots and tall grasses, consuming hundreds of kilograms of food a day. Travelling in herds of up to one hundred, they roam over no fixed living area and find enough water to drink up to 190 litres daily.

The mood of elephants can vary, and they have been known to kill people who are not kind to them. Years ago in Melbourne my twin sister and I were two of hundreds of children given rides on Melbourne Zoo's 'Queenie'. Back then we were unaware of the underlying mistreatment of the animal. The hidden abuse did not come to light until the day Queenie killed her cruel keeper. There was also the incident of elephants destroying the local crops of a small Indian village. In excessive retaliation, the men of the village killed the nearest elephant herd, including a baby elephant. Upon seeing the baby elephant dying, a herd of old elephant matriarchs returned to the village, destroying it and its adult inhabitants. They did not, however, kill a human baby. Tit-for-tat has its limits in the animal world. In contrast, human tit-for-tat, what should be a sensible no-no, has been historically used as a disaster for humankind.

We humans become angry for a wide range of reasons, but elephants have a gland between the eye and the ear which periodically produces an oily substance. When this happens the elephant experiences an excitable, dangerous state of mind, called *musth*, meaning madness. Such a condition occurs more often in males than in females, and suggests a state of sexual excitement. Man is not so well equipped. He must go to the pharmacist to buy a product which arouses this kind of excitement, the similar sounding musk, which he splashes on his skin and hopes for the best.

## Wildlife crime

African bull elephants, the largest land mammals, may reach a shoulder height taller than some home ceilings. Females are smaller than bulls and have more slender tusks. African elephants have enormous ears, measuring up to 107 cm in diameter, which they flap to keep themselves cool. Elephants talk mostly between early evening and early morning, using sounds as high as the top note of a clarinet to the lowest note of a concert piano (Warren 2004). Their voices can be so deep we cannot hear them at all. They pick up some ground vibrations with their feet.

Elephants sometimes adopt animals that are not of their own species—one adopted a buffalo herd—but love their own best. A matriarchal elephant strolling with her calf and herd on morning was attracted to one small orphan elephant, so much so that the big pachyderm kidnapped the calf from an adoptive mother. The little orphan disappeared into the depths of the jungle with its kidnapper.

"She knew she was doing wrong," said Catherine Tschanen, a wildlife vet, "and her own calf needed her milk."

Back at the orphan enclosure, the orphan's foster mother and the keepers were grieving. The orphan's adoptive mother trumpeted her concern, requesting return of the stolen calf. Subsonic rumbles, silent to human ears, augmented her audible cries of distress, registering the foster mother's agony fifty kilometres away. Next morning two young elephants appeared. Only 18 and 20 years old but respected by other elephants, they walked the kidnap victim between their trunks.

Compassion is part of an elephant's nature. There is a togetherness reinforced by rubbing each other while standing close in the dust. They have feelings of right and wrong, such as a dislike of bullying. On one occasion an older matriarch acted with kindness in the river when she saw large teenage elephants pushing a smaller one under the mud. She lumbered to the rescue, shoving the bullies to one side with her considerable body weight.

## Asian elephants

Once plentiful from China to Iraq, Asian elephants may be more in peril than those in Africa. The Thais owe a debt to the big grey giants. Elephant cavalry pushed back Myanmar (Burmese) tyrants in the 16th century, to give the Thais their freedom. Today the Thais remain free from Burma, but by replacing three quarters of the country's forests with logging and farming, the Thais have taken freedom away from their wild savior elephants. That's humankind.

Logging of natural forests was declared illegal in 1989, but illegal habitat removal continues. Men of little experience, attracted by what seems easy money, work as *mahouts* (handlers) in Thailand. Being a mahout requires understanding, as elephants kill one hundred inexperienced Thai keepers every year. Many Thais are concerned when worse things are recorded on camera. Journalist Jennifer Hile filmed the taming of Thai elephants by torture in her documentary *Vanishing Giants*. She showed villagers dragging a four-year-old elephant from her mother, depriving the infant of food, water and sleep for many days. If she took a false step, villagers stabbed her feet with bamboo sticks tipped with nails. Under this regimen the elephant is taught to work, to accept people on her back. Tourists from around the world paying top dollars to take elephant rides are in a diminishing habitat, unwittingly carried not on happy beasts but on diminished giants.

In 1901, Thailand had a population of 100,000 elephants. The country's remaining 3,000 elephants have lost their logging jobs but are too tame to be set free. They carry tourists instead of timber logs. One elephant called Jokia was forced to drag logs while pregnant, the strain and stress causing her to miscarry. Rebelling, she was beaten and shot by her mahout who, abusing one of the strongest human-animal bonds on earth, took to shooting her in the worst way, with a slingshot, blinding one eye. Jokia was upset. When her owner came up to try to control her, Jokia swung her trunk and broke her owner's arm. In revenge, the owner shot Jokia's other eye, totally blinding the animal. There was a witness to this abuse, however. A North Thailand travel agent, Sangduen Challert, who was a one-woman humane society in the city of Chang Mai, raised money to buy Jokia and took her to join seventeen other elephants in the Elephant National Park, a lush 955-acre forest reserve.

## Seeing-eye elephant

Things are now much better for Jokia. She has a friend to guide her—Mae Perm, the first elephant that Sangduen took under her care. The elephant-guide sends out warning squeals or blocks Jokia's way like a trained dog guide. At unexpected smells or noises, Mae Perm gives out deep rumbles and touches Jokia with her trunk to help her blind friend.

Jokia also has another friend, her Burmese refugee, a mahout called Kum, himself without one eye, the result of an accident in the forest. Kum sometimes hangs from Jokia's trunk, while she lifts him into mid air. He tells of how, when looking for Jokia in the jungle, his big friend often hides, trying to be quiet as a mouse, using her trunk to silence the clapper on the wooden bell she wears. "You're such a sweet girl," Kum tells her, "why must you also be so tricky?" (Chadwick 2005). Kum feels more than love for the elephants. He admires the disabled Jokia and enjoys the eight hectares of habitat Jokia needs to live. He feels protective of the wider savanna which eight to twelve close family members require to roam and explore with the local elephant matriarch.

In Cambodia, a UK charity increased local care for elephants forced to hobble about for 16 hours each day with no access to food and water. They were sunburned due to limited access to river mud, and with deep cuts and abscesses, injuries from ear ropes with metal hooks, and the pain of flies burrowing into the skin. There was no veterinary school in Cambodia. When Kum was sitting behind matriach Jokia's ears he looked at the busy forest floor, he did not realize he and Jokia had one of the closest bonds in the animal kingdom.

# 42 LONG WAY TO THE TOP

Patrick was a big man and his big hands were never more obvious than when he was on the football field marking the ball 50 yards out from the goal posts. Pat would drop the ball onto one large boot and firmly put it through for six points.

When he graduated as a veterinary surgeon, he found his big hands more than good enough for complicated bone surgery pulling fragments together when fractures threatened to be slow to knit. The vets around him would send their difficult smashed bones slow to heal. Pat's extra care suited everyone especially lame dogs needing four legs to race in the park chasing a tennis ball. Everyone noticed how fast dogs ran after Pat's top surgical skills.

It was not long before many difficult broken bones were referred to see the big gruff man who loved the park. The vet with big hands who threw the cricket ball from the cricket pitch to the boundary.

One day big Pat arrived at his Adelaide surgery to find a large Labrador mastiff mixed breed standing on three legs at the front door.

'What's the dog doing out there at the front? Better ring up the council and tell the dog catcher'. Pat was a top vet in a hurry and his appointment book was full.

Receptionist Moira was at the front desk. 'I think I remember that dog. He was brought in to see us three years ago when he was referred from the local practitioner because his broken leg did not heal. 'The dog is Buster'. Moira reminded Pat 'You put a pin in his leg, It was his humerus and we had to keep him here for weeks. He lives way out west the other side of Adelaide. 'I'll look up the records and see if I can find the owner.'

'Funny you should ask' said a squeaky voice full of emotion on the other end of the line,' He did not come home two nights ago and we were worried. 'It's good to hear.'

Certainly it was Buster's second leg to be badly smashed. For the second time, Pat pinned one of Buster's legs and used stainless steel screws to hold broken fragments closer together. Buster really liked his local vet with her soothing voice, and long golden hair. She was always gentle and made sore parts of his body better. Now one more leg had been crushed and he could not put it to the ground. Gentle Dr Goldilocks had once before sent him across the city to a get more treatment and have less pain. It was not an easy canine trip, as Buster had only done the journey once or twice and that was in a car. Yesterday he had walked a long way to return to Pat, the big vet whom Goldilocks had placed at the top.

Now he was safe again with the big man in the white coat, Buster settled in to rest.

Soon the leg would hurt no more. Before long his owners would arrive and Buster would go home.

*Acknowledgement:* Pat McCormack

# 43 SWIM WITH THE FISH

Angelo was a contented general practitioner in his adopted country looking after people in Ringwood. He was living some distance from his beloved sea but felt more at peace than when immersed in the middle of a big city of multi-story buildings such as Melbourne. Although he deeply cared about other species—they were never driven by money—it suited him to be looking after human families. The downside was that people on the other side of a big city sometimes did terrible violence to each other. Human violence, as bad as it was, had rarely eliminated a species. Even the Australian Aborigines had survived slaughter in the Southern Hemisphere. Angelo was aware of many Australian animal species lost—killed by animals introduced by people from the other side of the world. Angelo often thought about how vulnerable animals were with little or no voice to tell of pain. That's how it was for injured wild duck, shot on the water in the name of sport.

The doctor, surrounded by patients and plenty of kids, wondered whether he was kind enough to all beings. Angelo liked the children best for their unrestrained joy for life. And he could still get away to snorkel each summer afternoon.

He had met plenty of animal activists, however, and many challenges; shooters who wanted to kill duck wild life on the water.

At home Angelo noted with pleasure, people away for the day had begun to confine their cats outside in cat runs to stop bird loss. He must send that idea back to Italy. It might lead to more pressure from European groups trying to stop chained bears cruelly made to dance on the end of a knotted rope through the nose. Humane animal care should not be just for Greenpeace and PETA—People For The Ethical Treatment Of Animals. It was for all humanity.

Activists were not in existence when he was choosing his path in life. We needed new thinking how he could encourage children's enthusiasm to look after silent animal species? Outside his family and care of his patients, had he been thoughtful enough?

One afternoon after he finished his home visits, he pulled on his mask and goggles and slipped into the cool waters of the bay where he had swum before.

At last he was out of reach of the telephone.

Almost as soon as Angelo started to move underwater, he saw a multi colored striped fish as bright as a picture in the *National Geographic*, trying to attract his attention. He enjoyed colorful fish at the surface but noticed they lost their bright hues in deeper water. The fish swam to Angelo and away again. And did it again. The fish wanted to show Angelo something. Angelo followed until the big striped one showed off his pride hiding behind a big rock. Angelo was shown a group of little fish; they were color striped just like the big one. He was not surprised, one of his friends had a male cat who ran away and four months later returned home with four young kittens in tow. He showed them to his loving owners and disappeared again.

The doctor returned to his clinic with a smile on his face. He would do something new and visit local schools. He must tell the children in keeping with our need of food we must to go easy and keep up fish numbers, Perhaps they could write a story saying how we must do nothing to hurt where fish live and grow, and keep the seas free of chemical waste.

Other words, too, had come to him before, but not while he was swimming with the fish. Do we understand we are an ocean planet, the seas covering more than 70% of Earth's surface? In one of his waiting room magazines, he read that Australian seafood in large amounts is exported to Japan, China, USA and Europe (Pepperell 2011). He had often told his fellow doctors *we all need each other.* When he read that global commercial fishing between WW Two and the 1980's removed 90 % of larger fish, Angelo mentally added to the message about needing each other, *'we all need each other and be moderate in our fish eating.'*

In his mind, *Angelo* made a note to write on the white board of his waiting room. Words so the kids learned to put away the fishing line and swim with the fish.

*Ref: Pepperell J (2011) Slippery Subject in* Australian Geographic, Jan Mar 2011

**Further reading**
*Australian Geographic Jan* March *2011*
*Australia's Sustainable Seafood Guide* tells us what we can catch and what we must not catch *www.sustainableseafood.org.au*

# 44 A DOVE CALLED NOAH, A MARE CALLED SISSY

A dove has a much smaller brain than that of humankind but can show more than human compassion. Noah the one legged white dove in a Texan rescue ranch nevertheless knew needy beings when he saw them. In Texas, orphaned six-day-old baby rabbit bunnies came into the Animal Rescue after a dog attack. Noah parked outside their cage. The dove was not the only one impressed by being up close. The rabbits, too, liked what they saw. One of the bunnies sneaked outside the rabbit enclosure and joined the dove. Soon it was hidden under Noah. When a recuperating bunny moved and was protruding under the bird's feathers, Noah gently pushed the bunny back out of sight with his beak.

Noah sang his cooing song of comfort. Once the bunnies had disappeared under his feathers, Noah carefully stretched his wings to surround them to offer a good warm snuggle. The bunnies began to thrive.

Strange, Noah had not heard of Psalm 91 saying 'I will take you under my wing' nor had he heard the words 'under my wing you will find refuge.'

Larger animals look after the small but sometime small look after the large.

At Deer Haven Ranch, a private 300 rescue acres north of Yellowstone National Park, Michelle Feldstein runs with her husband, Al. She tells, of a blind grey mare, Sissy

"Sissy came with five goats and five sheep—and they take care of her," said Feldstein "The seeing-eye sheep and guard-goats are never far from the white mare, and they never lead her astray, shepherding Sissy to food and water, and guiding the mare into her stall amid blowing snows or driving rains'.

"They round her up at feeding time and then move aside to make sure she gets to the hay," Feldstein said. "They show her where the water is and stand between her and the fence to let her know the fence is there."

If we leave animals unfettered to nurture vulnerable others, perhaps wildlife will have a new reason to hope. When wildlife is healthy the planet is well.

**Acknowledgement**: Bob and Georganne Lenham of Wild Rose Rescue Ranch in Texas. Michelle and Al Feldstein of Deer Haven, and Joan Spittle, Dromana.

# 45 TOO SOON OLD, TOO LATE WISE*

*Animals are mainly here for our wonder and care rather than for our use. We need to be far more wise in caring for other species.*
**—David Suzuki the environmentalist, reminds us to be humble about and respect the unknown forces affecting us (Chandler 2010).**

All living beings are at our mercy, and we face challenges to make sure all beings on the planet get a fair go. While there is no easy way to measure the joy and unconditional love people feel with their domestic pets, it is easy to overlook that animals outside the house and garden are not merely property but have feelings much as we do. It is up to us to speak for them. What we do in front of young children is soaked up like a sponge.

Children are nurtured to high levels of self-esteem at home. We all know that's where it all begins. How much can the animal world help? Hearing the latest animal stories from kindergarten?

Geneticist Dr Alan Wilton, one of an international team of researchers, has suggested the dingo and the New Guinea singing dog may be the world's oldest dog breeds and are most closely related to wolves. Recent genetic evidence indicates dingoes and New Guinea's native singing dogs originated in South China and travelled through Southeast Asia and Indonesia to reach their destinations by land perhaps 5000 or 10,000 years ago—earlier than previously thought. (*Proceedings of the Royal Society B.* 2011).

We need more thinking about cruelty, especially for farm animals. Wildlife and farm animals are the next social cause. Children are intuitively aware that animals are not beneath us, only different. Animals depend on us for space on the planet and their day in the sun, free to run fast, breathe easy, and be with nature. Animals are looked after by a veterinary profession now mostly made up of women. We have massive challenges of care and a long way to go. If everybody's skill is well used, the planet is less likely to feel the disappointment of one young owner who consulting me observed 'I *was only a man*'.

We need to know more about animals dangerous to humans and human danger to our animals. The mosquito is the second most dangerous being to the planet after fellow humans and spreads diseases such as malaria, dengue fever and yellow fever.

The first people on the planet were worried finding tigers in the jungle. Now it is more serious, we are worried when we cannot find tigers in the jungle. Wild tiger numbers have slid from 100,000 a century ago to 3200 in year 2010 according to Save the Tiger Fund.

Can children learn that life is an exercise in respect and helping each other? How can they be better armed than being taught *before* mindless aspects of peer pressures, talk of drugs and sex loom (children can learn about sex in animals). Learn about nature before serious exams must be passed. We remember what our kindergarten teachers told us '*every being on the planet needs a fair go*'. It is a theme not heard much in later life.

Animals of the planet need us and we have much to learn from nature. *To whom can animals turn if we walk away?*

What's this in the heavens? You could not see much at first. There was a dot in the sky with a group of other dots. As the dots flew closer you could see many birds in formation. Closer, it was Azura wing to wing with snow geese looking for a safe haven for rest, food and flat water. From wetland to wetland, they had flown from the North Pole buffeted by storms and lightning. Now hungry and thirsty, the geese knew some wetlands rise and fall with the seasons, sometimes drying up entirely before the rains come.

Azura and friends landed safely and began feeding. Forget yesterday. There was lush grass. This was a new start.

*But in the streams nearby, freshwater animals were vanishing faster than those on land or in the sea (Chadwick 2010).*

*Acknowledgement: This chapter title is derived from "Too Soon Old Too Late Smart" in Dr Gordon Livingston's book "Thirty True Things You Need To Know Now".*
*Dr Livingston offers an excellent summary of a human life reflecting on working with people. There are far more than 30 'true things we need to know now' about animals.*

**Ref:**
Chandler J (2010), The Disciple of Nature, The Age 16/10
Chandler, and Chadwick, placed 1st

# 46 ONE MORE THING

I see the world differently now I am 80 years old. Animals have been there for us, are we always there for them?

A 2012 planet means we move towards not enough food and at times indifferent disease control in the Third World. The way we think is not always kind. People hold attitudes. such as 'I am above others' and 'I can do it so I will do it.' This applies to people living under a dictator but also to how we think about our wildlife habitat and farm animals.

Owners often remark as they show me their sick dog, 'People let me down, my dog never does.'

Freud explained the significance of affection, 'we need to love to stop going mad.' There are more reasons than Freud's to draw us closer to animals. How can we expect kindness for people if we do not treat animals gently?

Dame Phyllis Frost, dedicated social worker and champion for goaled women, told me and an audience of young Rotarian men 50 years ago 'you must be prepared to change your mind minute by minute if you wish to remain useful.'

I have not heard better advice.

# APPENDIX 1:
# SAVING HABITAT AND LEARNING FROM WILDLIFE

*Within 20 years 40% of wild animal species will have disappeared. We must leave wildlife alone except when their welfare is threatened. Villagers need dollars from eco-tourism rather than selling animal parts. Conservation can become the villagers' source of income.*

## Ten Commandments to Help Save the Planet

*With Dr. Catherine Tschanen, President of Terre et Faune*

1. Move towards becoming vegetarian, if you believe you need meat, eat it only once weekly.
2. If you must buy animal species, for example, buying fish from the market, select only from a source easily replaced.
3. In line with nature's design, support biological agriculture, plant native species to support fauna, use no plant poisons.
4. Stop buying exotic wood, the harvesting of which might lead to habitat destruction. Herbicides after tree felling remove vital cover of small species.
5. Recycle as much paper as you can.

6. Avoid buying products which contain palm oil, for example some peanut butter.
7. When you travel, do not buy animal hide, skin or other animal parts, such as turtle shells, feathers or claws.
8. Do not buy animals that were not meant to be pets, such as parrots, exotic tortoises and monkeys.
9. Do not take animal products as medicine, for example rhino horns. Double check with a recommended health professional. Traditional Chinese Medicine (TCM) may not be effective while at the same time threatening vulnerable animals.
10. Avoid restaurants which serve meat of wild animals which may be endangered for example shark fin soup, turtle soup, tiger steak.

# APPENDIX 2:
# SIMPLE EYE CARE

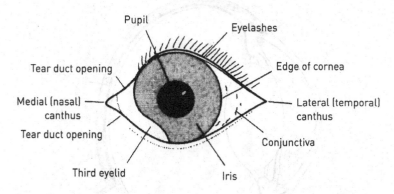

From Peiffer RL & Petersen-Jones' (1997)
*Small Animal Ophthalmology*, WB Saunders

*Let us breed out all inherited disorders and poor face design. Beware of dry eye. Learn from your vet to detect a serious red eye from a less serious red eye eg conjunctivitis. One red eye can be injury, or foreign body. A small pupil in the dark suggests uveitis.*

Do your homework before you acquire a new pet. The dog is affected by many inherited eye disorders which sometimes don't appear until later in the animal's life. Check with a veterinarian that the pup is not of a breed so afflicted. We must breed out all inherited threats to comfort and vision.

❖ *Before choosing an animal,* avoid prominent eyes and face wrinkles. Note if eyelids sit well on the cornea, not rolled in or falling down. Eyelids must fit snugly and not droop above or below the eye. Loose facial or forehead skin, ill-fitting eyelids, extra lashes, and long facial hair all threaten eye comfort and health. Veterinary advice is more value than your emotion. Fall in love with good head design.

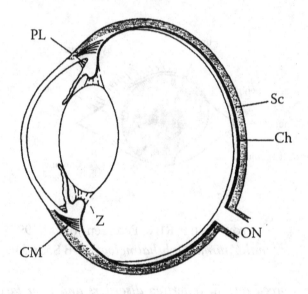

*The eye has structures susceptible to injury from trauma and the body's immune system.*

PL = pectinate ligament across drainage angle for aqueous internal eye fluid. Blockage causes glaucoma.
Eyelids fit to eyeball is vital. Cornea must be covered by eyelids when eye closed. Many dogs have a poor eyelid fit to cornea.
CM = ciliary muscle. when inflamed, spasm causes eye/head pain

ON = optic nerve. Disease, trauma cause vision loss. Some dogs are born with poorly functioning optic nerves.

Ch = blood rich choroid layer behind retina is exposed to immune reactions. Sick choroid = sick retina. Retina suffers from inherited atrophy—Progressive Retinal Atrophy (PRA), meaning thin retina and indicating degeneration.

The number of canine breeds affected could be over 100 breeds.

Sc = Sclera—seen as the white of the eye at the front around the cornea.

Z = zonules hold the lens in position. With chronic inflammation or trauma, zonules can break, allowing the lense to fall out of position. In some breeds there is an inherited weakness.

- ❖ *Eyes need shade and shelter.* In a treeless paddock, 'UV light is dynamite'. Plenty of pigment offers the animal protection. Avoid 'pretty' white eyelids, pink eyes, and albinos.
- ❖ Beware the one half closed or watery red eye. Two red eyes may be conjunctivitis serious if persistent. One red eye could be injury, internal inflammation (uveitis) or glaucoma.
- ❖ *Learn a home eye exam from a vet eye surgeon.* Animals do not complain, and we need to know more about animal eye examination than looking at the human eye. Examination of the eye is an owner's responsibility, not just the specialist vet's. Before eye injury occurs we need to know some basic first aid. (Treatment includes *keeping the eyeball wet perhaps with clean tap water as the lids are held open, ask your vet to show you). Tap all four corners of the eyelids with your fingertips* and watch that closing lids meet easily over central cornea. Incomplete lid

closure is an overlooked cause of discomfort and disease.

- ❖ *Be an owner who is wise to recognise the pupil size.* Learn how to look at the iris in dim light using a small torch shone obliquely through a shiny cornea. Small pupils in dim or dark light can suggest serious deep eye inflammation. Although less serious causes apply, call the vet immediately.

- ❖ Red eye: *two red eyes is probably conjunctivitis, possibly serious. A single red eye is always serious.* As a broad rule, one red eye suggests injury, foreign body, *deep inflammation (uveitis—*you-vee-eye-tis*)* or, more rarely, glaucoma, *Learn how you can tell a deeply red eye from conjunctivitis.*

- ❖ *Avoid flat faces, they indicate crowded teeth, less well-protected corneas and* show obvious whites of the eyes (scleras). Big whites suggest the corneas may not be fully protected by the lids.

- ❖ *Watery eyes* may not be comfortable but are easy to see; dry eyes are common and typically overlooked. If you suspect a dry eye, wet the eye with water squeezed from wet cotton wool and call the vet.

- ❖ *A caring owner must be wise and recognize the pupil size. Ask your vet to show how you can look at pupil size with a penlight torch in the dark.*

- ❖ *Vision loss* is easy to overlook. Push your horse without a halter through an obstacle course in light and dark with each eye covered in turn.

- ❖ *Glaucoma* (raised eye pressure) is among the causes of cloudy eye. Different types of glaucoma commonly affect at least 30 dog breeds and canine mixed breeds. Ask your vet eye surgeon.

- ❖ *Keep pups away from the family cat.* Cat claws destroy the eye.
- ❖ *Horses with chronic inner eye inflammation (uveitis)* may be part blind without the rider being aware. A fatal accident may follow. Test vision in light and dark, push the horse, without a lead, through an obstacle course with each eye covered in turn. *With a small torch in dim surroundings, learn to look past a shiny cornea at the iris.* A small pupil in dim light suggests chronic uveitis, which costs vision. Take your eldest children with you to the vet eye surgeon and record for 'Show and Tell' at school.
- ❖ *Learn eye treatment with a 'no touch the eyeball' from your vet.* Lift the nose up with one hand and rest your other hand holding the eye medication against the head, Hold the nozzle well away from the eye so that the eye is not touched even when the patient moves. Place one drop into the eyeball and hold the lids apart and the nose up for one or two minutes. Ask your vet to show you. The eye of small animals can only accommodate one drop. Two drops in an eye at one time is possibly wasteful. A match head size of warm ointment is placed on the eyeball.
- ❖ *Use antibiotic only when essential.* Save antibiotics for the rainy day of serious infection. Do NOT use antibiotic on the eye unless instructed by a vet and preferably a vet eye doctor to do so. From inappropriate antibiotic misuse and overuse resistant superbugs emerge and kill people.

*Natural non pharmaceutical medicine may be effective. Ask you vet.*

These rules are an introduction. People close to animals have a dedicated special lifetime of learning.

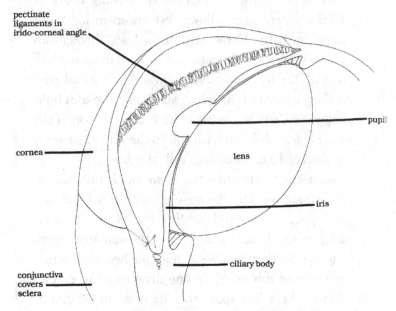

*Diagram of side view of animal eyeball.*
*Eyelids including third eyelid not shown.*
Image courtesy Dr Anita Dutton

# APPENDIX 3

## Glossary

**Greenpeace International:**
Based primarily in the Netherlands, supports study of climate change, sustainable agriculture, forests, oceans, polluting toxins, nuclear waste disposal, disarmament, and paths to peace.

**Vegan:**
A person who does not eat animals or animal products.

**Vegetarian:**
Noun. A person who does not eat meat or fish
Adjective. excluding animal food, esp meat
The best diet is described in Genesis: vegetables, grains, fruit and nuts.

**Total vegetarian:**
Reports from around the world show that many long-term total vegetarians (vegetarians who do not use any eggs, meat, fish, poultry or dairy products) are at risk of vitamin B12 deficiency.

Vitamin B12, an essential B vitamin, is of special interest to vegetarians since it is not found in any significant amounts in plant foods. Vitamin B12 deficiency can result in detrimental changes in certain body functions. It is required for the normal

317

maturation of red blood cells and also for the synthesis of the myelin sheath of nerve tissue.

1 cup of yogurt daily offers food rich in B12 (http://www.nal. usda.gov/fnic/foodcomp/Data/SR20/nutrlist/sr20w418.pdf)

Many older beliefs have been modified, many need to be changed. Keep reading.

# BIBLIOGRAPHY AND FURTHER READING

### Run Fast, Breathe Free, and Be With Nature

Blogg, R. and Allan, E. (1983), *Everydog: The Complete Book Of Dog Care*, Methuen, North Ryde.
Grandin, T. and Johnson, C. (2005), *Animals In Translation*, Scribner, New York.
BBC Television Program, 2009, *Pedigree dogs exposed*
Robertson, B. (2008), *ACES Breed Schedules*, Australian Canine Eye Scheme, Australian Veterinary Association.

### Passing of the Passenger Pigeon

Eckert, A. 1965, *The Silent Sky: The Incredible Extinction Of The Passenger Pigeon*, Little Brown & Co, Boston.
Readers' Digest Assoc, London (1997), *Protecting The Earth's Wild Animals*.

### Snow Geese—Friends and Foes

Elphick, J. (Ed) (2007), *The Atlas Of Bird Migration: Tracing The Great Journeys Of The World's Birds*, RD Press, Surry Hills.
Forbes, M. (2007), *'Warning of new bird flu danger, human-to-human spread in Sumatra'*, *The Age*, 31/8/07

Kowalski, G. (1999), *The Souls Of Animals*, New World Library, Novato, California
Pye, J. D. (2001), *Polarised Light In Science And Nature*, Institute of Physics Publishing, Bristol.
Whitman, L. (2008), *The High Life*, http://greennature.com/article620.html.

## The Vanishing Orang-utans of Borneo

Forbes, M. (2007) 'Human touch to seal boss' fate', *The Age*, December 2007.
Morell, V. (2008) 'Minds of their own: Animals are smarter than you think', National Geographic, vol 213, Mar 2008.
Randerson, J. (2007) 'Chimps outsmart humans in tests', The Age 5/12/07.
Schuster, G., Smits, W and Ullal, J. (2008) *Thinkers Of The Jungle: The Orang-Utan Report—Pictures, Facts, Background*, HF Ullmann, Potsdam.

## Communication From a Dolphin

Layton-Bennett, A. (2008) 'Whale Rescue', *The Veterinarian*, June 2008, Syd Mag Pub, Chatswood.
Morton, A. (2008) 'Mercury poisoning linked to dolphin deaths', *The Age*, 6/6/08.
O'Connor, R.C. and Peterson. D.M. (1994), *The Lives Of Whales And Dolphins*, Henry Holt and Co, New York.
Scheele, L. (1990) in *The Greenpeace Book Of Dolphins*, (May, J. (ed)), Random Century, Sydney.
Wyllie, T. (1993), *Dolphins: Telepathy And Underwater Birthing*, Bear & Co, Santa Fe, New Mexico.

320

## The Story of Slow Song

Carey, B. (2005) *'Ship noise drowns out whale talk, a threat to mating'*, http://www.livescience.com/animals/050220_whale_chatter.html.
Darby, A. (2009) *'Japan's whaling fleet facing cutbacks'*, The Age 14/11/09.
Khatchadourian, R. *'The wild man and the sea'*, *The Age*, Good Weekend Mar 1, 2008.

## Requiem For a Jungle Giant

Begley, S. (2007), *'Cry of the wild'*, *Newsweek*, August 2007.
Johnson, S. (2007), *'Guerrilla warfare'*, *Newsweek*, August 2007.
Kowalski, G. (1999), *The Souls Of Animals*, New World Library, Novato, California.
Stephens, A. (2009), *'Small sacrifice'*, *The Age*, 31/1/09.

## The Sheepdog and the Penguin

Coppinger, R. and Schneider, R. (1995), in *The Domestic Dog: Its Evolution, Behaviour And Interactions With People*, Serpell, J. (ed), Cambridge University Press, Cambridge.
Fox, M.W. (1971), *Integrative Development Of Brain And Behaviour In The Dog*, Chicago University Press, Chicago.

## To the Trenches

Gardiner, J. (2006), *The Animals' War: Animals In Wartime From The First World War To The Present Day*, Portrait, an imprint of Piatkus Books, London.

Mc Mullin, R. (2008), *'Australia's deadliest day ever'*, *The Age*, 29/5/08.

Nicholson, B. (2009), *'Military honours for Nova, a lost dog of war'*, *The Age*, 27/10/09.

Walls GL (1967) *The Vertebrate Eye And Its Adaptive Radiation*

## The First Caesarean

Kowalski, G. (1999), *The Souls Of Animals*, New World Library, Novato

## The Unspoken Bond Between Animals and People

O'Brien, S. (2008), *Wesley The Owl: The Remarkable Love Story Of An Owl And His Girl*, Free Press, New York

Roberts, J. (1972), *Seth Speaks: The Eternal Validity Of The Soul*, Amber-Allen, San Rafael.

Roberts, J. (1986), *The Unknown Reality*, Prentice Hall, New York.

Lagoni, L.S., Butler, C. and Hetts, S. (1994), *The Human Animal: Bond And Grief*, WB Saunders, Philadelphia.

## Animal Senses—What Do Our Animals See, Hear and Smell?

Duke-Elder, S. (1958), *System of Ophthalmology Vol 1: The Eye In Evolution*, Henry Kimpton, London.

Foster, S.J. (2000), *'Vision in the dog (Canis familiaris) with references to domestic cat (Felis catus)'*, *Veterinary International*, Nestec, Oxford.

Grzimek, B. (1968), in *Man and Animal: Studies In Behaviour*, Friedrich, H. (ed), MacGibbon and Kee, London.

Pascual-Leone A, Amedi A, Fregni F, Merabet L (2005) *The plastic human brain cortex*, Ann Rev Neurosci 28: 377-401

Land, M.F. and Nilsson, D.E. (2002), *Animal Eyes*, Oxford University Press, New York.

Walls, G.L. (1967), *The Vertebrate Eye And Its Adaptive Radiation*, Hefner, New York.

## Cocky Go to Bed

Duke-Elder, S. (1958), *System Of Ophthalmology, The Eye In Evolution*, Henry Kimpton, London.

Grandin, T. and Johnson, C. (2002), *Animals In Translation*, Scribner, New York.

Singer, P. (2002), *Animal Liberation*, Harper Collins, New York.

Weidensaul, S. (1999), *Living On The Wind: Across The Hemisphere With The Migratory Birds*, North Point Press, New York.

'Youth Alert On Bird Flu', *The Age*, 3/7/06.

## The Dangers of a Part Closed Eye

Blogg, R. (1987), *The Eye In Veterinary Practice: Eye injuries*, Chilcote Publishing, Malvern.

## Blind Dog for an ex-POW

Aguirre, G.D. and Acland, G.M. (1988), 'Variation in retinal degeneration phenotype inherited at the prcd locus', *Experimental Eye Research*, 46, 663-687.

Blogg, R. and Allan, E. (1983), *Everydog: The Complete Book Of Dog Care*, Methuen, North Ryde.

Rubin, L.F. (1975), *Atlas Of Veterinary Ophthalmoscopy*, Lea & Febiger, Philadelphia.

## Avoid a Moral Hangover—Say No to Tiger Wine

King, S.A. (2006), *Animal Messenger: Interpreting The Symbolic Language Of The World's Animals*, New Holland Publishers (Australia), Sydney.

## Your Friend Can Kill

Millan, C. and Peltier, M. (2006), *Cesar's Way: The Natural Everyday Guide To Understanding And Correcting Common Dog Problems*, Harmony Books, New York.

## Liar Liar, Cat On Fire

Fisher, C. and Painter, G. (1996), *Materia Medication Of Western Herbs For The Southern Hemisphere*, National Herbalists Association of Australia, Sydney.
Hall, D. (1988) Herbal Medicine, Lothian, Melbourne.
Scheffer, M. (1986), *Bach Flower Therapy: Theory And Practice*, Thorsons, Rochester.
Weinman, R.A. (1988), *Your Hands Can Heal: How To Channel Healing Energy*, Thorsons, London.

## A Shot For Tetanus

Hungerford, T.G. (1975), *Diseases Of Livestock* (eighth edition), McGraw-Hill, Sydney

## Go and Dance With the Stars

Roberts, J. (1972), *Seth speaks: The Eternal Validity Of The Soul*, Amber-Allen Publishing and New World Library, San Rafael.
Sheldrake, R. (2000), *Dogs That Know When Their Owners Are Coming Home*, Arrow Books, London.

## Cruelty of the Fur Trade

Kowalski, G. (2007), *The Souls Of Animals*, New World Library, Novato.
McEwin, E. (2008), *An Antarctic Affair*, East Street Publications, Bowden, South Australia.
Millar, S. (2001), *'Skinned alive: Seal cull shocks vets'*, *The Guardian*, April 2001.
*'Serbia's iron lady released from jail'*, The Age 29/10/09
Singer, P (1990), *Animal Liberation*, 2nd edition, Avon Books, New York
Smith, J.A. (2003), *'Judging The Buddhist World Fairly'* in *Sharing Jesus Holistically With The Buddhist World*, Lim, D.S. and Spaulding, D. (eds), William Carey Library, Publishers, Pasadena, California.

## Turtle Slaughter in Queensland

Allende, I. (1987), *Of Love And Shadows*, Bantam, New York.
Edwards, L. *'Non-stun killing hurts $10 billion industry, says Halal exporter'*, *The Age*, 13/8/07
Schemann, A.K., Hernandez-Jover, M., Hall, W., Holyoake, P.K., and Toribio, J-ALML (2010), *'Assessment of current disease surveillance act haconome he bingtivities for pigs post-farmgate in New South Wales'*, *Australian Veterinary Journal*, 88, No. 5.
www.animalsaustralia.org.

## For Heaven's Sake, Skip the Steak and Don't Bring Home the Bacon

Wade, M. *'India offers no-beef climate solution'*, *The Age*, 22/11/09.

## Elephant Life and Massacres

Chadwick, D.H. (2005), *'Thailand's urban giants'*, *National Geographic*, October 2005.
Edwards, L. *'Scales of justice'*, *The Age*, 19/8/07.
Katsikaros, J. (2009), *'The Elephant Valley project'*, *Australian Veterinary Journal*, vol 87, Oct.
Warren, L. (2004), *'Calls in the wild'*, *National Geographic*, Mar 2004.

## Too Soon Old, Too Late Wise

Chandler J (2010), *The disciple of nature*, *The Age*, 16/10
Livingston, G. (2005), *Too Soon Old, Too Late Smart: Thirty True Things You Need To Know Now*, Hodder, Sydney.

## *Further General Reading*

Stephen Coren (1994) *The Intelligence of Dogs* Simon & Schuster, London UK

Jane Goodall, Thane Maynard and Gail Hudson (2010), *Hope for Animals and Their World, How Endangered Species Are Being Rescued From the Brink,* Grand Central Publishing, Hachette Book Group, New York

Jonica Newby (1997) *The Pact For Survival Humans and Their Animal Companions ABC Books GPO Box 9994 Sydney*

Temple Grandin, Catherine Johnson (2009) *Making Animals Happy, How to Create the Best Life for Pets and Other Animals,* Bloomsbury, London

Philosophy underlying the Order of Australia:

The purpose of the Order of Australia is to recognise, by national honour, those who have made outstanding contributions that benefit their communities.

http://www.gg.gov.au/content.php/page/id/93

# EPILOGUE

I see the world differently now I am 80 years old. I had a charmed young life guided by animal ownership. Alas a 2011 planet means not enough food and ineffective disease control kills 20,000 children every day (Singer 2011). Surely we knew this was coming even when most beings are remote from our daily life. Are those who need us always remote? Bullying occurs at every level and even prolonged abuse is overlooked. When a young girl in a local workplace takes her own life, the bullies seem unrepentant.

As I matured I managed to get rid of the 'I am above others' and 'I can do it so I will do it' attitudes. Bullying animals and people has similar origins. An 'I am above you' approach is widespread towards wildlife and farm animals and copies the suffering of the down trodden living under a dictator.

The world watches as we ask for kindness to all other beings, but how can we expect kindness for people if we do not treat animals gently?

Meat is too expensive to feed the Earth and causes health problems. We need to know how little meat we can eat, not how much.

I repeat the question so many are asking. How do we better help our friends in the forest, the sky and the sea?

Dame Phyllis Frost, dedicated social worker and champion of goaled women, told me in an audience of young Rotarian men

I must be prepared to change my mind minute by minute if I wish to remain useful. I have not heard better advice.

*Ref:*
Singer, Peter (2011) ... *The Age*